TÜRKENHIRSCH
A Study of Baron Maurice de Hirsch

WITHDRAWN

Baron Maurice de Hirsch
1831-1896

TÜRKENHIRSCH

*A Study of Baron Maurice de Hirsch
Entrepreneur and Philanthropist*

BY

KURT GRUNWALD

ISRAEL PROGRAM FOR SCIENTIFIC TRANSLATIONS
1966

ISRAEL PROGRAM FOR SCIENTIFIC TRANSLATIONS

P. O. BOX 7145 / JERUSALEM / ISRAEL

COPYRIGHT © 1966
ISRAEL PROGRAM FOR SCIENTIFIC TRANSLATIONS
IPST CAT. NO. 2601

THIS BOOK HAS BEEN COMPOSED ON MONOPHOTO AT IPST,
PRINTED BY S. MONSON AND BOUND BY WIENER BINDERY LTD.,
JERUSALEM, ISRAEL

To the Memory of
ISRAEL B. BRODIE
*who still enjoyed reading the major part
of the manuscript*

TABLE OF CONTENTS

Foreword xi
Prelude xiii
Introduction xv
CHAPTER I: ANCESTORS 1
CHAPTER II: THE EARLY YEARS 1831-1855 9
CHAPTER III: THE BISCHOFFSHEIMS 13
CHAPTER IV: THE ASCENT: 1855-1868 20
CHAPTER V: THE STORY OF THE ORIENTAL RAILWAYS . . 28
CHAPTER VI: THE ENTERPRISE OF PHILANTHROPY 63
CHAPTER VII: BARON HIRSCH AND ZIONISM 76
CHAPTER VIII: FRIENDS AND ENEMIES IN HIGH PLACES . . 86
CHAPTER IX: BARON HIRSCH THE MAN 99
APPENDIX: I FOUR ENCOUNTERS 111
APPENDIX II: HIRSCH'S MEMORANDUM ON
PALESTINEAN COLONIZATION 122
Chronology 127
Bibliography 129
Index 135

CONVERSION TABLE

1 £ = 1 L.T. = 25 francs = 20 marks = 8 Florins = $ 5.-

FOREWORD

'THE badge of an economic historian is won by working with primary sources, not in making a synthesis of already synthetic material.'[1]

I am painfully aware of the truth of Professor C. P. Kindleberger's admonition. My original aim was to write a study of the entrepreneurial achievements of one of the great figures in Europe's railway development during the second half of the nineteenth century. But my hopes were soon dampened by the discovery that no archives whatsoever of Hirsch's had been preserved or are known to exist. Nor was there available, any helpful 'definitive biography' of Baron Hirsch, whose name, seventy years ago, was one of the most widely known in Europe. Therefore I had to rely on a number of widely scattered articles, references, and notes of various degrees of reliability in a great variety of publications, in order to reconstruct a picture of one of the most colorful personalities of his time.

I was greatly helped in this endeavor by my friend and collaborator Dr. J. O. Ronall of New York, who, apart from supplying much valuable material and advice, discovered in the Archives of the American Jewish Historical Society the fragment of a biography which the late Max J. Kohler started to write about fifty years ago but was prevented from completing by his untimely death. I wish here to record my thanks to the Director of these Archives, Dr. Isidore S. Meyer, and to Max J. Kohler's sister Lili, who graciously permitted me to use the fragment, as well as the letters to Kohler by Gustav Held, a secretary of Hirsch's and of the Hirsch estate, and some other correspondence. I felt greatly touched to find in the correspondence letters from my own grandfather, Dr. Joseph S. Bloch of Vienna, who had provided some material for the attempted biography.

I wish likewise to record here my appreciation of the assistance received from a great number of people in the form of advice, information, or material. These include the Banque de la Société Générale de Belgique, Brussels; Prof. Dr. Heinrich Benedikt, Vienna; Princess Eudoxia of Bulgaria, Friedrichshafen; Mr. F. H. Brunner, New York; the late Professor S. B. Chlepner, Brussels; Mr. E. Elath, President of the Hebrew University of Jerusalem; Mr. V. Girmounsky (Jewish Colonization Association), London; Mr. David Kessler *(Jewish Chronicle)*, London; Baron Donald v. Hirsch, London—Munich; Dr. Jacob Markus (American Jewish Archives), Cincinatti; Sektionschef Dr. F. Metznig (Bundeskanzleramt), Vienna; Dr. O. Rabinowicz, Scarsdale, N. Y.; Mr. G. H. Schlottmann (Deutsches Industrieinstitut), Cologne; Mr. Mark Uveeler (Memorial Foundation for Jewish Culture), New York;

---

[1] C. P. Kindleberger, *Economic Growth in France and Britain,* 1860-1950 (1964), p. 3.

and last, but not least, Mr. S. Adler-Rudel, my 'competitor' in the quest for Hirsch, with whom I enjoyed a most stimulating exchange of ideas.

As regards the technical aspects of preparing the MS., I wish to express my gratitude to Mrs. Olga Priester of New York and Mrs. Sylvia Farhi and Mrs. Gertrude Spitzer, both of Jerusalem, for typing the successive drafts of my book with unflagging and painstaking devotion. My thanks are also due to Dr. Alice Shalvi for her close and critical scrutiny of the MS. in general, and her valuable suggestions regarding the scholarly 'apparatus' in particular.

Looking for Hirsch, the entrepreneur, I felt entitled in this study to neglect or take less notice of Hirsch, the philanthropist, on whom a vast literature exists, and to whom S. Adler-Rudel has recently devoted his excellent Profile.[2] The same applies to the institutions Hirsch sponsored and supported.

This study could properly be styled 'Notes for a Biography,' in order to make clear the author's view that the material at present available does not justify the publication of what might be called a biography. It is only through Professor G. Jacquemyns of Brussels, and his admirable work on Langrand-Dumonceau,[3] that some information had incidentally become available on Hirsch's activities during the years 1855-1869. His impressive four volumes, and Jean Bouvier's delving into the archives of Crédit Lyonnais, which has so far yielded two important publications,[4] give reason to hope that new material will be unearthed that will make possible in the not too distant future the writing of a definitive biography of Baron Hirsch.

---

[2] S. Adler-Rudel, 'Moritz Baron Hirsch, Profile of a Great Philanthropist,' *Leo Baeck Institute Yearbook* VIII (1963).

[3] G. Jacquemyns, *Langrand-Dumonceau, Promoteur d'une puissance financière catholique*. 4 vols. (1960-1964).

[4] J. Bouvier, *Le Krach de l'Union Générale,* 1878-1885 (1960); Idem *Le Crédit Lyonnais,* 1863-1883. 2 vols. (1963).

PRELUDE

HABENT SUA FATA LIBELLI

IN THE Archives of the Jewish Historical Society of America there is a letter dated Paris, November 7, 1911, from G. Held, a secretary of the late Baron Hirsch, to the New York attorney and historian Max J. Kohler telling him:

> During my stay in my native town of Munich I spoke with a friend, Mr. David Wassermann. He has finished, after working on it for five years in all the archives of Bavaria, a history of the Jews in Bavaria up to 1860, when they were enfranchised. I heard from him that most of the American 'milliardaires'[1] are Jews from Bavaria with changed names. This work contains more than 10,000 names. Probably it will not be published because the cost of printing would be 40,000 marks, but it will be given after Mr. Wassermann's death to the Royal National Library of Bavaria.

On the Hill of Remembrance in Jerusalem in the Archives of *Yad Vashem*, the Jewish National Remembrance Authority, there are numerous notebooks, containing thousands of names of Bavarian Jews, which were received together with other remnants of the Central Archives of German Jewry. They are apparently the index of Wassermann's manuscript.

Was it just pure chance that Wassermann told Held of his manuscript, that Held wrote Kohler about it, that this letter was preserved in the New York archives, where the present writer, in search of material on Baron Hirsch, came across it, and quite incidentally mentioned it to one of the historians of the *Yad Vashem* archives who was now able to identify these hitherto mysterious fragments?

Wassermann's manuscript itself, alas, apparently disappeared during the Holocaust. The (Royal) National Library of Bavaria had never received it. This is a great pity because from it we might have learned more about the direct ancestry of Baron de Hirsch and about that group of the Bavarian *Landjuden* who, it seems, fathered the millionaires of America.[2] But it was not only millionaires who originated from that remarkable branch of the House of Israel. Oscar S. Straus, who as Secretary of Commerce and a United States Ambassador to the Porte served 'Under Four Admin-

---

[1] This is a literal translation from the original German of Held's letter; the English equivalent would be 'millionaires.'

[2] Cf. the interesting essay by Barry E. Supple on 'A Business Elite: German-Jewish Financiers in Nineteenth Century New York,' which shows that in the last century most of the noted Jewish financiers in New York hailed from Bavaria's rural districts and small towns. Most of them had arrived as youngsters between 1830 and 1850 with little or no money, but had earned their place in Wall Street by dint of arduous work, starting as peddlers in outlying parts of the Union and progressing through retailing, wholesaling and manufacturing to high finance.

istrations,' hailed from Otterberg in Rhenish Bavaria, and the noted New York attorney, Max J. Kohler,—to whom Held's letter was addressed, and who was working on a biography of Baron Hirsch,—from Munich. It was a veritable explosion of talent that preceded the *de facto* and *de jure* emancipation of Bavarian Jewry. But probably the most outstanding among them was Baron Maurice de Hirsch.

INTRODUCTION

THERE is practically no encyclopedia extant which does not devote an article to Baron Maurice de Hirsch. Hardly any economic historian of the nineteenth century omits mentioning Hirsch's role as entrepreneur, particularly of the Oriental Railway project. There is no book on Jewish history in modern times which does not refer to his attempt to solve the Jewish problem by settlement in the Argentine. Still, surprisingly, no full biography exists of this remarkable man.

The Viennese historian Professor Heinrich Benedikt, in a letter to me dated April 10, 1964, writes: 'If in Vienna today you were to ask a bank director or an historian who was Hirsch, the friend of Edward VII and Crown Prince Rudolf, you would be met by an embarrassed silence.' He adds: 'They don't even know the name. ...Fifty years ago one could still have collected the material.'

Fifty years ago—or more correctly, on March 15, 1910—Gustav Held, administrator of the Hirsch estate, wrote to Kohler, who wanted to write the biography of Baron Hirsch, that '...it was only on account of the pecuniary difficulties, that it [a biography] was not published in Europe; neither the heirs nor the many benevolent institutions [which he had endowed] were willing to contribute anything.' Matters have not changed much in this respect.

Three score years ago, Hirsch's name was revered by the Jewish people. Chaim Weizmann saw his picture at his father's house in Pinsk next to that of Maimonides.[1] Max Kollenscher remembered it hanging side by side with that of the Emperor Frederick in his parents' home in Posen.[2] And like Adler-Rudel on the eastern frontier of the Habsburg Empire,[3] Elkan N. Adler noticed it in many poor Jewish homes in Salonica, together with that of Moses Montefiore.[4] It had a place of honor even in some stately *comptoir* in Amsterdam.[5] But few people today, apart from those on his settlements in the Argentine, remember his name. Very few of those passing through the Baron Hirsch Street in Jerusalem or Petah-Tikva, or that in Mahopac, N. Y., or visiting Temple de Hirsch in Seattle,[6] know much about the man or his deeds. And if his name is remembered at all, it is because of ICA, the Jewish Colonization Association, and his other philanthropic endowments, some bearing

---

[1] Chaim Weizmann, *Trial and Error* (1949), p. 24.
[2] S. Adler-Rudel, *'Moritz Baron Hirsch'* p. 67.
[3] *Ibid.*
[4] E. N. Adler, *Jews in Many Lands* (1905), p. 90.
[5] Personal comment of Mrs. P. van Leer.
[6] Cf. Mary McCarthy, *My Catholic Childhood* (Penguin ed., 1963), p. 181.

his name, which he set up on a scale unheard of in his time and paralleled in our days only by Carnegie, Rockefeller and Ford. But just as we can learn little from the activities of these foundations about the contribution made by their founders to the economic development of the United States, so the story of Hirsch's philanthropic undertakings tells us little about Hirsch, the entrepreneur, whose daring eventually made him an international, though controversial, figure and one of the richest men of his time.

The crowning event in his business career was his great enterprise, the Oriental Railways, which, as Jenks says, 'were a factor in Balkan diplomacy for two decades.'[7] Of the preceding fifteen years, 1855-1869, we know only little for a full appreciation of the man. Hirsch did not write diaries; the archives disappeared. So one has to search for, and collect, 'circumstantial evidence' from secondary sources and scrutinize it carefully. Thus the writing of a definitive biography of Baron de Hirsch must be deferred until the lost archives are discovered.

Meanwhile the controversy about Hirsch has been reopened. Of late, historians of economic growth and entrepreneurial history are devoting increasing attention to the revelations of the last century. A number of them, such as Benedikt, Cameron, Hallgarten, Jacquemyns, and Landes, refer to Hirsch in their books, and usually not in a complimentary fashion. Some of their remarks seem to be based on inadequate source evaluation, others may be in place. The age of the entrepreneur had its own code of conduct, which may not be ours. As stated before a Viennese jury in those days, 'Railways are not built by morality sermons.' The defendant was, in fact, acquitted.[8]

It was the historical function of the nineteenth century to set free the productive forces which the Industrial Revolution had created. In the early part of the century this revolution had moved across the Channel to Belgium and France, and from there in stages south-east. This development became possible only under a regime of liberalism, which permitted a free reign to the entrepreneurial spirit. It was the entrepreneur, with his vision, daring, and risk-taking, who not only revolutionized industry, but created the markets for this industry and the distributive system for its products, as in the global expansion of railways. It was he who simultaneously revolutionized and adapted to the new needs the system and instruments of finance. The eventual failure of some of these instruments, like Pereire's Crédit Mobilière, does not detract from their historical merit in the speeding up of economic progress. And so we can only look back with admiration on Hirsch's device of the *Türkenlose* as a means to finance the Oriental Railways scheme.

The economic development since the end of World War II, particularly of what

---

[7] H. L. Jenks, *The Migration of British Capital to* 1875 (1927), p. 269.

[8] Cf. F. G. Steiner, writing on the Offenheim Case, 1873 (Lemberg—Czernowitz Railway), *Entwicklung des Mobilbankwesens in Oesterreich* (1913), p. 183.

In China at that time 'to obtain contracts and the like Jardine Matheson sought a position of influence with officials of the Imperial Household and the Board of Revenue in Peking, and obtained it by granting them loans on easy terms.' (cf. Maurice Collins, *Wayfoong: The Hongkong and Shanghai Banking Corporation* (London (1965), p. 59).

Introduction

are now known as the Development Countries, has dominated the economic-political thinking to such an extent that it has become, in the words of an American economist, the shibboleth of our times. More recently, like Molière's Monsieur Jourdain, who was surprised and pleased to learn that it was prose he had spoken all along, many of the advocates of economic development have learned that this process had been in progress even in the last century, and to a relatively greater extent than now. As Cairncross lately reminded us, 'If the same proportion of American resources were devoted to foreign investment, as Britain, out of a far smaller national income, devoted in 1913, the flow of investment would be thirty times as great. The entire Marshall Plan would have to be carried out twice a year.'[9]

Similar statements and comparisons raise important questions: why, today, with all the preoccupation with Foreign Aid, Point Four, and so on, does the flow of funds, public and private, into the Development Countries lag so far behind that of the economically less sophisticated past? There will be many explanations, both political and economic. But just as in development theory the emphasis has lately shifted from politics and economics to sociology, so we shall, in a study of the rapid development in the last century, usefully look to the personalities, whose vision, courage and pertinacity helped to bring this process about. And we shall have to judge these entrepreneurs by their achievements only, and not by their methods. There is indeed a strong prejudice today against the 'robber barons' of the 19th century and their methods. But we venture a guess that the productive economic net result of their enterprise was certainly not smaller than that of the vast foreign aid now being poured into many of the countries of the Far and Middle East.

It is this aspect which makes the lives of the great entrepreneurs, the pioneers of the economic development of the last century, so fascinating today. And Baron Hirsch was among the greatest, measured both by the scale of his enterprise and by that of his philanthropy.

Baron Hirsch lived in a time of transition. In the political sphere it was the struggle between the forces of Restoration and Legitimism against the rising Liberalism and Democracy. For the economic historian it is a period in which the Industrial Revolution swept over Europe, manifesting itself by the rapid expansion of the railway net over the Continent; and, closely connected therewith, the rise of the large joint stock banks, often with the backing and the experience of the old family banks, and the internecine struggle among the new giants for railway and other concessions. And finally, for the historian of the Jewish people, it was the Age of Emancipation, of the rise of modern Antisemitism, and of the pogroms and persecution in Russia. And we have tried to show Hirsch's response to these challenges of his time.

In the absence of a definitive biography, and in lieu thereof, it seems timely to present an admittedly incomplete monograph containing the material on Baron Hirsch so far available and to add, in possible future editions, such material as may meanwhile become available. In this way, we hope to prevent authors from using sources already proved unreliable, biased and outdated, and to prepare the ground

---

[9] A. Cairncross, *Home and Foreign Investment, 1870-1939* (1953).

for an eventual definitive biography. Moreover, it is hoped that the present publication will re-awaken interest in Baron de Hirsch, and thereby help to bring to light additional material, hitherto unknown.

This book seems to be a timely one, coinciding as it does with the seventieth anniversary of Hirsch's death. Moreover, in 1966 the Jewish Colonization Association, (ICA) London, is looking back on seventy-five years of activities, a period of history which has witnessed revolutionary changes in the life of the Jewish people. ICA is marking this jubilee by embarking on a large-scale colonization scheme in the Galilean hill country in Israel. This is a significant event, for it brings to a symbolical close and a practical conclusion a debate that began seventy years ago, in May 1895, between Dr. Theodor Herzl, the spiritual father of the Jewish state, and Baron Maurice de Hirsch, the founder of the Jewish Colonization Association.

CHAPTER I

ANCESTORS

THE years between the Peace of Westphalia, 1648, and the Congress of Vienna, 1814, form a fascinating chapter in the history of finance. It was the period of the Court Jew.[1] From the smallest principality to the Imperial Court in Vienna[2] Jews were entrusted with the management of the ruler's and the court's financial problems. As 'Hoffaktors' they took care of the supplies to the army and of the requirements of the court; they advanced the necessary funds against expected income from taxes on land, salt, or duties, and thus became tax collectors. Sometimes they became mint-masters, and sometimes they were simply court bankers. Occasionally they were entrusted with diplomatic missions.

After the Peace of Westphalia, in a Germany long split up into small principalities and self-governing cities, economic conditions made the Court Jew a universal phenomenon of the Age of Absolutism and of the Baroque.[3] At the very end of the period there appear on the scene the Hirschs of Gau-Königshofen, near Würzburg[4] whose scion Maurice takes a place in the Jewish history of the nineteenth century, equalled only by the proverbial Rothschilds.

The family appears first in documents in 1803, mentioning the 'Kurfürstliche Schutzjude Moses Hirsch von Gau Königshofen', as a man respected by the authorities 'wegen seiner persönlichen Denkart.' These words were used in a recommendation to permit 'Moses Hirsch & Söhne' to acquire real estate, first in Würzburg, and later in all Bavaria. The Hirschs were apparently the first Jews to receive this right.

Moses Hirsch was evidently a man of substantial wealth, but nothing is known about the source of this wealth. Military supply contracts over the preceding eighteen to twenty years may have been a principal source of this wealth and of the good name

---

[1] Selma Stern, *The Court Jew* (1954). Heinrich Schnee, *Die Hoffinanz und der moderne Staat* (1953).
[2] Max Grunwald, *Samuel Oppenheimer und sein Kreis* (1913).
[3] A similar development took place in the Ottoman Empire even before that time. A comparison between the social, political, and economic conditions which prevailed at these centers and favored such a development has still to be written. cf. Kurt Grunwald, 'The Bankers of Galata,' *Riv'on L'Bankauth* 6, (1962); Idem, 'The Sarrafs, the Bankers of Iraq,' *Hamizrach Hehadash* XI, 3 (1961).
[4] Joseph Prys, *Die Familie von Hirsch auf Gereuth* (1931). The origins of the Jewish population of Gau-Königshofen date back to the seventeenth century. An organized Jewish community existed from the early part of the eighteenth century. Jewish merchants from this place were recorded as visitors to the Leipzig Fair from the middle of the eighteenth century on. In 1830 a synagogue was built, and restored in 1920.

In 1816, the Jewish population was 108, out of a total of 546, i.e., 19.8%, but by 1900 it had dwindled to 91, or 14.6% of a total population of 622. In 1933, 53 Jews were left, 7.3% of a total population of 723, (cf. Yad Vashem, *Pinkas Ha-kehilloth* (in preparation)).

which Moses Hirsch apparently enjoyed with the authorities. However, Moses Hirsch remains a background name in the family's history. He probably passed away very soon thereafter.

It was the 'Handelsjude' Jacob, born in 1763 or 1764, who with his father's power of attorney acted on behalf of the family in 1803 in the acquisition of property in Würzburg. In 1806, addressed as 'Handelsmann' he received, because of his always evidenced loyalty and allegiance ('stets bezeugten Treue und Anhänglichkeit'), the freedom of movement in the kingdom, a valued privilege for Jews during a time of general civil disabilities burdening them. In 1812 he was spoken of as 'Hofbanquier' (court banker), and in 1818, after the acquisition of the 'Rittergut' Gereuth, the 'Hofbanquier und Grosshändler Jacob Hirsch' and his family were knighted with the title 'auf Gereuth.'

The estate of Gereuth was not only the basis for the knighthood; it was a place in which the family became rooted, and to the development of which as a model farm they were devoted.

Coat of Arms of the Hirsch family

Ancestors

No wonder that contemporary Jewish chronicles[5] took pride in Jacob von Hirsch, the first Jew in Bavaria permitted to acquire real estate, and to carry on farming; the man who rose from 'Talmudjünger' (he had the traditional Jewish education) to high rank and position. Without full rights as a citizen, he was a great patriot, who in the Napoleonic Wars equipped one battallion (75 men) of soldiers at his own expense. This fact, which is recorded in the Brockhaus *Lexicon* (1839), is surprisingly not mentioned in the edict granting the knighthood.

Jacob entered his father's business and soon developed it greatly, mainly through army supplies during the 1790-1800 wars.[6] In 1800 he opened a banking house in Ansbach. He became salaried court agent of Prince Loewenstein-Wertheim and, eventually, court banker to the Grand Duke of Württemberg. He was probably the first Jew in Germany to obtain the feudal right to hold a Court of Justice on his estate. He acquired a number of other substantial estates, apart from Gereuth.

In 1805 Jacob Hirsch signed contracts for the supply of horses to the army, and arranged various bond loans to the Bavarian Government between 1805 and 1817.[7] In 1821 (or 1819) Jacob left the House of Würzburg in the care of his son Joel Jacob (1789-1876) and settled in Munich, where until his death in 1841 (or 1840) he built up an important banking business. He also acquired the estate and manor house of Planegg near Munich, where he established a brewery. The Würzburg house added a sugar refinery to its activities. Thus agricultural industries were added to farming.

Jacob's death in 1841 was the end of the transition period from 'Hoffaktor' to private banker, which is aptly described in the following words:

> The war-economy and the financial exigencies of the State made a few bankers, and particulary the court-bankers, Aron Elias von Eichthal and Jacob von Hirsch, powerful figures in the State. They had made great profits on war-supplies, became large creditors of the State by deferring payments due to them and by cash loans, and subsequently also personally promoted the State's credit standing by advising the government and by the sale of State obligations. But with all the standing due to them as a result of their activities on behalf of the State finances, rewarded by new wealth and coats of arms, King Maximilian and King Ludwig I still saw in a Royal Court Banker a bit of the Elector's 'Hoffaktor' or Court Agent, who had not only to provide money for his prince, but to serve also as a target of coarse or malicious jokes.[8]

Jacob's death coincided with drastic political and economic changes. The Age of Absolutism gave way to the Age of Liberalism; and the Industrial Revolution spread from England to the Continent, with the consequent radical changes in financial organizations.

---

[5] See M. Kayserling, *Gedenkblätter* (1892), p. 31.
[6] H. A. Pierer (ed.) *Universallexicon* (1843).
[7] L. Hümmert, 'Die finanziellen Beziehungen jüdischer Bankiers und Heereslieferanten zum bayerischen Staat in der ersten Hälfte des 19 Jahrhunderts,' (unpublished Ph.D. dissertation, University of Munich, 1927).
[8] *Die Bayerische Staatsbank von 1780-1955* (1955), p. 96.

With the death of Jacob, the two branches of the House seem to have become independent units, the one in Würzburg, patriarchal in style, the other in Munich, more cosmopolitan and international in scope.

The inheritance which Jacob left to his widow, included a number of manorial estates, some of them with hunting reserves and one having a fishery, apart from Gereuth and Planegg, which he left to Joel Jacob and Joseph respectively. Among the bequests for charitable and religious purposes, was one for the 'Promotion of Agricultural Pursuits among Jews.'

Joel Jacob at Würzburg is in a way the most interesting of Maurice's forefathers; he revealed the entrepreneurial vision and drive which were to distinguish his nephew thereafter. He, too, was devoted to agriculture, which he helped to modernize. He mechanized farming and improved stock breeding. He added sugar-refining to beer-brewing on his large sugar beet plantation in Rottersdorf, which he kept busy in the

Joel Jacob von Hirsch—uncle of Baron Maurice—1764-1841

off-season with imported Indian crude sugar, alcohol being the by-product of this industry. A brandy-still may have been connected with his vineries, the products of his Franconian vineyards. Turf cutting and lumber were additional industries based on agriculture, as also was wool-spinning, for which in 1826 he imported 3,000 modern English water-drawn spindles to replace the traditional hand spindles.

He re-organized the Franconian lumber trade, thus breaking a Dutch monopoly, which hitherto had dominated this trade to the disadvantage of the producers; and he started to use the Danube-Main Canal for floating the lumber to the Rhine. He was active in the establishment of the Donau-Main Dampfschiffahrts Aktiengesellschaft and participated in various railway ventures.

The head of the Würzburg house also enjoyed the confidence of the ruler, who consulted him frequently. In 1835 he was one of the prime movers in setting up one of the mortgage banks, the Bayerische Hypotheken-und Wechselbank, for which he won the collaboration of the Rothschilds, who subscribed 1.5 million florin to Hirsch's 1 million florin. And he served on the committee which drew up the statute of this bank.

His progressive social ideas were shown by the establishment in 1863 of a Workers' Sick Fund, (possibly the first in Bavaria), for the employees of his sugar refinery at Rottendorf.

The synagogue in his house was a center for Würzburg's Jews. He participated in the efforts for the emancipation of Bavarian Jewry, reportedly established an art gallery and promoted industry and crafts in many ways.

The house in Munich probably was already in Jacob's last years predominantly under the management of his son Joseph (1805-1885), who had been appointed 'Hofbanquier' in 1840, (i.e., a year before Jacob's death) by King Ludwig I and was confirmed in this position by his successors Maximilian II and Ludwig II in 1848. For the position and confidence which he and the other court bankers enjoyed, an interesting testimonial is to be found in the History of the Bayerische Staatsbank,[9] which states that the government continued after the formation of the bank to entrust the court bankers of Munich and Rothschild with its current financial transactions. Eichthal, (a converted Jew, formerly Seligmann) and Hirsch, took care of salary transfers abroad, and repeated objections by the State Bank which wanted to handle this business were rejected; it was stated that the Court Bankers considered this as an honor and charged only their actual expenses. The Royal Bank (State Bank) would be considered only if it could undercut these charges; otherwise, preference would be given to the Court Bankers.

In 1856, the year after Maurice Hirsch's marriage to Clara Bischoffsheim— Joseph Hirsch, together with Bischoffsheim, Rothschild, and the State Bank, was among the founders of the Bayerische Ostbahn Aktiengesellschaft, on whose board he still appeared in 1869.

Joseph, like his father, excelled in acts of philanthropy, as when during the cholera epidemic of 1854, he organized soup kitchens, or when during the 1866 war, his castle of Planegg became a hospital for casualties of both warring parties, Austria and Prussia. Like his father, too, he endowed synagogues and institutes of Jewish learning. In 1869 he and his issue were elevated to a Barony. In 1855 he became Consul of Württemberg at Munich.

But it seems that he early left the House in Munich in the care of his son Emil, Maurice's junior by six years, while he became a gentleman farmer, devoting himself to the development of the estate at Planegg. Stories elsewhere recorded[10] seem

---

[9] *Ibid*, p. 100.
[10] Kohler Papers.

Joseph v. Hirsch

to indicate that his business acumen was not equal to that of his father or elder brother Joel.

The history of the Bayerische Staatsbank mentions the House of Hirsch as promoter, jointly with the Staatsbank, of industrial enterprises.[11] But the days of the 'Privat-Banquier' were numbered. With the rise of the corporate banks most of the

[11] *Bayerische Staatsbank*, p. 172.

The family manor at Planegg near Munich.

old and famous Houses like Hirsch lost their independence.[12] Soon after Joseph's death in 1885, his son Emil sold out to the Bayerische Vereinsbank.[13] (It is not clear whether the House of Würzburg sold out simultaneously, or how and when it ceased to operate.)

A student of this family record is struck by the unvarying devotion to the land, by a physiocratic philosophy, which sees in agriculture the source of all wealth, a philosophy typical of the romantic period rather than of the contemporary scene of rising industrialism and capitalism, of which, unwittingly perhaps, the family was an active agent. Their urge towards a 'Return to the Soil' was due, probably, to the yearning of the Wandering Jew, just escaped from the ghetto, to become rooted, 'bodenständig.' It is a way of thinking, a strong sentiment, which had an impact even on the 'footloose' citizen of the world, Maurice de Hirsch, and, incidentally, on a good part of Zionism—an interesting retrogression for Jews, who otherwise were in the avant-garde of modern capitalism.

Of Maurice de Hirsch his secretary, Gustave Held, reported that he had inherited his business acumen from his grandfather, and the pleasure in hunting and in sport in general from his father.[14] And elsewhere Held stated that after his retirement

[12] *Ibid,* p. 195.
[13] The Bayerische Vereinsbank was established in 1868 by the Anglo-Austrian Bank which, as we shall see, closely collaborated with Baron Hirsch in his various enterprises.
[14] See *Monographie du Palais des feu le Baron et la Baronne de Hirsch* (1906).

from business, following the death of his son Lucien, Hirsch had three passions: hunting, law suits, and evasion of income and inheritance tax which he considered unjust.[15]

From his grandfather Jacob, and even more so from his uncle Joel Jacob, he appears to have inherited his entrepreneurial spirit, and apparently also the zest for litigation where he felt wronged, and from his father the enjoyment of life as a country gentleman.

But there was another person who may have had an impact on the formation of his character: his mother.

---

[15] Held's letter to Kohler, March 15, 1910.

CHAPTER II

THE EARLY YEARS: 1831-1855

MAURICE von Hirsch was born in Munich on December 9, 1831, as a third child and second son. Frequently he is spoken of as the oldest son, probably due to the fact that his older brother died at the age of fifteen. There were nine children altogether—a modest figure compared with the seventeen children of his uncle Joel Jacob.[1]

Hirsch's mother, Caroline (Guttel), was the daughter of Zacharias Wolf Wertheimer, the Frankfort banker, a great-grandson of Samson Wertheimer (1658-1724), who as successor of his uncle Samuel Oppenheimer had become the banker (Hoffaktor) of Emperor Charles VI, who appointed him also to be Chief-Rabbi of Hungary. Through his mother Hirsch was related to many of the families, such as von Arnstein, Sulzbach, Bamberger, von Eskeles, Goldschmidt, Kaulla, Königswarter, von Schwabach, who during the 19th century became famous in the history of Austrian and German banking.[2]

As Straus remarks, 'His mother took care that he should have the best instruction in Hebrew and religion.'[3] His teachers, it is said, included the famous Rabbi Isaac Bernays, the 'Chacham' of Hamburg,[4] as well as Dr. Bär of Hamburg, who published a German translation of the *Tephilla,* a prayer book especially prepared for the use of the Hirsch children,[5]

But in spite of his upbringing and the orthodox religious tenets of his mother, Maurice was not religious. It was, as he once allegedly stated, the contrast between precept and practice on the part of one of his early teachers which alienated him from religion, so that he never entered a house of worship.[6]

As Straus says, 'His mind was very alert and quick of comprehension; but he did not have the disposition of a student.'[7] These last words are rather in the nature of an understatement; he had what practically amounts to an aversion to intellectual pursuits. He spoke almost mockingly to Margot Tennant of his son's intellectual interests.[8] To Herzl he said: 'I don't want to raise the general level. All our misfor-

---

[1] Cf. *Stammbaum* in J. Prys, *Familie Hirsch.*
[2] M. Grunwald, 'Deszendententafel der Familie Wertheimer,' *Mitteilungen zur Jüdischen Volkskunde* 1912).
[3] O. S. Straus, *Jewish Encyclopaedia.*
[4] This is questionable, as Bernays was Chief Rabbi of Hamburg from 1821.
[5] Kohler Papers.
[6] *Ibid.*
[7] *Jewish Encyclopedia.*
[8] Margot Asquith, *Memoirs* (Penguin Books ed., 1936), p. 86.

Caroline v. Hirsch

tunes come from the fact that the Jews aim too high. We have too many intellectuals, my aim is to discourage this tendency to push among Jews. They mustn't make such great progress. All the hatred of us comes from this.'[9] And in a letter of November 18, 1892 he declared: 'Je préfère infiniment un enfant capable de travailler le jardin de son père, de joindre ses boeufs et de travailler dans l'étable, à un enfant qui sait lire et écrire.'

Hirsch, brilliant as he was, was a man of action and not of words; intelligent, but not an intellectual. While his above-quoted statements apparently were exaggerations intended to make his point, undoubtedly they show an anti-intellectualism an explanation for which might possibly be sought with Freudian hindsight in the overpowering personality of his mother. Still, according to Sokolov,[10] 'he

[9] Herzl, *Tagebücher* (1921) Vol. I, p. 26.
[10] *History of Zionism* (1922), p. 248

The Early Years

cherished very affectionate recollections of his parents, and particularly for his mother.'

From his father, as we heard from Held, he had inherited his pleasure for hunting, and sports in general, which seems rather unusual for a religious Jewish house.

Of his father, who, as we have seen, preferred the life of the landed gentry to that of the businessman, it was told that, because of his poor judgment in business, old Jacob Hirsch had given an order to the stockbrokers always to reverse Joseph's orders, so as to prevent him from squandering his fortune.[11]

After his Bar-Mitzvah (confirmation) the bright and apparently strong-willed Maurice was sent to Brussels for his further education. We know nothing about his school, or his teachers. While in Brussels, we may assume, he was introduced to the Bischoffsheims, and there may have met their daughter, Clara, who was to become his wife.

At the age of seventeen he returned to Munich. According to Straus, 'while yet in his teens, he took part in several business ventures.'[12] Emden is more specific. 'At the age of seventeen, in 1848, he began to interest himself in railway enterprises and subsequently in speculations in copper and sugar. He always had the means to carry through his schemes.'[13] Emden, however, does not quote his sources, so we remain in the dark about the actual transactions, but remember the interest the family had in the sugar industry, an interest that Maurice seems to have inherited. As we learn from Lucien Wolf that Hirsch's fortune was partly derived from speculation in sugar and copper, it appears that his youthful enterprise in these lines led to an interest maintained over the years.[14] But folklore has it that he, like so many other Bavarian and South German Jewish bankers before and after him, served his apprenticeship in the cattle trade.[15]

In 1851 Maurice returned to Brussels and entered the services of the well-known banking house of Bischoffsheim & Goldschmidt, the latter being a relation of his mother. 'Though only a clerk, he soon became'—so Straus, possibly with some exaggeration, records—'the mastermind of this great international banking house.' And in 1855 he married the daughter of Senator Jonathan Raphael Bischoffsheim.

Hirsch's marriage to Clara Bischoffsheim (Antwerp, 1833-Paris, 1899) brought another striking personality into a family already abounding with impressive figures. About her we find some notes by Sara Straus, the wife of Oscar S. Straus.[16] Her mother's brother, Salomon H. Goldschmidt, had been for many years president of the Alliance Israélite Universelle. Clara had received a liberal education, spoke four languages, and had worked as her father's private secretary; she was well-versed not only in his business but also in his legislative and philanthropic work. Later she

---

[11] Kohler Papers.
[12] *Jewish Encyclopedia.*
[13] Paul Emden, *Money Powers of Europe in the Nineteenth and Twentieth Century* (1936), p. 320.
[14] Article on Hirsch in *Encyclopedia Britannica.*
[15] *Jewish Chronicle,* April 24, 1896.
[16] *Jewish Encyclopedia.*

often acted as her husband's secretary on their frequent trips abroad. It was she who guided Hirsch's interest to philanthropy, particularly to his fellow Jews.

At this point we may appropriately consider the question of Hirsch's financial resources. Emden's remark that Hirsch 'always had the means to carry through his schemes' is probably based on the frequently repeated assertion that, as Straus put it, 'having inherited from his father and grandfather a considerable fortune, which was largely augmented by his wife's dowry, he embarked on railway enterprises on his own account in Austria, in the Balkans and in Russia.'[17] The *Universal Pronouncing Dictionary of Biography and Mythology* (what a wise and fitting combination) likewise speaks of a large fortune left him by his father and a dowry of $20 million.[18] The *Neues Wiener Abendblatt* quotes the amount of his inheritance from his father as five million gulden, the dowry at 20 million francs,[19] while the *Augsburger Abendzeitung* lists these figures as 'approx.' 8 million and 20 million respectively, without giving the currency,—respectable figures in any event. They therefore deserve a closer examination.

Hirsch's grandfather Jacob died in 1841, when Maurice was ten. Jacob left four children, and 26 grandchildren by his two sons alone (almost all born after 1841), not counting those by his two daughters. So Maurice's share could not have been spectacular, though possibly sufficient to start out, at the age of 17 or 18, on some successful speculative ventures which increased the original inheritance.

When his father Joseph died in 1885, Maurice had amassed one of the great fortunes of the age. So, considerable as the inheritance from his father may have been in absolute figures, it was for Maurice, at best, marginal.

Apparently Maurice received from his father not an inheritance, but an 'appanage,' a settlement, in lieu of a share in the paternal firm to which he as the oldest surviving son would have been entitled.

To judge the magnitude of Clara's dowry, it is well to remember that Hannah de Rothschild on her marriage in 1878 to Lord Roseberry received a dowry of £2 million sterling, or $10 million, 'a fortune by the standards of those days even more enormous than it would be now.'[21] So it would probably be more correct to interpret Clara's dowry as having been 20 million francs or $4 million.

But no doubt, under Maurice's management, this fortune, must have been greatly increased between 1855, the year of their marriage, and 1869, when the Oriental Railway venture began.

---

[17] *Ibid.*
[18] 4th ed., 1915.
[19] April 21, 1896.
[20] April 23, 1896.
[21] Cecil Roth, *The Magnificent Rothschilds* (Pyramid ed., 1962), p. 54.

CHAPTER III

THE BISCHOFFSHEIMS

I

MAURICE'S marriage to Clara Bischoffsheim not only gave him a companion and counsellor, particularly in his humanitarian activities, but also provided him in many of his undertakings with the support of one of the most widely ramified and powerful financial organizations of that time. The Bischoffsheims, indeed, were considered second only to the Rothschilds.

Coming to Antwerp from Mayence in 1820, Louis Raphael Bischoffsheim (1800-1873) opened a banking firm which soon flourished, particularly after his marriage to Amalia, the sister of the well-known Frankfort banker Salomon H. Goldschmidt. He was joined in the bank by his younger brother Jonathan Raphael (1808-1880), who moved to Brussels when Belgium became independent. In Brussels, Jonathan in 1841 or 1842, established an investment banking business apparently semi-independent of his brother's firm. The latter known as Bischoffsheim & Goldschmidt, soon had offices in Antwerp, Brussels, Amsterdam and Paris (where Louis Raphael himself settled in 1848), in Frankfort, and, from 1846, in London. Jonathan may also have remained a partner in his brother's bank, which eventually was active in the formation of the great French banks, the Comptoir (Nationale) d' Escompte, the Société Générale pour favoriser le Commerce et l'Industrie, and finally the Banque de Paris et des Pays Bas, into which Bischoffsheim & Goldschmidt and the other family business merged in 1871.

The London house was managed by Louis Raphael's son Henry (1828-1907) who was married to Clarissa Biedermann of Vienna, who won the esteem of Queen Victoria and whose salon became a centre of London Society.[1]

Bischoffsheim & Goldschmidt were active in railway flotations in France and Italy, and joined Hirsch in the East-Hungarian Railway venture. They participated in the first foreign loan to Turkey in 1855 and in 1873[2] together with Société Générale (on the board of which Jonathan Raphael's son-in-law Cahen d'Anvers represented the family interests) the biggest foreign loan to Egypt. In 1872 jointly with the Ottoman Bank, they established a bank in Constantinople; they owned the Banque Franco-Egyptienne in Cairo, as well as the Bank of London and San Francisco.

Between 1866-75 the London house placed many loans to South American states, such as Costa Rica and Nicaragua, quite a number of which defaulted and proved worthless.[3] It became heavily involved in United States railway and Swedish mining

---
[1] Emden, *Money Powers of Europe*, p. 327.
[2] Jenks, *Migration of British Capital*, pp. 317-18.
[3] *Ibid*, pp. 269, 292.

J. R. Bischoffsheim
Hirsch's father-in-law

affairs—mistakes due to Henry Bischoffsheim's 'sanguine and energetic temperament,'[4] which eventually had to be cleared up by Ernest Cassel, another future tycoon who, like Hirsch, had started his career at Bischoffsheim & Goldschmidt. It was not only Bischoffsheim who appreciated what he did; Baron Hirsch, Bischoffsheim's brother-in-law, also admired Cassel's methods.

> The admiration of Baron Hirsch was of more consequence than that of Bischoffsheim. The latter was a man of the old school, enterprising, indeed, and ready to take risks, but no genius. Whether Baron Hirsch deserved to be called a genius is hard to determine, but anyhow he recognised genius wherever he found it. His admiration drew him towards Cassel. He sponsored him in business as well as socially, and promised him that whenever he wanted to do some big thing on his own account he would support him financially to the fullest extent. From that moment Cassel became a power in the City.[5]

In Paris, Louis Raphael was assisted during the years 1853-1866 by Ludwig Bamberger,[6] a son of his sister Amalia, who was to become famous as an initiator and co-founder of the Deutsche Reichsbank, the Deutsche Bank, as a father of the German currency, and as a parliamentarian. Bamberger's younger brother Heinrich, who had married Maurice Hirsch's sister Amalia, steered the Banque de Paris et des Pays Bas during its first difficult years.

---

[4] *Ibid*, p. 269. Cf. G. Myers, *History of the Great American Fortunes* (Modern Library ed., 1935), pp. 577-8.
[5] S. Japhet, *Recollections from my Business Life* (1931), p. 127. As a result of the friendship between the two men, both of whom were intimates of the Prince of Wales, Cassel became one of Hirsch's executors.
[6] Cf. Bamberger, *Erinnerungen* (1899).

While Hirsch apparently served his apprentice years in Bischoffsheim & Goldschmidt under Louis Raphael, it was Jonathan Raphael's daughter whom he chose as his life-companion. In contrast to Bischoffsheim & Goldschmidt, some of whose transactions have been severely criticised by contemporaries as well as by historians, no adverse remark was ever levelled against Jonathan Raphael, who appears to have been a real *grand seigneur,* a 'founding father' of the Belgian economy, who had become a senator, and in whose memory one of the main avenues of Brussels was named.

Jonathan Raphael 'became a personage in the Société Générale de Belgique, prospered as a railway magnate and became part-owner of Société John Cockerill and other metallurgical enterprises in Belgium.'[7] He helped the Banque de Belgique out of an embarrassing situation in 1841; assisted the Minister of Finance in 1847 in converting 5% bonds into bonds of $4\frac{1}{2}$%; and made large advances to the Treasury, was active in the formation of the Banque Nationale and the Union du Crédit de Bruxelles, an initiator of the Crédit Communal and of the Société Nationale des Chemins de Fer Vicinaux, 'une des créations les plus originales.'[8]

He served on the board of these and many other concerns as director or 'administrateur,' and was Treasurer of the Liberal Party. He concerned himself particularly with education and endowed several schools. 'There were few important financial operations during the first half of the nineteenth century in which the name Bischoffsheim does not appear as advisor or participant.'[9]

Was it the twilight of private banking or the lack of suitable successors which induced the Bischoffsheims to merge their firms with one of the banking corporations they had created? This was the Banque des Dépôts des Pays Bas in Amsterdam, of which Louis Raphael was a co-founder in 1863,—with branches at Geneva and Paris, where the actual management resided. Louis Raphael's nephew, Henri Bamberger, in charge of Bischoffsheim & Goldschmidt at Antwerp from 1850-1863, arrived in Paris in 1863 to take over the management of the new concern. After the merger in 1871, first with the Banque de Paris and then with Bischoffsheim & Goldschmidt and Bischoffsheim & Hirsch, Brussels (to which we shall refer later) this bank became the powerful Banque de Paris et des Pays Bas.

In anticipation of the later story, it ought to be mentioned here that 'the first venture of this bank was into the morasses of Spanish credit, directly connected with the restoration of the Bourbons.'[10]

Only one small 'offspring' of this once powerful family concern remained: Leopold, the son of Louis Raphael's partner Goldschmidt, had in 1855 married Regina,

---

[7] Jenks, p. 269.
[8] Chlepner, *L'Etranger dans l'Histoire Economique de la Belgique* (1932), pp. 31-32.
[9] I. Kauch, 'Jonathan Raphael Bischoffsheim,' *Revue de Personnel, Banque Nationale Belgique* (January, 1950), p. 2.
[10] Jenks, p. 269. cf. also: 'The brilliant start of the Banque de Paris et des Pays Bas was based largely on speculation in shares, issues for the Chemins de Fer de la Turquie in 1872.' (A. Pose, *La Monnai* (1942), p. 239). The Banque also held the majority of the shares in the Société Générale. (cf. Hallgarten, *Imperialismus vor 1914* (1963), Vol. II. p. 368). Its Austrian affiliate was the Bodenkreditanstalt, Vienna, which later sponsored the Wiener Bankverein.

Jonathan Raphael's daughter. Their son Maximilian, who in 1878 had married Minna Caroline de Rothschild of Frankfort, opened a banking firm in that city under the name Goldschmidt-Rothschild. For many years this bank had only one account: Maurice de Hirsch.[11] When it was liquidated in 1900, it was still a first-class house.

II

In 1851, Maurice entered the services of Bischoffsheim & Goldschmidt. He was just twenty when he returned to Brussels and he had probably known the families of his new employers socially when he was at school in Brussels. 'Though only a clerk—so Straus records—he soon became the mastermind of this great international house.' The story is told,[12] how an accident drew Bischoffsheim's particular attention to Hirsch. The head of the house had to work out a complicated combination of government finance, but had not succeeded in doing this when young Hirsch, with impressive clarity, modestly offered an ingenious, practical and simple solution. Kohler records this story as related by Baroness de Hirsch herself. After this incident, her father gave his agreement to her engagement with Hirsch, which he had previously withheld.

Although, according to various sources,[13] Hirsch upon his marriage became a partner and manager of the Paris office (where Louis Raphael had resided since 1848), Straus[14] stresses that although he had become the son-in-law of a senior member of the house, he never became a partner, for he was regarded as too enterprising and aggressive in his plans to meet the conservative ideas of the heads of the firm. (Somewhat ambiguous and, therefore, apparently contradicting his own story is Straus's version elsewhere,[15] that Hirsch on his marriage 'became a member of the firm'—whatever that may mean).

These statements on the conservative outlook of the Bischoffsheims do not ring true. Ludwig Bamberger, a nephew of the Bischoffsheims who, living as a political refugee in Paris, served his early years in banking in the Paris office of Bischoffsheim & Goldschmidt reports that both his uncles, in Paris and Brussels, while very conservative in credit operations, fell easy prey to the fantastic investment schemes of unscrupulous promoters.[16] To Bamberger's objections to his uncle lending his ear to such people, Bischoffsheim replied: 'Do you think Rothschild will come to me with business propositions?' It speaks well for the profitability of the banking business at that time, that Bischoffsheim & Goldschmidt could absorb the resulting heavy losses without difficulty.

'After marriage, he was related to both partners of the house who were…always pleased to allow him the use of the organization of Bischoffsheim & Goldschmidt for

[11] Cf. Katznelson (ed.), *Juden im Deutschen Kulturbereich* (1959), p. 753.
[12] *Neue Freie Presse*, April 21 1896.
[13] *Encyclopedia Jüdaica, Jüdisches Lexicon*, etc.
[14] *Jewish Encyclopedia*.
[15] *The American Spirit* (1913), p. 323.
[16] *Erinnerungen*, p. 367.

Maurice de Hirsch

his transactions, and at times also left the management in his hands, but, a little afraid of his all too great spirit of enterprise, they did not take him into partnership.'[17]

It is due to Ludwig Bamberger that we have some characterization of the young businessman.[18] Hirsch, he says, possessed that rare financial genius that succeeds rather through diplomatic skill than through economic reasoning. Under different conditions of birth and antecedents he might have become a famous statesman. To illustrate Hirsch's resourcefulness and shrewdness under embarrassing circumstances, he tells the story of how Hirsch, in 1865, [?] handled the matter of the William Luxembourg Railway, in which Bischoffsheim & Goldschmidt held a substantial interest, but which was then facing ruin: the French railway line, which had operated it hitherto, had dropped it for financial reasons. Hirsch thereupon went to Berlin and drew Bismarck's attention to the strategic and political importance the line could have for Prussia, if operated under a Prussian traffic agreement. With a favorable Prussian reaction in his pocket Hirsch hurried to Paris, where, now under pres-

[17] Emden, p. 333.
[18] *Erinnerungen,* p. 365. Cf. story on p. 26

sure of the government and with its guarantee, the French line entered into a new agreement, advantageous to the Luxembourg company. A victory, though at a price. As Hirsch was to find out in later years, Bismarck never forgave him.[19]

Thus, as we see, Hirsch was active in 1865 on behalf of Bischoffsheim & Goldschmidt though since 1862 or so he had had his own firm, Bischoffsheim & de Hirsch, Brussels, with his brother-in-law Ferdinand as his partner. It was probably this similar sounding name which gave rise to the story of Hirsch having become a partner in the firm of Bischoffsheim & Goldschmidt; but he did apparently cooperate closely with them in some fields, as we have seen. The story seems unfounded also for another reason: after their marriage, so Sara Straus tells us, the young couple moved to Munich, where a year later their son Lucien was born.

In that year, 1856, we find the two family concerns, Joseph Hirsch, Munich, Bischoffsheim (Antwerp), the Bayerische Staatsbank, Rothschild, and others, among the founders of the Bayerische Ostbahn Aktiengesellschaft.[20] It may be assumed that Maurice had not been idle in this transaction, although on his return to Munich he seems to have gone into business on his own. Kohler relates that some of his engagements resulted in heavy losses, which even jeopardized Clara's dowry.

In view of Madame Bischoffsheim's eagerness to have her daughter close by, the young couple moved to Brussels a few years after the marriage, and Maurice acquired Belgian nationality.[21] Here he seems to have done well quickly, because the wife of the Dutch diplomat, Baroness Ainis de Wilmar, in her reminiscences of Brussels in 1862, remembers him 'as a very rich man and a real gentleman.'[22] As the *Neues Wiener Tageblatt* said on April 22, 1896: 'He belonged to the Croesuses of Europe, even before he entered upon his Oriental Railway venture.' But we have no record of his business here, and can only surmise that in the atmosphere of the Bischoffsheim house, congenial to railway financing, he was encouraged in pursuing this old interest of his.

Between 1848, when as a lad of seventeen Hirsch began to interest himself in railway ventures, and 1869, when he obtained the concession from the Ottoman Government which was to turn him into one of the tycoons of the century, he apparently had acquired widespread railway interests, of which, however, only a few are known.

Held[23] speaks of Hirsch's railway interests in Germany, Belgium and Holland; Straus[24] and Sokolov[25] refer to his embarking on railway enterprises in Austria, Russia, and, with most success, in the Balkans, prior to his big venture, adding that they were 'mainly light railways' (feeder lines), and Emden mentions Hirsch's railway constructions in Austria, Hungary, and Russia.[26] These light railways, 'Klein-

---

[19] Cf. Kohler Papers.
[20] Bayerische Staatsbank, p. 175.
[21] Kohler Papers.
[22] Baronne Wilmar, *Souvenirs de Bruxelles* (1862), p. 125.
[23] Monographie.
[24] *Jewish Encyclopedia*.
[25] *History of Zionism*, p. 248.
[26] Ibid., p. 230.

Clara de Hirsch née Bischoffsheim

oder Vicinalbahnen,' of which Sokolov spoke, Hirsch handled alone. Probably they were profitable ventures, particularly when they eventually were sold to the larger trunk lines, or amalgamated into larger networks. During these activities Hirsch became a partner in Bischoffsheim's Société Nationale des Chemins de Fer Vicinaux. It may be assumed that the valuable experience Hirsch gained in these undertakings stood him in good stead when he obtained the Ottoman concession.

CHAPTER IV

THE ASCENT: 1855-1868

THE period from 1855, when Hirsch married and associated himself with the Bischoffsheim family, to 1868 when he obtained the concession for the East Hungarian Railways—only a year before the decisive concession for the Oriental Railways—has hitherto been a blank in Hirsch's history. However, thanks to Jacquemyns[1] some information had incidentally come to light on Hirsch's activities during this period, and we now know some of the sources, archives and publications from which further information can be obtained.

The conflicting statements as to whether or not Hirsch became a partner in his father-in-law's firm can now be at least partly explained. We now know that in about 1862 he, together with his brother-in-law Ferdinand, opened the Banque F. Bischoffsheim-de Hirsch in Brussels,[2] although, according to Jacquemyns, a Belgian *Almanac du Commerce et de l'Industrie pour* 1862 lists only Hirsch's name among the bankers.[3] But Jacquemyns tells us that in 1860 Bischoffsheim-de Hirsch had delegated a certain F. de Brouwer to serve as general manager of the Russian Moscow-Riazzan Railway. The bank which acted for the Langrand enterprises was absorbed in 1870 by the Banque de Dépôts des Pays-Bas, a Bischoffsheim interest, which in turn, in 1872, merged with the Banque de Paris into the Banque de Paris et des Pays-Bas.[4]

Who was Langrand-Dumonceau? Few people today remember his name, although the collapse almost a hundred years ago of his financial empire, comprising 32 banks, mortgage, insurance and real estate concerns, was an international event of no less a magnitude than that of the Kreuger scandal in more recent days. Still, his name does not appear in the *Encyclopedia Britannica* or in Chambers. Only the *Grosse Brockhaus* (1932) records, 'Langrand-Dumonceau, count, Belgian adventurer, born Vossem, died Rome 1905. Of low background, became bank clerk, won clergy by his plan to 'christianize' capital, established numerous private and public companies, made a count by Pope Pius IX; 1870 collapse of concerns, escaped to Brazil. Delay

---

[1] Jacquemyns, *Langrand-Dumonceau, promoteur d'une puissance catholique*.
[2] Letter from Banque de la Société Générale de Belgique to the author, November 14, 1963.
[3] Jacquemyns, Vol. I, p. 225.
[4] *Ibid.*, Vol. II, p. 187. It was the increasing magnitude of the very enterprises sponsored by the private bankers, and their financial requirements, exceeding their sponsors' resources, which brought about the formation of the large joint-stock banks, which were often promoted and controlled by these private bankers, cooperating or merging with the new giants.

It took some time for this process to affect the provincial centers which financed local rather than international enterprise. Thus it was only in 1885 that Hirsch's paternal house sold out to the Bayerische Vereinsbank.

of proceedings caused political scandal. Sentenced in absentia to 15 years' imprisonment.' The question as to criminal intent has never been quite clear. Sir Henry Drummond Wolff, the British diplomat who was the liquidator of Langrand-Dumonceau's International Land Credit Company, London, states that no illegality could be proved and that sound schemes often fail in incompetent hands.[5]

Hirsch, who collaborated with Langrand in various schemes, and was joint manager with him of one company, was as Bizemont wrote to Langrand on November 11, 1866 '...sceptical of you; he believes you won't stop living with illusions. He thinks you have a lively imagination, and an optimism that does not know obstacles, and which may land you in success or the reverse.'[6] The bankers F. Bischoffsheim, M. de Hirsch and Jacques Ervers Oppenheim testified to the excellence of Langrand-Dumonceau's ideas, and to his inability to carry them out.[7]

As Jacquemyns states, 'The collaboration between the "financier catholique" and the scion of the "haute banque israélite" did not bring about the union of which mutual sympathy and friendship form the basis. Though together in important business, each is always on the defensive for his own interest.'[8] And the final break came over the Turkish railway concession.

It is, to say the least, surprising to see the protagonist of a 'christianized capital', of Catholic versus Jewish and Protestant financial organizations, collaborating closely throughout with those whom he claims to fight. As Jacquemyns puts it, there is the 'Thesis' and the 'Hypothesis': 'La Thèse: en principe, opposition irreductible aux banquiers juifs—La Hypothèse: vu les contingences financières, collaboration avec eux.'[9] Anyhow, there was hardly a name among the 'haute banque juive' of that time, such as Rothschild, Goldschmidt, Bischoffsheim, Königswarter, and Hirsch, which did not appear as in some way connected with one of the Langrand enterprises.

Hirsch's first connection with Langrand seems to have been the Viennese Insurance Company, 'Der Anker,' founded on December 1, 1858, when Hirsch, on behalf of a Belgian group, subscribed 172 out of 500 shares, and joined the board.[10] Barely a year later, on August 8, 1859, Langrand-Dumonceau and Hirsch together formed the Association Générale d'Assurances. Mercier, a former Belgian Minister of Finance, Langrand-Dumonceau's mentor and collaborator, had for a long time pressed Langrand-Dumonceau to collaborate with Hirsch and his associates. 'It is good to have a Crœsus behind you.'[11] The Association Générale was a holding company, an investment trust for shares of insurance companies, established by Langrand-Dumonceau. Their total number was to be six, and some, such as 'Der Anker,' still survive today.

Of the large nominal capital of 20 million francs in 10,000 shares, only 4,000 shares

---

[5] *Rambling Recollections* (London, 1908), Vol. II, p. 370.
[6] Jacquemyns, Vol. III, p. 27.
[7] *Ibid.*, Vol. III, p. 49.
[8] *Ibid.*, Vol. I, p. 229.
[9] *Ibid.*, Vol III, p. 495.
[10] *Ibid.*, Vol. I, p. 178.
[11] *Ibid.*, Vol. I, p. 14.

were subscribed and half paid up, by two groups, one consisting of Jonathan Raphael Bischoffsheim, Maurice de Hirsch, and Henri Bamberger, the head of Bischoffsheim, Antwerp; the other of Mercier and members of the Langrand group. Langrand-Dumonceau and Hirsch became joint managing directors, the former responsible for external affairs and trading in shares, the latter for accounts and internal administration.[12] All the books of the company were kept at Hirsch's house.[13]

The company was originally established for a period of seven years, but was liquidated in September, 1863. There was always the conflict 'between financial orthodoxy and the New Men.'[14] Hirsch was critical of Langrand-Dumonceau's over-optimism in wanting to cash in profits before they were earned. Mercier, too, advised prudence,[15] but meanwhile enjoyed the taste of the 'forbidden fruit.' In 'Der Anker,' too, Hirsch pressed for a reduction of the excessive general expenses. Mercier supported him. Though he did not completely trust his new Israelite associate, he thought it wise to pacify the powerful banker.[16]

At about this time, Association Générale bought shares of the Royale Belge, another Langrand-Dumonceau creation, at high prices, bringing the quotation from 300 to 750, and Bischoffsheim and Hirsch were accused by other board members of selling their holdings at these high prices.[17] Usually Mercier, Langrand-Dumonceau and Hirsch speculated on joint account, buying and selling at rising prices and cashing substantial profits. When prices fell, they unloaded the shares to Association Générale.[18]

The first new concern formed by Association Générale on September 3, 1860, was the Vindabona Mortgage Insurance Company, Vienna. Langrand-Dumonceau, Mercier and Hirsch together subscribed to 471 shares and formed a syndicate with 280 of these. By the time the company was finally constituted, each of the three members of the syndicate had netted a profit of 100,000 francs,[19] and substantial management and directors fees were paid.[20] But the profits of the company did not come up to the optimistic expectations and promises that had been made in order to drive up quotations. Hirsch advised a merger with 'Der Anker,' Mercier and Langrand-Dumonceau opposed it. Mercier believed Hirsch 'wishes to enjoy the chestnuts pulled out of the fire by others.'

Finally, on August 21, 1863, Langrand-Dumonceau formed the Banque de Crédit Foncier et Industriel, of which he became the sole manager. The bank absorbed the Association Générale, with profit to the latter's shareholders, but not to those of the

---

[12] *Ibid.*, p. 222.
[13] *Ibid.*, p. 239.
[14] *Ibid.*
[15] *Ibid.*, p. 235.
[16] Letter from Hirsch to Langrand-Dumonceau, dated Munich, September 29, 1860, cited by Jacquemyns, Vol. I, p. 192.
[17] *Ibid.*, pp. 126-127.
[18] *Ibid.*, pp. 216-217.
[19] *Ibid.*, p. 269.
[20] *Ibid.*, p. 252.

new concern.[21] Thus ended the first collaboration of Langrand-Dumonceau with the 'haute banque internationale juive,' an experience which had been, perhaps, not without friction, but profitable to both parties, though not quite so to the outsiders.

It was this company, the Industriel, which by the end of 1866, was in serious trouble. By paying excessive prices for real estate in Hungary and Spain, and over-generous salaries and commissions to hangers-on, it had lost its entire capital and its precarious position endangered also its associate concern, The International Land Credit Co., which had a substantial holding of shares in and advances to Industriel.[22]

Hirsch, consulted by Langrand, recommended immediate radical steps to avert the catastrophe, but was sceptical about the idea that Count Bisemont and he should become joint-managers with Langrand.[23] Other Langrand concerns, too, were heavy losers, and the members of the London board of the International Land Credit Co. started to resign, one after another, under all kinds of pretexts.[24]

Meanwhile, in order to finalize a promising business with the Italian government, Industriel had to deposit £500,000 in Italian bonds as a performance guarantee. Unable to put up this deposit, Langrand approached Bischoffsheim & de Hirsch, who provided £375,000. On the liquidation of this affair a dispute arose and Langrand, on the advice of his advocates, submitted Industriel's claims to court on July 9, 1867. Bischoffsheim & de Hirsch responded on July 19, by submitting to court a request to interrogate the claimant on 'facts and figures', which would have brought into the open the embarrassing situation of the company. The board, therefore, hastened to have the dispute settled by internal arbitration, although Langrand seems to have had a strong case.

Jacquemyns comments: 'the whole affair shows that Hirsch wanted to help Langrand in certain difficult circumstances, but he made himself paid for these services and did not hesitate, if necessary, to defend his case with arguments which threatened the downfall of the promotor of a catholic financial power. The latter, subsequently, went on more than ever to vituperate the Jews. But that did not prevent him from maintaining close business relations with Hirsch. *Business First.*' Bischoffsheim & de Hirsch, Jacquemyns adds in a documented footnote, did undertake a great number of stockmarket transactions for Langrand and his concerns.[25]

But prior to this step, Langrand-Dumonceau, in order to feed the mortgage insurance companies with business, had established mortgage banks everywhere. The first, the Banque Hypothécaire Belge, (November 16, 1863), which was also authorized to operate in Austria, had the more immediate purpose to absorb the ailing Vindabona Company. Hirsch and Bischoffsheim were slow in making up their minds. So Langrand-Dumonceau closed the deal with Dechamps and de Decker; both, like Mercier, were Catholics and former cabinet members, 'thus making this new institution a purely Catholic power.'

---

[21] *Ibid.,* p. 239.
[22] Jacquemyns, Vol. IV, pp. 82-87, 250-255.
[23] *Ibid.,* Vol. IV, pp. 82-83.
[24] *Ibid.,* Vol. IV, pp. 87.
[25] *Ibid.,* Vol. IV, p. 251.

This did not prevent Langrand-Dumonceau from continued collaboration with Jewish high finance. In 1863, he and Hirsch were again together in the 'Algemeene Maatschappij vor Handel en Nijverheid,' (Société Générale de Commerce et d'Industrie), Amsterdam, a kind of Crédit Mobilier, founded and headed by Mendel. On the board was 'Maurice de Hirsch auf Gereuth, de la maison Bischoffsheim et de Hirsch,' together with other notables, many connected with other Langrand-Dumonceau enterprises.[26] One of the early deals of the company, which proved to be troublesome, was the purchase of 7,000 debentures of the Rustchuk-Varna Railway Company.[27] The British contractors for the Rustchuk-Varna railway in Rumania, Messrs. Pete, Betts & Crampton, bought material in Belgium, paying for it with bonds of the railway company, which were sold to the Belgian public through a Bischoffsheim syndicate.[28]

The first subsidiary was the 'Maatschappij tot Exploitatie van Staatspoorwegen,' which in 1863 obtained the concession to operate the Dutch State Railways. The most influential member in the management of this concern was one of Hirsch's men, the Belgian Florentin de Brouwer de Hogendorp, a former vice-president of the Belgian Railways Permanent Commission, and Member of Parliament, whom Hirsch had sent to Russia in 1860 to manage the Moscow-Riazzan Railway,[29] and who was now called back.[30] He was 'intimately involved in the "tripotages bancaires," the underhand banking transactions—"of the House of Bischoffsheim-de Hirsch, and particularly those referring to the Compagnie des Chemins de Fer Liègeois-Limburgois"'[31] with which the Dutch railway company entered into agreements on the extension of lines from Liège to Eindhoven.

The Société Anonyme du Chemin de Fer Liègeois-Limburgois was another Hirsch-Langrand-Dumonceau partnership. Hirsch was chairman of the board; another member, in addition to Langrand-Dumonceau, was Van der Elst (Cyrin), an entrepreneur from Brussels, whom we shall encounter again in connection with the Ottoman concession. The bankers were obviously Bischoffsheim-de Hirsch.

By being on the board of the Société Générale, and by having his protegé, Brouwer, on the management of the Dutch railway company, Hirsch, as chairman of the Société Anonyme, allegedly knew how to make all agreements between them to the exclusive benefit of the company in which he had the principal interest.[32] Jacquemyns

---

[26] *Ibid.*, Vol. I, p. 174.

[27] *Ibid.*, Vol. II, p. 183.

[28] Jenks, *Migration of British Capital*, p. 177.

[29] The Moscow-Riazzan Railway, according to J. N. Westwood (*A History of Russian Railways* (1964), p. 43) was the only bright spot in the generally grim railway situation of the mid-'sixties (in Russia). It had Belgian support (i.e., Hirsch?). Originally (1856) planned to reach the Volga at Saratov, financial difficulties enforced a more moderate programme. But in the hands of a certain 'crafty von Derviz' the company obtained the right to raise the necessary funds by a bond-issue in Germany, so that Derviz did not need to sell the shares in the prosperous concern which he appropriated for himself (and his Belgian backers?).

[30] Jacquemyns, Vol. II, p. 187.

[31] H. P. G. Quack, the Secretary of the Dutch State Company (1863), later Professor of Economics and Governor of the National Bank, quoted by Jacquemyns.

[32] Jacquemyns, Vol. II, p. 187.

here repeats Mercier's remark that Hirsch, 'likes to enjoy the chestnuts pulled out of the fire by others,' and adds that this was neither the first time, nor the last, that he deserved such reproach. The Société Générale eventually collapsed; its manager, Mendel, escaped without being prosecuted. At one time its shares were traded at a high premium; Langrand, selling 6,000 shares through Bischoffsheim-de Hirsch, made a profit of 300,000 francs on one sale alone.[33]

Time and again we find Bischoffsheim-de Hirsch mentioned as paying agent for Langrand-Dumonceau concerns. And when a Papal loan was offered in 1864, Langrand-Dumonceau had to use the Jewish bankers Bischoffsheim-de Hirsch to place it on the stock exchange of Brussels and Paris at 75-77, owing to the indifference of the Catholic circles in buying on tap.[34]

Langrand, always hunting for railway concessions, had to spend large amounts on 'commissions', for which he lacked the funds and had to be aided by backers such as Bischoffsheim-de Hirsch.[35] He finally obtained the Ottoman Concession (1868) and the one for the Kaschau-Oderberg railway (1867). He claimed to have brilliant offers for the sale of the Ottoman Concession. The Anglo-Austrian Bank and Hirsch asked him for participation in these two concessions.[36]

From Jenks we learn that 'at the end of 1868, the East Hungarian Railway concession was awarded to a syndicate comprising Charles Waring and the "Austrian" Baron Hirsch, backed, there is reason to suppose, by the Belgian Bischoffsheim. The Anglo-Austrian Bank organized the company with a glittering board of Hungarian notables. Eighteen thousand tons of rails were ordered in England, twelve locomotives in Bavaria, thirty-five passenger coaches in Switzerland, and five hundred freight cars in Austria.'[37]

Jacquemyns refers to an important railway line in Transylvania (Eastern Hungary), from Arad to Karlsburg, under construction in 1867 by the Belgian firm of Riche frères, the concession for which was held by a consortium of which Bischoffsheim-de Hirsch were members.[38]

The Anglo-Austrian Bank, which, as we shall see later on, always closely cooperated with Hirsch, played a considerable role in the crisis years of the Langrand empire, 1866-1870, and advanced him large sums. It took over from him the Kaschau-

---

[33] *Ibid.*, p. 297.
[34] *Ibid.*, Vol. III, p. 538.
[35] *Ibid.*, Vol. IV, p. 218.
[36] *Ibid.*, p. 305.
[37] *Migration of British Capital*, p. 177. Although Jenks cites the pamphlet by Ludwig Schönberger (*Die Ungarische Ostbahn-Ein Finanzskandal*, Vienna, 1873) in his bibliography, he does not make use of this apparently biased and unreliable source. Schönberger, editor of the *Börsen und Finanzberichte*, states in his violent attack that the concession was granted in December, 1868, to Charles Warren (Jenks correctly speaks of Waring, a member of the well-known British firm of railway builders), a concession hunter and swindler, a 'Strohmann,' i.e., a dummy for Bischoffsheim-de Hirsch, or rather for 'Türkenhirsch' himself, backed by the Anglo-Austrian Bank, whom he accuses of practically owning the leading Viennese daily *Neue Freie Presse*.

On the first board, so we incidentally learn here, there served Ralph Earle whom we shall meet again later on.
[38] Vol. IV, p. 223.

Oderberg railway and helped Hirsch to snatch ('enlever') the Ottoman concession from Langrand-Dumonceau.[39] Hirsch obtained the concession for the Oriental railway from Vienna to Constantinople in 1869. 'He was reputed to hold Count Beust, the Austrian Prime Minister, in his hand. And his interests were a factor in Balkan diplomacy for two decades.'[40]

In a previous chapter the story was told of young Hirsch's diplomatic skill in negotiating the agreement of operating the William-Luxembourg Railway. The original charter for this line had been obtained by a Belgian banker, Adolphe Prost, who went bankrupt in 1858. The company was reorganized under the management of Jules Van de Wynkele, a former commercial director of the French Eastern railways, and under an operating contract with that line, apparently the very one negotiated by Hirsch.[41]

In 1863 the French Eastern succeeded in obtaining from the Netherlands State Railway Operating Company, then in financial difficulties, an operating lease on the Liège-Luxembourg (Liège-Hasselt-Eindhoven) railway, a Belgian company controlled by French capital. The French Eastern agreed on the condition that it might run its trains over the Dutch State lines from Eindhoven to Rotterdam, i.e. through-trains from Basle to Rotterdam.[42]

The French Eastern was controlled by Crédit Mobilier (with whom J. R. Bischoffsheim had collaborated in the construction of the Chemins de Fer de Midi). Was it just by accident that Hirsch, by his negotiations with the Eastern in 1858 and again in 1863 had brought about an almost 'continental' through-service or was this part of a larger idea, of a greater concept? However before coming to his larger scheme, we should like to complete the record of Hirsch's business interests, meager as it is and probably apocryphal as many of the stories seem to be.

There are no indications that Hirsch speculated regularly on the stock exchange, although after the 'Krach' in 1873 he acquired cheaply a substantial parcel of Viennese municipal bonds and profited handsomely on their subsequent redemption in full.[43] Hirsch also kept away from the copper trust (Kupferring), but on at least one of the periodical downturns of this commodity he bought stock in distress and profited on its recovery.[44]

Enthusiastic biographers have ascribed to Hirsch large-scale ownership of industrial enterprises reportedly employing 'hundreds of thousands' of workmen. This was generally assumed to be the main source of his wealth, particularly since it was his ambition to make each of his enterprises as efficient and profitable as possible.[45]

At the end of the 'seventies he owned a *brasserie* near the Paris Opera, where he

---

[39] Jacquemyns, Vol. II, p. 69.
[40] Jenks, p. 269.
[41] Rondo E. Cameron, *France and the Economic Development of Europe,* 1800-1914 (1961), p. 310.
[42] *Ibid.,* p. 311.
[43] *Neues Wiener Tageblatt,* April 22, 1896, and *Neue Freie Presse,* April 21, 1896.
[44] *Neue Freie Presse,* April 21, 1896.
[45] *Neues Wiener Tageblatt,* April 22, 1896.

sold his Bavarian beer.[46] He was upset when the manager of this *brasserie* retired because he had made enough money. 'What, he does not want to make another million?' was allegedly Hirsch's shocked reaction. In addition he allegedly owned extensive real estate in France, Bavaria, Austria, Hungary, Galicia, Turkey, Palestine[47] and the Americas,[48] including the lands of his settlements.

---

[46] *Ibid.*
[47] *Neues Wiener Abendblatt,* April 21, 1896.
[48] *Ibid.*

CHAPTER V

THE STORY OF THE ORIENTAL RAILWAYS

PRE-HISTORY

By an agreement of April 17, 1869, and by the firman of October 7 of that year, Baron Hirsch obtained a concession from the Imperial Ottoman Government for the construction and operation of a railway network in European Turkey which was to connect Constantinople with Vienna, and from there with the rest of Western Europe.[1]

It is by this Turkish enterprise that Hirsch suddenly emerges as a European figure, and that his nickname 'Türkenhirsch' becomes proverbial on the Continent.[2] It was a gigantic enterprise for those days and it was to keep Hirsch fully engaged for almost two decades. It needed courage to undertake it: European Turkey in those days was largely a *terra incognita,* visited only by daring explorers whose records still make fascinating reading.[3] Little experience had been gained in dealings with the Porte, which just a decade before had begun to enter the Western orbit.[4] Hirsch in 1869 certainly could not anticipate that his enterprise would embroil him in diplomatic intrigues on a continental scale or that his project would become deeply entangled in the sensitive 'Eastern Question' which kept the chancelleries of Europe alert for many years.

Thus, as one historian sees it, the Oriental Railways became the Rhinegold of a new Nibelungen Song: 'the overture of which were Hirsch's speculations,' which, continuing in the Baghdad Railway scheme, ends with the conflagration of Europe as the 'Twilight of the Gods.' It is a story of 'cunning, force, robbery and deceit.'[5]

Hirsch as a businessman, a man of action rather than ideologies, could not foresee that his ventures would become an international *cause célèbre* in an act almost symbolic for what was to become known as the Age of Imperialism. He only saw the

---

[1] See G. Young, *Corps de Droit Ottoman* (1906), Vol. IV, pp. 66-103; Charles Morawitz, *Les Finances de la Turquie* (1902), pp. 375-385; A. du Velay, *Les Finances de la Turquie* (1903), pp. 250-260; R. M. Dimtchoff, *Das Eisenbahnwesen auf der Balkan-Halbinsel* (1894), p. 25.

[2] *Neue Freie Presse,* April 21, 1895.

[3] F. von Kanitz, *Donau, Bulgarien und der Balkan.* 3 vols. (1877); E. de Laveleye, *The Balkan Peninsula* (1887).

[4] Hitherto only two smaller railways had been built in this area: one, a 60 km. line from the Danube to the Black Sea, from Tchernavoda to Küstendje (Constanza), built by an English group led by Thomas Wilson under a concession of 1856, had been in operation since 1860; the other, from Rustchuk to Varna, 224 km., also from the Danube to the Black Sea, concessioned in 1861, was opened in 1866. Its concessionary, too, was an Englishman, William Gladstone. The first line was sold, after the Congress of Berlin, to the new Rumanian government (1882), the latter to the Bulgarian government (1888). In neither case were the relations with the Turkish government 'satisfactory.' (cf. R. M. Dimtchoff, p. 7 ff.).

[5] G. W. F. Hallgarten, *Imperialismus vor 1914,* Vol. I, p. 212.

advantage for an expanding world economy that would accrue from such an undertaking, and thereby to the undertaking itself.

The idea of a rail connection with the East was not entirely new. In 1856, the year which, with the end of the Crimean War, saw Turkey's entry into the 'Concert of Europe', Palmerston, who opposed the idea of a Suez Canal, wrote that the real communication with India must be a railway to Constantinople, and from there through Asia Minor to the Persian Gulf: 'a provision of the Baghdad Railway in 1856 is creditable to any man of seventy-two.'[6]

But he was not the only one to think along these lines. For instance as Cameron shows[7] the railway age had hardly dawned when Michel Chevalier (the Pereires' friend and fellow Saint-Simonian), in his outline (written in 1832[8]) of a 'Mediterranean System' which would link Europe, Asia and Africa by means of railways, steamships and the Suez Canal, envisaged a railway from the Channel to the Persian Gulf. In the 1840's and 1850's French, English and Austrian promoters offered to build a railroad from Constantinople to Belgrade. The Ottoman Government, however, looked upon such projects as on the offer of a Trojan horse, and not quite without reason.[9] Only after 1855, encouraged by her Western allies in the Crimean War, did Turkey actually solicit proposals from European entrepreneurs. The first results of these endeavours, the railways linking the Danube with the Black Sea, did not serve as encouraging examples. Incidentally, the Bischoffsheims placed the bonds of the Rustchuk-Varna line, given in payment for Belgian supplies.[10]

But there were more ambitious schemes, too. In 1857 we find the British engineer Layard working on a link between Constantinople and the West, but only in 1865 did the Porte approve of a layout of the line which was practically identical with the one later on embodied in the actual concession, signed in 1868.[11] Meanwhile negotiations with the Crédit Mobilier, carried on by the engineer, Galant, bore no fruit.[12]

It was not until almost fifteen years after the Crimean War that the Rothschild-financed South-Austrian and the Pereire-sponsored Austrian State Railways extended their lines to Croatia and the Banat of Temesvar respectively, and now both companies took an interest in a further extension of their lines to Constantinople. But they could not agree between themselves on the construction and operation of one common line, the Rothschilds favoring Sisek in Croatia as the junction, the Pereires preferring a route via Hungary-Belgrade. And so the Ottoman time limit ran out.

To these projects, all of which had originated in England or France, was now added Austria's direct interest. She had begun to feel the effects of competition of cheap

---

[6] Philip Guedalla, *Palmerston* (1926), p. 386.
[7] Cf. references in R. E. Cameron, *France and the Economic Development of Europe,* 1800-1914, p. 320.
[8] *Ibid.,* p. 134.
[9] Cf. also Dimtchoff (p. 17) who quotes Engelhardt, a member of the Serbian regency council, as saying to the French Consul: 'Les Chemins de fer vaincront la Turquie, ils feront plus pour le solution du problème oriental que les canons rayés.'
[10] Jenks, *The Migration of British Capital,* p. 177.
[11] Dimtchoff, p. 20.
[12] Cf. Dimtchoff, p. 21.

sea freight from England, France, and Belgium on her traditional Turkish market and hoped to be able to meet this competition by the proposed rail-line.[13] Bismarck backed such ambitions partly for similar economic considerations, partly to direct Austria, which after her defeat by him in 1866 had ceased to be the leader of the German Empire, towards a 'civilizing function' in the East. Had not Metternich said that the Orient started at St. Marx, Vienna's eastern gates?

But it was von Beust who, as Austria's Minister of Foreign Affairs and Chancellor, became the main protagonist of the project. In 1867, on the visit to Vienna of the Sultan Abdul Aziz and his Grand Vizier Fuad Pasha, the Sultan was persuaded that such a railroad would help cement his Balkan dominions. On Beust's recommendation, a concession was, on May 31, 1868, granted to the Belgian firm Van der Elst & Cie., Entrepreneurs, an associate of Langrand-Dumonceau, to build the railways of Roumelia (Bulgaria), i.e. through the Balkans to Constantinople. A letter from von Beust to Langrand-Dumonceau indicated that the recommendation was to compensate the financier for losses he had suffered in Austria.[14]

However, not only von Beust backed the project. With him and after him there were Andrassy and all the diplomats and consuls who formulated Austrian foreign policy. And they had the blessings of all the European powers except Russia. Von Beust's steadfast support of the project seems to have caused some comment.

It is interesting to read, in this context, a book anonymously published in Germany

---

[13] *Neue Freie Presse,* April 21, 1896.

[14] According to Rechberger, *Geschichte der Orientbahnen* (unpublished Ph. D. dissertation, University of Vienna, 1958, p. 48) the concession of 1868 had been granted to the Belgian 'banking firm' van der Elst with whom were associated the Paris Credit Foncier, and a London consortium. The group was headed by Count Zichy, of Vienna.

It is not known whether van der Elst sold the concession to Langrand-Dumonceau (with whom, as we know from Jaquemyns, he was associated in various deals) or was his 'agent' and 'front' from the very beginning of the concession. But Langrand-Dumonceau negotiated in Turkey, apparently as van der Elst's representative, until, finally, he openly claimed ownership of the concession.

Count Zichy had some years earlier made proposals for a Serbian railway (cf. Dimtchoff, p. 5). Under the proposed concession, the concessionary was to obtain mining rights for a strip of two German miles wide along the railway track, for quarries, bricks and other materials, particularly coal. Should no coal be found, Serbia was to supply wood at a fixed price. (This point should be remembered as a precedent for the subsequent, so widely criticized, rights which Hirsch obtained on the Bellova forests).

Langrand apparently started out insufficiently financed. He seems to have obtained from Hirsch the promise for an advance of 500,000 francs on completion of the work on the railway to Tshermedje, and on the basis of this promise borrowed heavily. When Hirsch did not pay, (because the work was not completed) Langrand defaulted. After the collapse of the Langrand concern, Beust invited the Porte to send representatives to Vienna to open negotiations with alternative entrepreneurs. Daoud Pasha came and contacted two interested groups, the Anglo-Austrian Bank and the Consortium Creditanstalt, Banque Impériale Ottomane, Crédit Foncier, and Südbahn. While Daoud was negotiating in Vienna, Sady Pasha made progress in Paris with Bischoffsheim-de Hirsch, and their associates, the Anglo-Austrian Bank and the Südbahn.

Serbia, hearing of the Paris agreement which provided for a track favoring the Südbahn, hurried to grant a preliminary concession to the Staatsbahn jointly with the Franco-Austrian and the Franco-Hungarian Banks, and a consortium of the Viennese bankers Oppenheim, Todesco and Dumba.

Later Staatsbahn was ready to join in Ottoman Concession, jointly with Eichthal and Mallet, and approached Alphonse de Rothschild.

Oriental Railways

in 1870 'by an Englishman', who, it was learned later, was Baron Henry de Worms, from 1895 Lord Pirbright.[15] Worms, who in 1864 had married the daughter of the Viennese banker, Baron Tedeschi, in this book emphasizes that Beust's policy was identical with that of Britain, particularly concerning the trans-continental railroad, eventually leading to Basrah, which was to make Vienna the center between East and West. This was to help more than agreements on paper to strengthen Turkey against Russia, to bring European civilization and progress to Turkey, and to improve the position of the Slavs in the Balkans. However, at the time of the discontinuation of Hirsch's concession in 1872 by the anti-Western Mahmoud Pasha, who preferred a Russian connection, German nationalist writers such as Dehn and Dimtchoff claimed that England was supporting Mahmoud's anti-Austrian policy.[16]

ENTER BARON HIRSCH

'Tout le monde içi demande une concession, l'un demande une banque, l'autre une route. Çe finira mal,—banque et route—banqueroute.' This *bon mot* of Fuad Pasha,[17] was to be proved true in the history of the Balkan railways more than once. Soon after the signing of the concession it became clear that the concessionaries were unable to live up to its terms; their backer, Langrand-Dumonceau's concern, had collapsed. On April 12, 1869 the concession was cancelled, and five days later, on April 17, a new agreement was signed with Baron Hirsch.

When it had become clear towards the end of 1868 that the original group was unable to fulfil the terms of the agreement, the Turkish Minister of Public Works, Daoud Pasha, was ordered to go to Europe to find another group or person to take up the concession. Only one had the courage to do so: the banker in Brussels, Baron Hirsch.[18]

Somewhat different is the story as told by Sokolov and Straus.[19] According to them Hirsch had acquired the concession from a banking firm in Brussels, evidently Langrand-Dumonceau, which had been unable to carry through the project, and then went to Turkey successfully to renegotiate the terms of the concession. Emden, who deals at length with the history of Langrand's International Land Credit Co. and its bankruptcy, claims that Hirsch had bought the concession with other valuable assets from the company's liquidator and receiver, Drummond-Wolff.[20] It was indeed, a peculiar deal: the remnants of that tremendous concern, which with the Vatican's backing had tried to build a Catholic financial power, in opposition to

---

[15] Anon. ('Von einem Engländer'), *Die Oesterreichisch—Ungarische Monarchie und die Politik des Grafen Beust* (1870), pp. 153-155.
  Worms in later years translated into English the memoirs of von Beust, whose policy was anti-Prussian and pro-Western. We find Pirbright, together with Hirsch, in a photograph depicting the leaders of Anglo-Jewry in 1895 (see p. 82).
[16] Cf. Dimtchoff, p. 34.
[17] Kohler papers.
[18] Morawitz, *Les Finances de la Turquie*, pp. 375-415; du Velay *Les Finances de la Turquie*, p. 251.
[19] N. Sokolov, *History of Zionism;* O. S. Straus, *Jewish Encyclopedia*.
[20] Emden, *Money Powers*, p. 320. cf. *Times*, April 22, 1896.

that of the Protestants and Jews, was sold by a Protestant of Jewish origin to a Jewish financier!

Here one cannot help asking why Hirsch should have bought a worthless concession, already declared in default and due to be cancelled. Did he consider the possession of even so doubtful a contract a 'pied à terre' for a re-negotiation with the Porte? An answer to that question is probably given in the fifth volume of Jacquemyns, who indicates that Hirsch had snatched ('enlever') the concession from Langrand with the assistance of the Anglo-Austrian Bank.[21]

The idea of a rail connection between Vienna and Constantinople, according to the *Oesterreichisches Biographisches Lexikon,* had preoccupied Hirsch in Paris. A Viennese paper claimed that he learned about the Turkish project in Paris, referring to the Bischoffsheim connection there as having kept him informed.[22] But knowing, as we do, of Hirsch's close connection with Langrand, we may presume that he was informed of all the developments in Brussels, where the Van Elst concern was also located. Another Viennese paper[23] claimed that Hirsch obtained the concession because of his Turkish connections. (Bischoffsheim and Goldschmidt had placed the first Turkish loan in Paris in 1854 and jointly with the Ottoman Bank had established the Crédit Générale Ottoman.)[24]

In any event, we may give credit to the story that, while Daoud was negotiating in Vienna with the Rothschilds and the Bodenkreditanstalt, he was, according to the Kohler Papers, approached by Hirsch through an emissary, 'a young Belgian named de Laveleye and the Belgian Minister in Vienna.' De Laveleye who was soon to become well-known in Europe as an economist, was apparently another one of the bright young men around Hirsch, like Cassel and Morawitz.[25] Thus Hirsch seems

Anselm Freiherr von Rothschild

---

[21] Jacquemyns, Vol. II. p. 69 (see footnote 14 on p. 30).   [22] *Neue Freie Presse,* April 21, 1896.
[23] *Neues Wiener Abendblatt,* April 21, 1896.   [24] Jenks, *Migration of British Capital,* p. 177.
[25] Emil Louis Victor de Laveleye (1822-1892), noted Belgian economist; Christian-Socialist of the school of François Hult. Interested in the revival and preservation of small nations.
Karl (Charles) Morawitz (1846-1914). After serving with Banque de Paris and Ottoman Bank joined the Oriental Railway Co. as financial director in 1871. In 1885 moved to Vienna. From 1893 served on board of Anglo-Austrian Bank and was its president from 1906.

to have secured the concession independently and, though he later obtained the backing of the Austrian government, not through Austrian interests initially, as is often claimed. Dimtchoff, basing himself on letters by Baron Hirsch, published by one of his secretaries, Herr Budde, in the 'Kölnische Zeitung' of March, 1883, claims that Daoud had been bought by Hirsch; that he soon thereafter had to resign and take refuge in Western Europe, never to return to Turkey.[26]

Obituaries recall that Hirsch originally wanted to carry out the project in co-operation with the Austrian State and the Southern Austrian Railways. They refer to the sensation created by Hirsch's conferences with the Viennese financiers, whose jealousy of one whom they considered an upstart prevented an agreement.[27] In Paris Hirsch had already been in contact with Pereire, the French director (governor) of the Austrian State Railway who had been favorably inclined, when the company's president Baron Wodianer[28] arrived from Vienna to oppose such collaboration. He allegedly rebuked Hirsch in parables: 'I have a house in the heart of Vienna, you want to build one in a distant suburb and suggest that we should be equal partners in that joint property!' and 'You invite us out on a drive. You want us to sit in the back, while you hold the reins in your hand. If we go, it is we who must hold the reins and see where we go.'[29] *Si non è vero, è ben trovato*. It would have been quite in line with Wodianer's 'typical Viennese *bonhommie*' thus to snub Hirsch.

Somewhat mystifying is another story told by the same source: Daoud Pasha apparently, on his previously mentioned mission in Vienna, tried to win Wodianer for the project by offering him a cadeau of five million francs, which Wodianer courteously declined. Whereupon Daoud exclaimed 'You want to be a businessman and reject five million francs?!'

'If it had depended upon the late Baron Hirsch,'—so *The Times* sums up this period[30]—'his connection with Austria-Hungary would probably have been of still greater benefit for the Monarchy.' His first idea as to the construction of the Balkan railways, through which he mainly acquired his enormous fortune, was to extend the Southern and State lines connecting them with the Turkish system and thus establish a direct connection with Constantinople under Austrian auspices. He failed however to receive the necessary support in Vienna for the plan, owing, it is said, to local jealousy, and was obliged to take another course and enter into negotiations with the Ottoman government. After he received the concession from the latter, notwithstanding the advantages which were offered to Austrian commerce by the new railroad (which had their headquarters in Vienna) and the circumstances that Hirsch and most officials were Austrian subjects, the project met with considerable opposition in the country.'

[26] Dimtchoff, p. 33.
[27] *Neue Freie Presse*, June 21, 1896.
[28] Moritz Wodianer, son of the Budapest wholesale merchant and banker Samuel Wodianer (and allegedly grandson of an old-clothes merchant in Pressburg), had changed his religion before changing his residence. He refrained from social intercourse with Jews, but his accent and appearance betrayed his Jewish origin. (Sigmund Mayer, *Wiener Juden* (1930), p. 292.
[29] *Neues Wiener Tageblatt*, Finance Section, April 22, 1896.
[30] April 22, 1896.

'TÜRKENHIRSCH'

The concession of April 17, 1869 provided for the construction of a main line from Constantinople to the Austrian frontier via Adrianople (Edirne)—Philippopolis (Plovdiv)—Sophia—Nish—Pristina—Sarajevo to Sisak and four connecting branch lines: one from Adrianople to Dedeagatch (Alexandroupolis) on the Aegean Sea; a second from Philippopolis to Burgas on the Black Sea; a third from Nish to the Serbian frontier; and a fourth from Pristina to Salonica,—altogether about 2,500 km, though calculations of the subsidy, as we shall see, were based on 2,000 km.

The concession covered both the construction of this railway network in European Turkey and its operation. Simultaneously Hirsch negotiated with the South-Austrian Railway concerning a lease by the company as operator of the entire network for the duration of the concession, i.e. 99 years. The construction was expected to take five to seven years.

To cover his costs the concession-holder was assured: a) of an annual rental of 14,000 francs per completed kilometer, payable by the Ottoman government, for the entire period of 99 years, to be paid out of a state loan, and b) an annual rental of 8,000 francs per kilometer from the operator. This rental of 22,000 francs (14,000 + 8,000) represented 11 per cent on 200,000 francs, which was the expected construction cost per kilometer. During the construction period, however, the government was obliged only to provide the land for the railroad at a cost of 10,000 francs per kilometer. In view of the particularly high cost of construction of the line over the difficult terrain of Bosnia, the Turkish government agreed to pay three-fourths of the construction cost in excess of 250,000 francs per kilometer.[31] The government was to share in the profits of the enterprise. The concession apparently also provided for the exploitation of natural resources along the railroad, such as minerals and forests, on a royalty basis.

As the South-Austrian Railway company claimed to be able to pay the 8,000 francs only out of the operation of the completed railroad, the government undertook to pay this amount during the expected construction period and the three years thereafter, i.e. over a period of 10 years. For this purpose the government was to create a guaranty-fund in semi-annual cash installments over ten years, totalling 65 million francs. During this transition period the operator was to receive out of gross income the first 12,000 francs per kilometer for his costs, and one fifth of the excess, with four-fifths going to the government. Any income exceeding 22,000 francs was, both in the transition period as well as thereafter, to be divided between the operator (five-tenths), government (three-tenths), and the concessionary (two-tenths).

But, contrary to initially promising progress, and after the approval of the agreement by a general meeting of the South-Austrian Railway, in Paris on July 18, 1869, negotiations failed unexpectedly in August owing to divergent views within the board, as it was said,[32] but actually owing to the resistance of the Viennese House of Roth-

---

[31] Kohler Papers; Dimtchoff, p. 25.
[32] Morawitz, *Les Finances de la Turquie*, p. 375.

Oriental Railways

schild.[33] Thus the entire concession was suddenly jeopardized. But Hirsch quickly rose to the occasion and, in this first crisis of the still unborn new enterprise, showed his full determination, courage and resourcefulness, of which he was to be in need, again and again, throughout its history.

Originally Hirsch did not wish to engage in operating the railroad, a business to which he did not want to devote his life;[34] but now he was forced to act. With the aid of his friends, and particularly of Paulin Talabot, another of the great railway tycoons of that time who had carried on the negotiations on behalf of the South-Austrian Railway, a new operating company was formed by January 1870, the Companie Générale pour l'Exploitation des Chemins de Fer de Turquie d'Europe, with head offices in Paris, until its conversion into an Austrian company in 1879. Its shareholders were the Société Générale, Paris, the Anglo-Austrian Bank, Vienna, Banque Bischoffsheim-de Hirsch, Brussels, Baron Hirsch and some others. Talabot,[35] director-general of the Paris-Lyon-Mediterranée Railway, (1862-1882) and active on the board of the South-Austrian Railway, was chairman and negotiator with the Turkish authorities on behalf of the new company which entered into the rights and obligations originally provided for in the agreement with the South Austrian Railway. Its other board members were: Edouard Hentsch and Edward Blount, on behalf of the Société Générale; Count Kinsky, a co-founder of the Anglo-Austrian Bank,[36] and Baron Hirsch. Blount, like Talabot, belonged to the founders of the South Austrian Railway in 1858; Hentsch was an occasional associate of the Bischoffsheims in banking enterprises.[37]

At the same time Hirsch organized another company, the Société Impériale des Chemins de Fer de la Turquie en Europe (in brief, the construction company) to which he assigned his concession. He became its president, the Comte de Chatel its vice-president; the other directors were Messrs. K. Mayer, Seidler and Springer of the Anglo-Austrian Bank, and Florentin de Brouwer de Hogendorp, president of the Société d'Exploitation des Chemins de Fer Nederlandaise, a Hirsch interest. Mr. Cezanne, former chief-engineer of the South-Austrian Railway, was director-general.[38] And W. v. Pressel, the famous builder of the South-Austrian Railway, was to be its chief-engineer[39] and prepared the first designs.[40] Max Springer was a co-founder of

---

[33] Idem., *50 Jahre Geschichte einer Bank* (1913), pp. 15 ff.
[34] Kohler Papers.
[35] Paulin François Talabot (Limoges, 1799-Paris, 1885), pioneer in French railways and maritime communications, also in exploitation of iron deposits in Donetz Basin. Financier with interests in Société Générale.
[36] The Anglo-Austrian Bank, which, as we have seen, had collaborated with Hirsch from the very beginning of the venture in all its phases, and had acquired a substantial interest in the company, 'impatient to realize its profit on the construction business, had sold its shares in the early years of the enterprise.' (Morawitz, *Geschichte einer Bank*, p. 19.)
[37] Concerning the personalities associated with Hirsch here, and their activities, cf. Cameron, *France, and the Economic Development of Europe, 1800-1914*; also 'Ein Jahrhundert,' Creditanstalt Bankverein, Vienna 1957; on Blount, cf. Emden, *Money Powers* and Blount, *Memoirs* (1902).
[38] Cf. A. du Velay, p. 252.
[39] Kohler Papers.
[40] The connection between Pressel and Hirsch requires still further examination. The claim that Hirsch,

the Austrian Bodenkreditanstalt in 1863, and of its offspring, the Wiener Bankverein, in 1869, i.e. a collaborator of the Pereires, while Talabot and Blount were 'anti-Pereires'—an interesting re-alignment of forces. Karl von Mayer, a writer (*Schriftsteller*), director of the Anglo-Austrian Bank, is reported to have been an intimate friend of Hirsch's.[41] Each of the two companies was registered with a capital of 50 million francs of which one quarter was paid up.

If Hirsch's in-laws were not prominent in either of these companies this may be explained by the story that Bischoffsheim (Louis or Jonathan?) declined all but a nominal participation claiming that this business would make its entrepreneur either a beggar or a multi-millionaire, and it was doubtful which.

—AND 'TÜRKENLOSE'

In view of Turkey's poor finances the country's undertaking to pay an annuity of 14,000 francs per kilometer for 2,000 or 2,500 kilometers had to be ensured. The market was saturated with Turkish government loans, which were traded at heavy discounts. Hirsch therefore agreed with the Ottoman government on a novel form of finance, namely bonds carrying a low interest of 3 per cent, payable over 99 years,

---

starting his Oriental Railway venture, engaged Pressel as chief-engineer or planner of the line, in about 1870—is partly borne out by E. M. Earle (*The Great Powers and the Baghdad Railway* (1924) p. 18), who mentions that the famous German railway engineer, W. v. Pressel, had been retained in 1872 (?) to elaborate an overall railway plan for Turkey (by the Turkish Government?), and a few years later took a prominent part in the construction of the Trans-Balkan lines of the Oriental Railways. This would mean that Pressel came in at a later stage of the construction.

Different altogether is Friedjung's version of the story. He writes: 'The honourable and upright man [Pressel], did not allow himself to be used as a tool by the finance-baron Hirsch, and left Constantinople in order to find in Vienna a backing for his scheme to cover the Balkan Peninsula with railways. But he passed away, and 'ein Grösserer erst' [sic] a bigger man [than Hirsch] eventually realized his ideas.' (See H. Friedjung, *Zeitalter des Imperialismus* (1922), Vol. I, p. 249).

It is difficult to understand who this 'Grösserer' was, since Hirsch in fact built the railways. After reading a more recent account on von Pressel and his plans, (Joan Haslip, *The Sultan—The Life of Abdul Hamid II* (1958), pp. 202-203), one might argue that this 'Grösserer' was the Emperor William II, in whom von Pressel had found an 'enthusiastic disciple' of his plan for what was to become 'one of the most famous and disputed railways in the world,' viz. the Baghdad Railway. It thus seems that the notorious German nationalist fervour of this Austro-Jewish historian may have led him astray.

Friedjung's implied stricture of Hirsch, however (and also Haslip's remark that Hirsch, by 'distributing baksheesh in the right quarters had succeeded in obtaining a concession with kilometer guarantees so absurd that the Rumelian railways had come down in history as one of the major financial scandals of the nineteenth century,' are contradicted by no less an authority than von Pressel himself. Writing in 1902 on his plans for building railways in Asiatic Turkey, he complained about the (false) prejudices concerning the cost of railway construction in Turkey. 'I still remember the debates I had to carry on in 1869-1870, on this point. The financiers who had come to the aid of Baron de Hirsch *(one of the rare men of initiative at that time)* in his enterprise of the Rumelian Railways, imbued with wrong notions, were forced to yield in the face of the evidence.' (Wilhelm v. Pressel, *Les Chemins de Fer en Turquie d'Asia,* (1902), p. 35. In other words, Hirsch had shown that one could build railways in Turkey at a reasonable cost.

It is surprising that authors such as Friedjung and Haslip, writing after 1902, should have overlooked this most authoritative evidence.

[41] *Neue Freie Presse,* April 21, 1896.

but participating in bi-monthly drawing of prizes, three of them as high as 600,000 francs. These highly speculative bonds were soon known as 'Türkenlose.'

The Ottoman government issued to Hirsch 1,980,000 such bonds of a nominal 400 francs each, totalling 792 million francs but at a 'market value' of 32.15 per cent, i.e. equivalent to 128.50 francs per bond,[42] a total of 254.43 million francs (or 264.25 million, i.e. 129 francs per bond.[43])

To become marketable the bonds had to be introduced, first of all, on the Viennese stock exchange, a step vehemently opposed by the Austrian Finance Minister, Baron von Brestel. But finally Chancellor von Beust, who was, as we have seen a strong protagonist of this railway project won out, and the permission was finally granted. The rumor then had it that Beust had received 800,000 francs for this service.[44]

For the sale of the bond Hirsch now formed an underwriters syndicate. The composition of this syndicate is variously described by du Velay and Bouvier, as follows:

DU VELAY	BOUVIER
Société Générale	Société Générale
Anglo-Austrian Bank	Anglo-Austrian Bank
Crédit Général Ottoman	Wiener Bankverein
Banque de Crédit et de Dépôts des Pay Bas[45]	Haute Banque
F. A. Seillière	
Sulzbach, Goldschmidt & Co.	
Max Springer	
Oppenheim	
Albertis & Co.	
Emile Erlanger & Cie.	
The Ottoman Bank refused to participate.	

Bouvier's mentioning of the Wiener Bankverein seems to be due to the identification in his sources of this institute with its founder, Max Springer, whom du Velay mentions, while the various private bankers are grouped together as 'Haute Banque'.

Both the Crédit Général Ottoman and the Banque de Crédit were Bischoffsheim affiliations. The latter Bank was due to emerge, two years later, as Banque de Paris et de Pays Bas, in the formation of which Baron Seilliére of the private banking firm F. A. Seillière, a long time director of Crédit Mobilière participated with the largest shareholding.[46] With Sulzbach, Goldschmidt and Oppenheim there existed, apart probably from joint business interest, also family ties.

---

[42] Bouvier, *Le Crédit Lyonnais*, Vol. II, p. 688.
[43] Cameron, *France and the Economic Development of Europe*, p. 321.
[44] Benedikt, *Die wirtschafliche Entwicklung in der Franz-Josephs Zeit* (1958), p. 121.
[45] A. Pose (*La Monnaie*, p. 239), refers to the brilliant start of Banque de Paris et des Pay-Bas, which was largely based on speculation in rents, issues for the Chemins de Fer de la Turquie in 1872.
[46] Cameron, p. 197, n.

In March 1870 Hirsch sold to his syndicate at 155 francs the first series of the bond issue of 750,000 bonds, which was offered to the public at 180 francs. Due to a spectacular propaganda campaign in which advertising expenses probably included editorials as well, the issue was a full success, in spite of the outbreak of the Franco-Prussian War. Subscriptions were accepted at twenty-eight centres in Europe, but not in London or Paris.[47]

From Bouvier's story[48] we learn that the Société Générale which had underwritten 100,000 bonds, ceded 3,750 bonds to Crédit Lyonnais as sub-underwriter, for which they received 581,000 francs, and, on liquidation of the syndicate in January, 1872 paid Crédit Lyonnais 59,045 francs as their share in the commission. Thus it appears that Hirsch netted not 155 francs but about 141.50 francs per bond.

In September, 1872 the second series, this time of 1,230,000 bonds, was offered through the same syndicate, but at lower prices: 150 francs to the syndicate, 170 francs to the public. Crédit Lyonnais again received a quota of 3,750 bonds, but its head, Henry Germain, wanted more. He pressed Hirsch's brother-in-law, Ludwig Bamberger of 'Paribas' (Banque de Paris et Pays Bas), and received a total of 18,075 bonds, of which he kept 1,800 for himself. But times were bad, the public bought only 460,000 out of 880,000 bonds under-written and Crédit Lyonnais was left with 16,275 bonds. In July, 1873, 742,000 unsold bonds were with the syndicate. By October the price at Paris was down to 130. Crédit Lyonnais disposed of its parcel in time at a loss of 279,000 francs.

In Vienna, in January, 1872, prices did not exceed 143, but after having reached a quotation of 183, they tumbled down, after the 'Krach' at the end of 1873, to 115, slowly recovered to 130 and kept on this level until the suspension of payments by Turkey in 1875.[49]

What were Hirsch's proceeds from these issues? Rejecting all exaggerated estimates Morawitz rated them at approximately 290 million.[50] Cameron, calculating that Hirsch obtained the bonds at 32 per cent (i.e. 253.44 million) and sold them to the syndicate at 38.5 per cent, arrived at an additional profit of 40 million for Hirsch and of 50 million for the syndicate;[51] i.e. about the same figure as Morawitz. If, however, as seems from Bouvier's figures, Hirsch received only slightly more than 140 francs per bond, his net proceeds would have been approximately 280 million. This would also be more in accord with du Velay who stated that Hirsch received 30 per cent of the syndicate's profits.[52] But Hirsch himself is said to have admitted a cash yield of only 254,545,454 francs![53]

When Turkey in 1875 suspended payment on her debts, the Türkenlose were likewise affected. Some bond-holders tried in a Viennese court to make Hirsch personally

---

[47] du Velay, p. 255.
[48] Vol. II, pp. 577 ff.
[49] du Velay, p. 255.
[50] *Les Finances de la Turquie*, p. 381.
[51] Cameron, p. 321.
[52] du Velay, p. 255.
[53] Dimtchoff, p. 43.

responsible for payment; they lost their case. Payments were resumed later within the general settlement of the Ottoman public debt. And some of the big prizes drawn of 600,000 francs, of 300,000 francs, and so on were surprisingly never collected.[52]

'MAHMOUDOFF'

The funds were now available, but even before this stage all steps had been taken to ensure the efficient and rapid progress of the construction, apparently with the Anglo-Austrian Bank's interim finance.[54] The construction of the first part of the lines proceeded during the years 1870 and 1871 under most difficult conditions. The outbreak of the Franco-Prussian war not only caused financial worries, but created difficulties in the provision of experts and skilled manpower and in the delivery of materials ordered in France. In the Turkish provinces the population was hostile towards the 'giaours,' the unbelievers, while in Bosnia an open revolt broke out against the Ottoman government. Still determined and undiscouraged, Hirsch went on with the work. Construction had started at the eastern seaboard: from Constantinople to Adrianople, from the Aegean coast to Adrianople and from Salonica to Uskub. By 1872 some of the lines were already in operation. By the time the second bond issue was put on the market 387 kilometers were in operation, 102 ready for operation and 661 under construction,—altogether 1,150 kilometers.[55]

Now an event took place which seemed to endanger the entire enterprise, but Hirsch's determination and diplomatic skill averted a calamity and exploited a potentially dangerous situation to advantage.

In September 1871 the Western-oriented Grand Vizier Ali Pasha, who had favoured the rail link to Western Europe, died. His successor, the reactionary Mahmud Nedim Pasha, who had been appointed under the influence of the Russian ambassador Ignatieff, preferred links with Russia via Rumania to rail connections with 'unbelieving' western Europe via Austria. Ottoman attempts to cancel the agreement with Hirsch failed, but a revision was eventually agreed upon, mainly due to the endeavours of Ralph Earle, a former member of the British parliament and a onetime secretary to Lord Beaconsfield.[56] Apparently Earle had replaced Paulin Talabot as agent for the operating company. Under the revised agreement the lines completed or under construction were to remain isolated and disconnected, and the total kilometrage was to be reduced to 1,179 kilometers, according to the table on p. 40.

The construction of a line from the Austrian frontier through Bosnia was originally a condition for admitting the Türkenlose to the Vienna exchange, presumably because Austria had an eye on these Turkish provinces which in 1878 in fact came under Austro-Hungarian administration, but this condition was apparently dropped.

---

[54] Morawitz, *Geschichte einer Bank*.
[55] du Velay, p. 256.
[56] Ralph Anstruther Earle (Edinburgh, 1835—Soden, Germany, 1879), secretary to Disraeli while Chancellor of Exchequer, 1854; M.P., 1859 and 1865-68; Parliamentary Secretary to Poor Law Board, 1866-67.

In	From	To	Kilometers	Total	Completed
WESTERN TURKEY	Constantinople	Adrianople	318		
	Adrianople via Philippopolis, Sarambey	Bellova	243		June 1873
	Adrianople	Dedeagatch (Aegean Sea)	149		Aug. 1873
	Tirnova	Jamboli	106		Dec. 1874
				816	
MACEDONIA	Salonica	Uskub	244		Aug. 1873
	Uskub	Mitrovitza	119		
				363	
				1,179	
BOSNIA	Banjaluka	Doberlin	102		Dec. 1872
				1,281	

Turkey preferred the connection via Bosnia not only because it facilitated the control of this rebellious, difficult part of the Ottoman Empire, but because they feared that a rail connection between Serbia and the West would strengthen the tendency of this autonomous state towards complete independence. In this context, it is interesting to read in Count Mijatovich's *Memoirs of a Balkan Diplomatist*[57] of his intervention in Vienna, in 1869, on behalf of the Serbian government, in order to have Serbia substituted for Bosnia on the railroad from Constantinople to Vienna. He was told that Russia, unable to prevent the granting of the concession, had persuaded Turkey to insist on the link via Bosnia, hoping that the physical difficulties there would frustrate the completion of the project. Mijatovich told Andrassy and Beust that in Bosnia, Serbian bands would during the night destroy what was constructed during the day. Andrassy resented this threat, which he considered almost a declaration of war, but Beust counselled patience and advised Mijatovich privately that the concession with Hirsch should and indeed would, be modified in this manner, with Austria's co-operation.

To appreciate the political scene at that time, we must remember that Serbia's relations with Austria were more friendly than with Russia, which backed Bulgaria. One may wonder to what extent Hirsch was aware of this secret diplomacy and influenced by it in his decision to start work at the harbours. At the same time he had built part of the Bosnian line, from Banjaluka to Oberlin, which was completed and in operation at the end of 1872. But as the Ottoman government did not proceed with a connection to the Austrian or the Macedonian line, the operating company handed the Bosnian line back to the Ottoman government in January 1876. After a few months of Ottoman operation, the line was abandoned.

Under the new agreement Hirsch and his construction company were no longer concessionaries but contractors to the Ottoman government. The agreement with

[57] Kohler Papers.

the operating company was taken over by the Ottoman government. The proceeds of the bonds remained with Hirsch in payment of the construction costs and loss of profit.

The rights for the exploitation of natural resources along the line were cancelled but replaced in specific instances such as the forests of Bellova, by individual concessions.

Now Hirsch, as even his friends admit,[58] was not too unhappy to be forced into this settlement. It relieved him of building the most difficult and costly part of the line, that through Bosnia. But it is wrong to say, as Cameron does, 'that Hirsch was unable to fulfill his obligations,'[59] or, as Feis states, that 'the task began to frighten Baron Hirsch's company [which] asked for and obtained a revision of its concession.'[60] The initiative for the change had come from the Ottoman government, as is admitted even in the anti-Hirsch publications.

The Ottoman government had, under the revised agreement, undertaken the completion of the lines as envisaged in the original agreement (with the exception of the Bosnian junction?). Among other minor changes in the agreement, the concession for the operating company had been reduced from 99 to 50 years.

Between August 1872 and December 1874 all five sections of the railroad were completed. At Adrianople on July 17, 1873, the Grand Vizier officially opened the Constantinople-Bellova line and Hirsch's brother James, who represented him on this occasion, was decorated by the Sultan.[61] All the lines entrusted to Hirsch were completed, but not those which were to be built by the Turks. Thus the railway project meanwhile consisted of three isolated lines.

Dimtchoff claims that Mahmoud Pasha, according to his own confession before an Imperial Court at Constantinople, had received a baksheesh of L.T. 400,000 from Hirsch upon the revision of the concession agreement on May 18, 1872.[62] He was sentenced on this count, but pardoned by the Sultan.

Blaisdell tells us that Mahmoud Nedim had been Grand Vizier in 1871 (the new agreement was signed in 1872) and was succeeded by Midhat Pasha who, in fixing the blame for the disappearance of certain funds, traced their peculation to his predecessor.[63] This information did not prevent Mahmoud's re-appointment in 1875.

Ignatieff, appointed Russian ambassador to Constantinople in 1864, had a thorough knowledge of eastern psychology combined with remarkable ability and unscrupulousness; he was known to the public as 'Father of Lies.'[64] As Poulgy tells us, Mahmoud was so completely under Ignatieff's influence that he was popularly known as 'Mahmoudoff.'[65] Ignatieff, who 'aimed at the destruction of Turkey by every means,' advised Mahmoud in 1875 on the suspension of debt services, osten-

---

[58] Morawitz, *Geschichte einer Bank*, p. 18.
[59] Cameron, p. 322.
[60] H. Feis, *Europe, the World's Banker, 1870-1914* (1930), p. 295.
[61] *Times*, July 2, 1873.
[62] Dimtchoff, p. 35, citing *Augsburger Allgemeine Zeitung*, Nos. 197 and 211 of 1873.
[63] W. H. Blaisdell, *European Financial Control in the Ottoman Empire* (1929), p. 79.
[64] Sir Henry G. Elliott, *Some Revolutions and Other Diplomatic Experiences* (1922), p. 186.
[65] G. Poulgy, *Les Emprunts de l'Etat Ottoman* (1915), pp. 66-67.

sibly a patriotic, anti-Western act, knowing well that any such suspension of payments would be equal to a declaration of state bankruptcy with consequences even more serious for Turkey.⁶⁶

'Türkenhirsch':Photomontage cartoon,c. 1875

Hirsch was thus twice affected by Mahmoud's acts: in 1871, by the cancellation of the 1869 concession; and in 1875, by the suspension of payments on his 'Türkenlose'.

Of particular interest is the interpretation which Friedrich Engels gave to this turn of events. Writing from London on April 21, 1882, to Eduard Bernstein, Berlin, with reference to an article in the *Kölnische Zeitung* which was, apparently, critical of Hirsch, he explains:

'Mohamed Nadin Pasha, like Mahomet Dauat Pasha (the Sultan's brother-in-law),

---

⁶⁶ 'Mr. Morgan Foster, the Director General of Ottoman Bank, a man whose repute is beyond cavil, hearing rumours that the Turks were about to repudiate, called on the Grand Vizier to learn the truth. He was assured upon the Minister's honour, that the Government had no idea of doing anything of that kind. The very next day the Decree of Repudiation was issued, and Foster declared that he had trustworthy information that it had already been signed by the Grand Vizier himself, before he visited that functionary.'
Sir Edward Pears, *Forty Years in Constantinople,* 1873-1915 (1916), p. 54.

Oriental Railways 43

is Russia's principal paid agent in Constantinople. As the Russian Poliakoff, who also wanted the Turkish railway concession, could not get it (because the Russians could not simultaneously start war against Turkey and exploit (einseifen) the Turks), the Russians were eager to obtain such conditions for the Austrian Hirsch, the only competitor, backed as he was by Austria, as would make him, and Austria with him, hated in Turkey, and prevent Turkey from getting a continuous railway network. Any financial weakening of Turkey, relatively speaking, was in any event to Russia's advantage. Thus Nadim made his bargain, Hirsch paid him for selling him Turkey, and the Russians paid Nadim again for his very readiness to sell Turkey. The Russian diplomacy does business on a large scale, not with the competitor's envy of a petty trader, and thus, if they can't help it, they even permit an opponent like Austria to gain an apparent or temporary advantage, and still draw an advantage therefrom themselves.'

—AND POLYAKOFF

Nevertheless, Hallgarten (according to whom Hirsch's transactions were responsible, in the last resort, for the entire German Orient misfortune,[67] but who had to admit that Hirsch, in spite of the for him advantageous change in the original concession, was apparently more the 'Geschobene' than the 'Schieber,'[68] the pushed one rather than the pusher) still accuses Hirsch of having only too willingly fallen in with Mahmoud's Russian inspired policy. Others even went so far as to accuse Hirsch of having inspired Mahmoud in this direction, and not to Mahmoud's disadvantage. As Dimtchoff claims, Mahmoud received a handsome bribe for it.[69] According to Hallgarten this policy was influenced by 'a close relative' of Hirsch,[70] the Russian railway tycoon Polyakoff, who was, Hallgarten alleges, Hirsch's brother-in-law, and who also had an interest in blocking the westward completion of the railway.[71]

---

[67] *Imperialismus vor* 1914, Vol. II, p. 345.
[68] *Ibid.*,Vol. I. p. 230.
[69] p. 41.
[70] Vol. I, p. 235.
[71] *Ibid.*, pp. 237-238. If, as Hallgarten insinuates, Hirsch had really worked hand in hand with his 'close relative' Polyakoff, the exponent of the Russian interests, the Russians would not have objected to Alexander of Bulgaria as 'under the influence of Hirsch and the Austrians,' as W. Langer claims. (*European Alliances,* 2 nd edition (1962), p. 340).

The L. S. Polyakoff, to whom we are first introduced by Hallgarten, who, together with Baron Gunzburg, wanted to open a bank in Bulgaria, was not the railway tycoon, nor a relative of Hirsch's, as Hallgarten erroneously states, but his younger brother, Lazar, (1842-1912), who had a bank in Moscow and other banking interests, as well as industrial interests in Persia, where he also built roads. He was the head of the Jewish community in Moscow, while his oldest brother Jacob, (1832-1919), a banker and philanthropist, headed the Petersburg community. He became a Vice-President of Hirsch's Jewish Colonization Association. Both were knighted Russian and Persian barons. (*Cf. Jüdisches Lexicon*).

It was the second brother Samuel (1836-1888), who became one of the great railway entrepreneurs. In his *History of Russian Railways* (1964), Westwood tells us how Polyakoff, "a former plasterer in Kiev,' in 1861 presented himself 'in full Jewish regalia' to the Moscow-Yaroslavl Company, asking for a rail transport contract, which was refused (p. 70). By 1862 he was coal supply contractor for the pumping

This family connection, to which Hallgarten attributes 'the highest importance,' was however, slightly different. Polyakoff was not Hirsch's brother-in-law, but the father-in-law of his younger brother James, who on April 29, 1880 married Zenaide, daughter of the *Kaiserlich Russischen Wirklichen Geheimrats* Samuel Polyakoff.[72] Thus the family connection was not as close as Hallgarten claimed, nor did it as yet exist at the time under review.

The non-completion of the line to the Austrian border was also in the interest of English trade in the Balkans, and, therefore, Hallgarten asserts, favoured by Hirsch because of his intimacy with the Prince of Wales. Hallgarten ignores the fact that Hirsch met Edward for the first time in 1886, i.e. fourteen years later. (These examples indicate the questionable reliability not only of Hallgarten, with his 'numerous assumptions, assertions and combinations,' as Wilhelm Treue puts it,[74] but of much of the anti-Hirsch literature, which even sound historians all too often use uncritically.)

Hallgarten likewise accuses Hirsch of using the non-completion of the line as a pretext for withholding from the Turkish Government the annual payment of 8,000 francs per kilometer under operation by the Betriebsgesellschaft,[75] and of (fictitiously) claiming damages for roads and port installations, which in spite of their contractional obligation the Turks had not built. He was, therefore, interested in the continued *status quo,* in which he was helped by the continuous revolts in the Balkans, (1875-1878). It does not seem to occur to Hallgarten, that the earnings of the completed line would have been considerably higher than the fee withheld. It was for this reason that Hirsch persisted in his efforts, throughout the years, and particularly at the Congress of Berlin, 1878, to achieve this completion, which Turkey actually had

---

stations of Moscow. Contracts for highway construction in the Moscow area brought him into contact with Count Tolstoi, Minister of Posts & Telegraphs, who entrusted him with the post offices on his estates. Soon he had the means to become the contractor for the Ryazan-Kozlov Railway. (Hirsch was interested in the Moscow-Ryazan Railway!). This brought him together with the engineer-speculator Von Merk for the Kozlov-Vononef line. Derviz, Hirsch's 'partner' refused to associate with them. Tolstoi apparently was holder of a parcel of 'baksheesh' shares.

Later on (p. 91), we find 'the notorious Polyakoff' transferring a rail-supply contract to Hughes. He is partner in the Orenburg, the Urals and, by 1876, in the Fastov Railways, together with Varshavski and Yubovain, and only internal dissension prevents them from securing control over the Vistula Co. as well.

The *Jüdisches Lexicon* mentions that Kozlov-Voronezh and the Orel-Grydz and the Kursk-Kharkov-Asov lines as among those built by him, as well as the Bendery-Galatz Railway. This was apparently the only line of his approaching the Balkans.

He was the founder of the Moscow Agricultural Bank and of the Agricultural Fund, which was the origin of ORT. He had been offered the Finance Ministry of Pobjedanoszev, if he would accept the Christian Faith.

Indicative of the intellectual climate of that time is a letter of 1868 by Kleinmann, the emissary of the recently founded Crédit Lyonnais to his principals, describing Polyakoff (Jacob?) as... 'a typical example of a Russian parvenu, bourgeois entrepreneur, a specimen of the capitalist class in formation, a former butler to an elevated personage, held in low opinion by the Society of the Capital, a type one does not consort with... but whom it is useful to know if one wants to invest money.' (Bouvier, *Crédit Lyonnais,* p. 739).

[72] Gotha, *Gen. Taschenbuch der freiherrlichen Häuser* (1887).
[73] Vol. I, p. 233.
[74] In 'Tradition' 4 (1965), p. 147.
[75] Vol. I, p. 230.

Oriental Railways

taken upon herself, and which was no longer his obligation. But these efforts were to Hallgarten just double-faced manoeuvres,[76] though it is not clear what purpose they should have served.

A TURKISH-BUILT RAILWAY?

Those who hoped that Turkey would now proceed, in accordance with the revised agreement, to build the missing rail-links, were to be disappointed. It was not due to Turkey's financial difficulties that she failed in doing so; rather, the nature of the Ottoman regime prevented the completion of such an undertaking. This is clearly shown in contemporary evidence.

Emil de Laveleye, the noted Belgian economist, during the 1880's reported from his trips in the Balkans (Rumelia):

> From time to time we came across traces of the railway, commenced ten years ago, to connect Sofia with the line Sarambey-Constantinople; in the ravines were the piles of half-finished bridges, or stones lying on the ground, also embankments and cuttings furrowed by the rains, even some rails buried under the weeds and shrubs. It is a lamentable history which shows plainly the impotence of Turkish rule and the causes which have hindered reform.[77]
>
> Having quarrelled with Baron de Hirsch, the Porte decided to finish the railway system by an agent under its own control. A Pasha was appointed. He found the post pleasant and lucrative, but the work did not advance; so he was recalled and replaced by another Pasha, who followed his example. The government was tired of the expense, and the work was given up, after it had cost more than half of what was required to finish the line.

The Viennese explorer of the Balkans, F. v. Kanitz, had a similar story to tell a decade earlier of a 'most recent illustration of the Asiatic regime,' when he came across the collapsed understructure for a railway line, started a few years before by Midhat Pasha, (Grand-Vizier, 1872-1874), then governor (*Vali*) at Rustchuk.[78] Midhat intended to connect Plevna, the centre of a rich agricultural district, by an American-type rail-track with the Danube, on the banks of which a new town, 'Sultanieh,' was to be built as a trade centre at the Osem inflow into the Danube. Twenty thousand peasants from the districts of Nikopoli and Plevna were indentured without pay for many months to build the under-structure. More difficult operations were postponed, as timber had to be brought from far away in the Balkans. Meanwhile Midhat was replaced as Vali of Rustchuk by a successor, who had little understanding for Midhat's idea. Replaced in turn by the Vienna-educated Omar Fewzi Pasha as Vali, the plan was revived, engineers put on the job to build the Plevna-Nikopoli line, and negotiations started with a German construction firm.

---

[76] *Ibid.*, p. 235.
[77] *The Balkan Peninsula*, p. 265.
[78] *Donau, Bulgaria and the Balkans*, Vol. II, p. 196.

But soon Omar Fewzi was transferred to Crete, and thereafter, in 1871, the plan was buried.

HIRSCH CARRIES ON

Hirsch had finished his construction enterprise and could have retired from the scene, satisfied with his profits. But he remained deeply involved in this concern. First of all, there was his interest in the operating company; the restricted business was no adequate substitute for the larger project of a Trans-Balkan railroad. But it was not this material aspect alone which during the next few years drove Hirsch to further involvement.

As Mazerat of the Crédit Lyonnais, Paris, wrote to his colleague Mercier in Constantinople on March 21, 1876, Hirsch, in spite of Turkey's suspension of debt services in October, 1875, 'is always busy trying to find money for Turkey to continue the railway construction.' Hirsch accepted a plan of action based on Austrian influence, for which he tried to enlist the support of financial groups in Paris and London, as well as of the Ottoman Bank, which however remained reserved.[79] In accordance with this plan, and despite French counter-action in Constantinople, Hirsch in 1878 transferred his operating company from Paris to Vienna and replaced the French directors with Austro-Hungarians. Meanwhile the political events in the Balkans—the revolts in Bosnia in 1875, those in Bulgaria in 1876-78 and, finally, the Russo-Turkish war in 1877-78—prevented the commencement of construction until after the Congress of Berlin in 1878.

Hirsch endeavoured to protect the interests of the bond-holders. 'He made a good bargain in his combining the interests of the holders of the consolidated and the floating debt.'[80]

'Meanwhile one should not under-rate Hirsch's strength; he can attract, combine and reconcile various groups [of interest], to be set up. If division continues, Turkey will get accustomed to paying nothing.' As the Crédit Lyonnais archives show, there was indeed a struggle between the holders of the different types of debt, represented respectively by the Imperial Ottoman Bank; by Hirsch, backed by the Banque de Paris et de Pays Bas and the Jewish *haute banque* (Camondo, Cahen d'Anvers, Bischoffsheim & Goldschmidt); and by Crédit Mobilier. Early in 1876, prior to Hirsch's visit to Constantinople, an Austrian, Herr Schenk of the Wiener Bankverein (a Paribas associate) negotiated on behalf of Hirsch, on the occasion of a meeting of representatives of the English and French bond-holders' committees held in the city.[81] Another five years passed however, before a settlement was reached under the Decree of Moharrem, on December 20, 1881 which set up the Debt Publique Ottoman. It seems that Hirsch's interests were taken care of by Herr Justizrath Primker, officially delegated by Bleichröder to represent the German interests on the board of

---

[79] Bouvier, *Crédit Lyonnais*, Vol. II, p. 703.
[80] *Ibid.*
[81] *Ibid.*

Debt Publique Ottoman, presumably with the approval of the German Foreign Ministry whose legal counsellor Primker had been.[82]

Here we can record one of Bismarck's little 'revanches' on Hirsch. As Moritz Busch, one of Bismarck's friends and his biographer, records: 'On 19th July [1882] [Lothar] Bucher [one of Bismarck's assistants] sent me an article from the *Deutsche Tageblatt* of 16th July entitled 'Hirsch-Bleichröder-Rothschild and Germany in Constantinople.' It discloses the financial intrigues of this group of bankers, 'chosen members of the chosen people' who exploit Turkey under the pretence that they are protected by the German government in the persons of its representatives. It energetically protests against this trio and particularly against Bleichröder who knows how to take advantage of the credit which Germany enjoys at the Golden Horn, in association with persons who only manifest their national sentiments and their patriotism where these can be turned to account for their own transactions. Bucher notes 'I send you this article for your memorabilia. It will be mentioned hereafter. Justizrath Primker of Berlin is Bleichröder's agent here referred to.'[83] Two days after the publication of this apparently inspired article Bismarck declared that 'as to the Austrian government... they had committed themselves too far with Hirsch.'[84]

In the Holstein Diaries (November 27, 1882) we read that in spite of this warning Bleichröder informed Bismarck of his readiness to buy shares in Hirsch's railway and to participate in the construction of the link with Austria, provided he were given the same protection as formerly in Rumania, but Bismarck rejected this condition.[85]

The Diaries also tell us that on December 29, 1882, the Austrian Ambassador handed Busch notes from Vienna stating that as Bleichröder was to become the dominant partner in the railway project it was hoped Bismarck would support the undertaking. The Ottoman Bank, too, was to become a partner in the new consortium.

Bismarck informed Austria that the German Foreign Ministry would support the project on the political level, but could not concern itself with its finance or use its political credit to influence the Sultan. Since the name of his private banker was involved he also advised caution in order to prevent scandalmongers from exploiting this affair, and for this same reason Bismarck also asked Bleichröder to withdraw from the project. Bleichröder asked Holstein whether this was the real reason for Bismarck's demand, or whether it was his intention to harm Austria. In the former case, Bleichröder could arrange with another bank to act on his behalf.[86]

But this is to anticipate our story.

A CATALOGUE OF COMPLAINTS—AND DISAPPOINTED HOPES

Germany and Austria had put great hopes on the early completion of the Trans-Balkan rail connection with Turkey as a means of competing with the cheap sea

---

[82] Blaisdell, *European Financial Control in the Ottoman Empire*, pp. 90 and 280.
[83] Moritz Busch, *Bismarck, Some Secret Pages of his History* (1898), Vol. II, pp. 62-63., cf. also p. 74.
[84] Quoted in Kohler Papers.
[85] N. Rich and M. H. Fisher (ed.), *The Holstein Diaries* (1957), p. 18.
[86] *Ibid.*, p. 23.

freights from the Western countries; they were greatly disappointed by the delay in completing the railway. Hirsch became the target of vociferous attacks particularly by German nationalist and antisemitic writers and pamphleteers. He was particularly accused of having started construction where it was cheapest, i.e. of building his railway from the coast inland, from Constantinople, Dedeagatch and Salonica, and of not having taken into account the justified, or allegedly justified, Austro-Hungarian demands for a connection with their railway net. Thus, it was claimed, Hirsch harmed Austrian and German commercial interests more effectively than could have been done by a hostile Turkish regime.[87] British ships dominated the Turkish ports from which Hirsch's railways now facilitated the entry of British goods into the interior. British ships almost exclusively also went up the Danube as far as Widin, until the regulation of the 'Iron Gate', in 1896. Moreover, the fact that an Englishman, Ralph Earle, negotiated the revision of Hirsch's agreement was considered evidence of Hirsch's representing British interests.

Austrian interests had indeed been badly affected by the recent developments. Writing on his visit to the Balkans, only about two or three years after the opening of Hirsch's railway 'stumps,' Kanitz[88] reports that Sofia, an age-old emporium for an active trade with the Adriatic coast, now received its goods by sea and rail via Salonica. Although in Sofia Austro-Hungarian goods coming down the Danube still balanced those from Britain, France and Switzerland, they had lost the profitable markets east of Philippopel and Uskub. Even after the completion of the railway via Belgrade, Kanitz feared, it would be difficult to re-conquer these markets. Kanitz speaks here only of Austro-Hungarian commerce. But what about Germany, whose spokesmen were so particularly vociferous? Young states that while British merchants held a virtual monopoly of Constantinople's foreign trade before the Crimean War (1856), during the latter half of the century the commerce of Turkey was passing steadily from British into German hands, partly due to the growth of the German merchant navy.[89]

What hurt the Austrians and Germans more was the fact that the bulk of the Türkenlose had been absorbed in Austria and Germany. But, as one of Hirsch's critics admits, the best and most natural plan for the projected railway, was the one worked out by the noted Austrian engineer W. von Pressel, and adopted by Hirsch, which started at the harbours of the Balkan Peninsula and led via Nish north to Belgrade.[90] It is therefore wrong to accuse Hirsch, as Zimmerer did, of having started construction at the ports, where it was least costly, without intending to connect it with the Austro-Hungarian rail-net.

That Hirsch was really doing everything in his power to have the railway completed at an early date is shown in a confidential memorandum by the Ballhausplatz to Bismarck, a copy of which was sent with a covering note, dated September 29, 1881

---

[87] Cf. Heinrich Zimmerer, *'European Turkey,'* in Helmholt's *Weltgeschichte*, Vol. IV (1920).
[88] Cf. Kanitz, p. 25, and Dimtchoff, pp. 40-41, 47.
[89] *Constantinople,* p. 206.
[90] Dimtchoff, p. 20.

Oriental Railways

to Baron Calice,[91] the Austrian Ambassador to the Porte. Here we learn that Turkey, while admitting her responsibility to complete the Constantinople-Bellova line to the Bulgarian frontier (Vacarel), tried to evade her responsibility concerning the connection of the Salonica-Mitrovitza line to the Serbian frontier, due, it seemed, to the Sultan's fear that that would facilitate Austria's march on Salonica. But, as the memorandum pointed out, this line, so important for Austria's and Germany's commerce, was not essential for the feared military operation, should such be contemplated.

The Turks, too, were unable to build these lines themselves, but did not want to entrust Hirsch with the job. In the absence of any other applicant, Austria, anxious to see the job done, was backing Hirsch's company, now an Austrian concern, hoping for a settlement of the dispute between Turkey and him. Hirsch, in fact, had confidentially informed the Austrian government that he was ready to build these two connecting lines without any financial burden for Turkey.

FAULTY CONSTRUCTIONS

Although Hirsch had completed his commitment under the 1872 agreement, the Turkish government refused to accept the work. Its Technical Committee appointed for this purpose declared the work defective and estimated that it would cost 27,000 francs per kilometer to make the lines operative.[92]

The report of the committee which, as Morawitz claims,[93] consisted of officials hostile to Hirsch, was countered by the Company report written by a group of outstanding European engineers and chaired by a famous German expert, Hartwick, who stated that the line was in good operating order and built according to the specifications of the agreement.

The Turkish government, thus pushed to the wall after many procrastinations, applied to the British government for the nomination of impartial experts. As their report was never published by the Turkish government it stands to reason that it was not unfavourable to Hirsch. As Morawitz adds, the heavy military use without breakdown of the railway during the Russo-Turkish war showed its solid construction.[94] Moreover, the operating company annually spent considerable amounts on improving the rolling stock and the roadbed to achieve greater speed and comfort.[95]

Nevertheless, as a British intelligence report in 1917 noted 'The service of trains is or was slow and inefficient. The laying of the line left much to be desired; neither the permanent way nor the engines permitted of any rate of high speed.'[96] In 1909 and after, bridges had been strengthened to permit the passage of heavier locomotives. The speed of the Orient Express was 28 miles per hour from Constantinople to

---

[91] Austrian State Archives.
[92] Poulgy, *Les Emprunts*, p. 59.
[93] *Les Finances de la Turquie*, p. 378.
[94] *Ibid.*, p. 383.
[95] *Ibid.*, p. 378.
[96] Admiralty War Staff, Intelligence Division, *A Handbook of Turkey in Europe* (1917).

Pavlo, and 31 miles from Pavlo to Adrianople. The road was apparently originally adequate for the type of locomotion available in the seventies, and was later adjusted to improving locomotion. In contrast to these intelligence reports, Sir Edwin Pears, a long-time resident of Constantinople, writes in the very same year, 1917, that 'it is sufficient to say that during the last quarter of a century the service of this train (i.e., the Orient Express) was one of successful management.'[97] Up to the opening of this line in 1888, as Pears recalled, the best connection between London and Constantinople was either by boat from Marseilles, or by railway via Berlin and the Russian frontier, from Podvolocheskoff to Odessa and thence by boat to Constantinople, journeys of 7 and $4\frac{1}{2}$ days respectively.

FAULTY LAYOUT

Not only the construction, but also the very layout of the line was criticized. Thus Mears: 'In European Turkey the Oriental Railway is poorly laid out, with no attempts to avoid severe curves, since an underlying plan was to obtain as large a mileage as possible in order to obtain the benefit from the kilometer guarantee. Thus, although Constantinople is only 148 miles from Adrianople by highway, the railway has a length of 198 miles, including 24 miles inside Bulgarian territory.'[98] The same complaint of excessive mileage is made by another writer on Turkey[99] who, however, perhaps unwittingly offers an explanation other than lust for money: 'As the railway gets nearer the lines of Tchataldja, the outermost fortification of Constantinople, it begins to loop itself round the barren downs in apparently meaningless meanderings. These writhings represent the wranglings of the promotor, Baron Hirsch, to increase his kilometer guarantee, and of Baron von der Goltz, the fortifier of Constantinople, to bring the line nicely under the fire of his batteries. But we, weary with a long dull journey ...will curse impartially both the Austrian Jew and the Prussian Junker.'

Turkish strategic considerations, rather than Hirsch's financial calculations evidently determined the lay-out of the railroad. This military aspect of the railway, which prompted Turkey to have it built, is also incidentally mentioned in the previously quoted British intelligence report. It was constructed with the intention of strengthening the Turkish military position in the Vilayet of Tuna (Danube), now Bulgaria. And the Porte, wishing to be independent of the sea transport of troops outside the Dardanelles, granted the concession for prolonging the line to Dedeagatch with that objective in mind.

Thus the charge of excessive mileage, which originated at Hirsch's time and was still repeated half a century later, can be discarded. It was apparently never raised by the Turkish government which had approved of the layout.

Another complaint was that, instead of providing towns along the line with con-

---

[97] Sir Edwin Pears, *Life of Abdul Hamid* (1917), pp. 152-153.
[98] Mears, *Modern Turkey* (1924), p. 224.
[99] G. Young, *Constantinople*, p. 6.

veniently situated stations, the company often located the stations some kilometers distant even from the main cities of the provinces in order to avoid difficult construction. Thus one finds along the line stations without towns, and towns without stations,[1] the very same complaint as was levelled against the Rustchuk-Varna railway.[2] It is difficult now to judge whether such a layout was chosen for reasons of economy or whether again military considerations suggested keeping the stations somewhat distant from concentrations of an often disaffected population.

UNPAID LABOUR AND PROPERTY

Another complaint against Hirsch, 'the well-known benefactor when concerned about his co-religionists,' is that his company did not pay for part of the earthmoving work which was done by indented labour provided by venal pashas.[3] In the case of the Rustchuk-Varna railway we hear the same story[4] though it is the 'company' and not the main concessionaire, Mr. W. Gladstone, on whom the opprobrium falls. It may well be that the payment made by the company remained in the pockets of the pashas and did not reach the labourers. No documentary proof is at present available for either claim. The case of expropriated property was similar. As de Laveleye was able to relate, on entering Constantinople by train, along an eight kilometer stretch from the Seven Towers to the central station, one passed on both sides dilapidated and half-collapsed houses. The railway had to destroy hundreds of dwellings for which they had paid compensation to the government which had pocketed the money instead of passing it on to the thousands of homeless and destitute.[5]

Oscar Straus apparently refers to this event when reporting how some of the dispossessed complained to the Baron who referred them to their government. On hearing of this the Baroness insisted on paying these people out of her private funds to enable them to build new houses.[6]

'BAKSHEESH'

There were wide-spread rumours regarding the lavish 'gifts' Hirsch made to the appropriate persons. Count Beust allegedly received 800,000 francs for obtaining approval of placing the Türkenlose,[7] and Mahmoud received 400,000 Turkish pounds for the change of the concession.[8] Dimtchoff claims[9] that Daoud and Nedim Pasha suddenly became rich and escaped prosecution only by permanently retiring

---

[1] Dimtchoff, p. 45.
[2] *Ibid.*, p. 11.
[3] *Ibid.*, p. 44.
[4] *Ibid.*, p. 11.
[5] de Laveleye, p. 313.
[6] Straus, *Under Four Administrations*, p. 95.
[7] Benedikt, p. 122.
[8] Dimtchoff, pp. 35-36, See above, p. 41.
[9] Dimtchoff, p. 32.

abroad: some of Hirsch's letters prove that he had bought Daoud.[10] Even 'the highest person in the land was himself a recipient of the largesse of the Austrian Baron.'[11] Midhat Pasha, who insisted on the restitution of the sums received, was duly dismissed as Grand Vizier.[12]

Hirsch allegedly spent 100 million francs on bribes but, as Benedikt who mentions this rumor adds,[13] this must be expected of a man who had available a 'private ledger' of which there are no accounts.

It can be safely assumed that Hirsch had to pay his way in Turkey, as was customary.[14] Moreover, the custom extended beyond Turkey. Bontoux, for instance, negotiating for a Serbian railway concession in 1881 reportedly spent 6 million francs in Belgrade.[15] The financial prowess of Balkan royalty was, indeed, proverbial. But 'let it be stated in justice to de Hirsch that the popular belief that he provoked the change in the concession, and that, having executed the easier part of the line, he threw up the more difficult, is wholly at variance with the facts. It is said that de Hirsch bribed the Porte to be quit of the 1,220 kilometers which were abandoned; the exact contrary is the case, the Porte paid a heavy premium to de Hirsch to forego what he gave up.'[16] This compensation was paid out of a saving of £T. 5 million made by reducing the length of the line. The money thus came partly out of the pockets of the shareholders, and partly from the Turkish tax payers. The Porte received part of this sum of £T. 5 million; the Sultan's personal share was £T. 350,000, and Mahmoud was probably not forgotten (are these the bribes Midhat refers to?). 'But the Turks and the Russians, to mask their own questionable conduct, spared no pains to propagate the belief that de Hirsch, having made his profit out of half of the concession, bought himself off the rest by paying a heavy premium. That is totally false.'[17]

THE BELLOVA FORESTS

'To have obtained a contract giving unlimited control over the richest forests in the world on the pretext of cutting sleepers...,' as Midhat Bey phrased it, was another one of the accusations levelled against Hirsch. Apart from profiting from the additional mileage he allegedly extended his railroad by eight kilometers from Sarambey to Bellova for no other reason but to carry his timber.[18] This accusation, however, seems to have been baseless, as the government had granted Hirsch, under a special agreement, a 99 year lease on 900 square kilometers of forests in the mountains near Bellova.[19]

[10] Reproduced in the *Kölnische Zeitung* of March, 1883.
[11] Cf. Hallgarten, p. 231.
[12] A. H. Midhat Bey, *Life of Midhat Pasha* (1903), p. 65.
[13] Benedikt, pp. 119-120.
[14] Dimtchoff (p. 15) mentions the bribe Daoud Pasha received from the Rustchuk-Varna Co.
[15] Bouvier, *Krach*, p. 90.
[16] *Times*, August 21, 1888.
[17] *Ibid.*
[18] A. H. Midhat Bey, *Life of Midhat Pasha*, p. 65.
[19] Dimtchoff, p. 37.

Oriental Railways

Hirsch's lease, obtained in 1872, and not as part of the original concession, was not restricted to limited lumbering rights for the construction of the track, such as those mentioned in other contracts.[20]

De Laveleye, who travelled in this region in 1884, mentions meeting buffalo wagons carrying wood for fuel and carpentry from the forests of Bellova, 'belonging to Baron Hirsch,' to the railway—a journey which took four to five days.[21] And elsewhere he tells the story[22] of the head manager of the Bellova forest, 'belonging to the Oriental Railways,' who had been carried off by brigands and had to be freed by a ransom of £6,000 sterling. These notes, written ten years after the completion of Hirsch's railway, indicate that Hirsch and his company had long-term contractual rights in this district, and lead us to infer that Midhat Bey's book, too, must be used with reservations.

THE EASTERN QUESTION—THE ROAD TO BERLIN

The beginning of the Oriental Railway construction coincided with a renewal of Russia's pressure on Turkey. This was probably not purely accidental. Russia, in pursuit of her political plans, wanted a railway running from north-east to south-west, from her Rumanian border to the Adriatic Sea and the Mediterranean. Austria, however, apart from the West-East line from her borders to Constantinople, wanted also one running south-east, to Salonica, not through Serbian territory but rather through the Turkish provinces of Bosnia-Herzegovina, and the Sandjak Novipazar.[23] Russia expected the Black Sea coast and Constantinople as her main spoils of a partition of Turkey and she was prepared as a *quid pro quo* to agree to an Austrian hegemony over Serbia and the Western Balkans as far as Salonica. But Austria considered the preservation of the Ottoman Empire as essential for her own existence. As Andrassy, the Austrian foreign minister, stated in 1876, 'If it were not for Turkey, all these [nationalistic] inspirations would fall down on our heads... If a new state should be formed there [in the Balkans] we should be ruined and should ourselves assume the role of the "Sick Man."' Austria was not eager to be saddled with Slavs, unmanageable after their long resistance to Turkish rule. Moreover, such a partition of European Turkey would have put under Russian control the mouth of the Danube and the exit from the Black Sea, still Austria's most important economic life-line, and would have destroyed an economic unit which offered much scope to the penetration of German capital.[24]

Bismarck's Germany had no special interest in Turkey which might justify a clash with other powers. It was not for her to prevent Russia from marching on Constantinople. That was to be left to England and the Habsburg Monarchy

---

[20] Cf. the 1899 contract with the Baghdad Railway Company. Herschlag, *Introduction to the Economic History of the Middle East* (1964), p. 49.
[21] *Balkan Peninsula*, p. 264.
[22] *Ibid.*, p. 318.
[23] L. S. Stavrianos, *The Balkans Since 1453* (1958), p. 417.
[24] Cf. particularly A. J. P. Taylor, *The Habsburg Monarchy* (Penguin edn., 1964), pp. 164-165.

(though Germany was committed to the maintenance of the latter's integrity). Nor was it for Germany to help Russia in her plans.[25]

But it was England, wary of Russia's ambitions in the Straits, who had been the main guardian of the Ottoman Empire, while Russia, skilfully using the Pan-Slavist movement, ignited the Eastern question. It started with the 1875-76 revolt in Bulgaria in which Christian atrocities against the Moslem ruler provoked an even more atrocious suppression. Europe was shocked. The 'Gallant Turk' of the Crimean War days became the 'Unspeakable Turk' in Gladstone's speeches. England and Austria sought without avail to repair the situation by pressing for internal reforms in Turkey. In 1877 Russia went to war until she was stopped at the gates of Constantinople by England's intervention.

The Peace Treaty of San Stefano returned to Russia her losses in the Crimean War, and created a new, large, Russian-dominated, Bulgaria. This was unacceptable to Austria, who became alarmed by Bulgaria's gains in the Western Balkans and the Russian control over her Danube life-line. Nor was it acceptable to England, who feared that the satellite Bulgaria would give Russia an overland route to the Aegean Sea and the Mediterranean. A greater Bulgaria blocking the way to Salonica was not only unacceptable to Austria, but also obstructed Serbia's south-east expansion. Thus a European conflict threatened to break out which Russia could not face and in 1878 she therefore, accepted Bismarck's offer to be an 'honest broker' when he invited the powers to a Congress in Berlin.

These political developments obviously greatly affected Hirsch's interests. His largest lines, particularly the one from Mitroviza to Salonica, were now in the area of Greater Bulgaria. Who would pay the annual kilometer fee (subvention)? Indeed, many of the banks holding shares in the operating company, such as the Ottoman Bank and Crédit Lyonnais, approached the Great Powers concerning these rights. At a much later date a Viennese rumour had it that Hirsch's fortune after the Treaty of San Stefano was practically lost, and only his close connection with the Prince of Wales, who was financially obligated to Hirsch, and, through him, with the British representatives at the Congress of Berlin led to revision of the peace treaty, which would have been rather disadvantageous to Hirsch.[26] As Hirsch met Edward only in 1886, this story and its malicious implication can be disregarded.

Better documented, however, is Hirsch's appearance at the Congress of Berlin accompanied by Altgraf Franz von Salm-Reiffenscheidt,[27] a member of the Upper House *(Herrenhaus)* and president-designate of the Turkish-Roumelian Railways, and his immediate approach to Andrassy, the leader of the Austrian delegation.[28] The interests of Andrassy and Hirsch were identical. Andrassy asked Serbia on

---

[25] Cf. K. Helfferich, *Georg von Siemens* (1923). Vol. III, p. 18.

[26] Letter from S. H. Wechsberg, Vienna, to Kohler, January 24, 1922. Kohler Papers.

[27] An Altgraph Hugo v. Salm-Reiffenscheidt is mentioned as one of the holders, in 1868, of the concession for the Austrian Nordwestern (together with L. v. Haber, I. v. Liebig, Parisian and Viennese banks (cf. *Creditanstalt,* p. 35).

[28] *Aufzeichnungen und Erinnerungen aus dem Leben des Botschafter Josef Maria von Radelin* (1928), Vol. II, p. 84. Benedikt, *Die Wirtschaftliche Entwicklung i.d. Franz-Josephs-Zeit,* p. 120.

Hirsch's behalf for the right to build the connections to Constantinople and Salonica through her territory. But Ristich, Serbia's premier, firmly refused. Andrassy finally succeeded in having inserted in sections 10, 21, and 38 of the final protocol the obligation to complete the trans-Balkan lines.

The Berlin Protocol granted independence to Serbia and established an autonomous Bulgaria, but reduced it in size by what was to be the autonomous Turkish province of Eastern Roumelia. The Turkish provinces of Bosnia and Herzegovina came under the administration of Austria-Hungary which also obtained the right of maintaining garrisons in the Sandjak of Novipazar.

Bulgaria, Serbia, and Turkey were committed to complete the parts of the railway within their respective territories as far as the Austro-Hungarian frontier. The implementation of this resolution was entrusted to a 'Conférence à quatre', but it was not until five years later, in 1883, that the four states concerned ratified a final convention.

THE COMPETITORS ACT

Eight years had passed since Hirsch had completed his construction contract with the Turkish government, and five years since the Congress of Berlin had decided on the completion of the 'Oriental Railway,' before the 'Conférence à quatre' met. Hirsch had not been idle during these years; neither had his competitors.

By 1874 the Austrian State Railways *(Staatsbahn)*, a concern in which Austrian and French capital participated, and whose president was Baron Wodianer, had 1,646 kilometers of track stretching from the Saxo-Bohemian frontier via Vienna, Pressburg, and Budapest to the Hungarian plain, from where it was ready to branch out to Rumania on the one side and to Serbia on the other. The arm to Rumania, via Szeged-Temesvar to Orsova, the Iron Gate on the Danube, was completed in 1874. And within Rumania the company, on behalf of the Bleichröder-Diskonto Bank syndicate, was operating the Crajova-Bucarest-Braila-Galatz-Yassy line which had originally been built by the unfortunate Strousberg. By 1876 the connection between Orsova and Crajova was completed, bringing the line to the Black Sea.

In its attempts to establish a connection with Serbia, the company was less fortunate. Its repeated requests for a concession for a line via Kikinda to Semlin (Belgrade) were rejected by the Hungarian government, which did not want the line in the hands of a foreign company with French capital and Austrian jurisdiction. Even French political pressure and the threat to Hungarian credit on the Paris market could not influence the Hungarians who also preferred a line along the right bank of the Danube from Budapest via Peterwardein to Semlin rather than the proposed left-bank line. It was for the right-bank line that Hirsch in 1878 asked for a concession, but without success.[28]

In view of this failure, the Austrian State Railway in 1880 considered a new scheme, namely to connect Constantinople with its existing network through a line from Hirsch's railway to Crajova or Rustchuck, and negotiations were started with the

[28] Bouvier, *Le Krach*, pp. 73-92.

governments concerned. This idea was backed by French diplomacy, which opposed a line via Belgrade to Salonica as liable to harm the trade from France's Mediterranean ports. Eventually this project, too, was dropped.

Meanwhile a new personality appeared on the scene: Paul Eugene Bontoux (1820-1904).[29] Originally a railway expert of the French, then of the Austrian State and finally of the South Austrian Railroad Company, he had had to resign in 1878 because of some mistakes and thus broke with the Rothschilds. By the end of that year he had successfully organized the Union Générale in Paris, a Catholic group which was to free the country from financial domination by Jews and Freemasons. Like Langrand-Dumonceau before him he succeeded in rapidly attracting large funds from those French and Austrian circles to whom the objective appealed, and rallied behind him particularly the French Legitimists. In Vienna, with the moral support of the new Taaffe cabinet, he started the Kaiserliche und Koenigliche Privilegierte Länderbank, with the Böhmische Union Bank and the Ungarische Länderbank as subsidiaries. On January 20, 1882 the Union Générale defaulted; the Länderbank survived, though weakened for a while due to the sluggish financial markets in Paris and Vienna. In May 1881, Bontoux's Länderbank obtained an agreement to build and finance the line to Semlin with a connection to Belgrade, on behalf of the Hungarian Government. Bontoux was planning a Vienna-Budapest line via Komorn to compete with the somewhat longer left-bank line of the Austrian State Railroad.

He soon opened negotiations in Belgrade for the concession to build the lines which under the Berlin Protocol Serbia was obliged to construct. Backed by France, Bontoux met with British, Russian and Panslavistic intrigues. There were also competitors: the Russian Baronof and a mysterious Franco-Belgian group (with Hirsch in the background?). While Andrassy, the Austrian Foreign Minister who had retired in 1879, had backed Hirsch, Prime Minister Taaffe backed Bontoux. Hirsch, he saw, had neither the support of the Jewish bankers in Vienna, nor of the Parisian banks which were behind the Austrian State Railroad. Therefore he advised Belgrade to disregard Hirsch's rights under the Turkish concession of 1872, which Serbia as successor had to respect. But Turkey objected.

At this point we must counter suspicions of a secret agreement between Bontoux and Hirsch on the Bulgarian and Turkish lines. These suspicions are based on Auguste Chirac's book, *L'Agiotage sous la IIIe République,* Vol. II, but the author's antisemitic pamphlet, *Les Rois de la République* (1883), seems to disqualify him as a reliable source.[30] Nevertheless, Hallgarten,[31] who speaks of 'Hirsch who jointly with his friend Bontoux and his Union Générale tried to exploit the Balkans' notes 'Strange! Bontoux the prominent antisemite, pride of the French monarchists, and Hirsch, most prominent of Semites, financier of Jewish settlements,—arm in arm.' Hallgarten

---

[29] Cameron, pp. 198, 220, 322.

[30] In this pamphlet, sub-titled a 'Histoire des Juiveries,' a chapter (pp. 218-227) is devoted to Hirsch, who is described as hailing from Mannheim—an agent of German interests!

[31] Hallgarten, Vol. I. p. 212.

apparently does not know of the close connection between Hirsch and the Orleans. But even Bouvier's thorough research of documentary evidence revealed only Bontoux's wish, shortly before his fall, to meet with Hirsch in January 1882, then in Rome; the meeting did not materialize.

In 1881 Bontoux suddenly faced a powerful new competitor. The Banque de Paris et Pays Bas joined the syndicate of Austrian State, of which Henry Germain, the president of Crédit Lyonnais, had become vice-president, to expedite the previously mentioned Rumanian project which they considered economically sounder than the Serbian-Bulgarian line since it led through a more densely populated territory. This powerful syndicate commanded French government support and the confidence of the market. Still, Bontoux succeeded in obtaining the contract from the Serbian government for the construction of the 365 kilometer Belgrade-Nish-Vranje line at 198,000 francs per kilometer (the cost to himself was 150,000 francs) and the Nish-Pirot line at 210,000-225,000 per kilometer. The government subsidy was to be 7,800 francs per kilometer operated.

In April 1881, the cornerstone was laid, but in February 1882 Union Générale folded up. By May 1882 the Comptoir d'Escompte de Paris under the chairmanship of Edouard Hentsch, jointly with the Länderbank and some German banks including Erlanger, formed the 'Compagnie de Construction et d'Exploitation des Chemins de fer d'Etat Serbe,' with a capital of 16 million francs, to take over the Bontoux contracts. Thus Comptoir d'Escompte won out over Paribas and Austrian State, both of them incidentally Bischoffsheim creations.

FROM THE 'CONFERENCE A QUATRE' TO THE 'FIRST TRAIN,' VIENNA-CONSTANTINOPLE

Austria-Hungary and Serbia had thus taken all the steps to carry out the obligations of the Berlin Protocol. But Bulgaria, influenced by Russia, used delaying tactics, and so did Turkey. Only in December 1882 did the four powers convene in Vienna, and on May 9, 1883, a final agreement was signed on the completion of Hirsch's line from Bellova via Sofia, Tzaribrod, Nish, Belgrade to Semlin, and of a connection from Nish via Leskovatz and Vranje to join up at Mitrovitza with Hirsch's line to Salonica.

Things did not move smoothly and swiftly. Considerable diplomatic pressure was needed before Turkey began to act. In 1885 the Turks contracted for the construction of the 46 kilometers from Bellova to Vacarel on the Bulgarian frontier, and the 85 kilometers from Uskub to Zibevce on the Serbian frontier. Contrary to agreement, the contract went to a French concern at a price which was a third higher than the bid of Hirsch's operating company, and the operation of the lines to a concern of the Ottoman Bank. But in 1888 an arbitration award returned the operation of these lines to Hirsch's company.

When in 1888 the Bellova-Vacarel line in Eastern Rumelia was completed it was taken over by the Bulgarian government by force and operated by them as 'tenants' of the Turkish government.

The delay in the implementation of the 1883 convention was partly due to political developments: in October, 1885 Bulgaria occupied Eastern Rumelia, which under the Treaty of San Stefano was to be part of Greater Bulgaria, but under the Berlin Protocol had become an autonomous Turkish province. Turkey mobilized, but had no money to see such a costly military venture through. In this emergency Hirsch came to Turkey's assistance and through his operating company advanced to the Turkish government a million Turkish pounds (23 million francs), secured by the annual rent of 8,000 francs per kilometer operated which was due to the government from the company, and which so far had been withheld because of Turkey's failure to meet her obligations. By an agreement of December 22, 1885 this rental was reduced to 1,500 francs per kilometer as long as the income was below 10,333 francs per kilometer; it was to be increased by 45 per cent of the gross income above that amount. Other outstanding points of dispute were to be submitted to arbitration, which finally took place in 1888. This established a new *modus vivendi* between Hirsch and the Turkish government, whose relations had been deadlocked for some years. On August 12, 1888, almost twenty years after the signing of the original concession, the first train left Vienna for Constantinople.

FINAL ACCOUNT — HIRSCH SELLS OUT

Towards the end of 1887 when Oscar S. Straus, the United States Minister at Constantinople dined with the Sultan, the latter asked him to act as arbitrator between the Porte and Hirsch. Hirsch had suggested first the French and then the Austrian ambassador, but neither had been satisfactory to the Sultan; however, both agreed on Straus. Despite the Secretary of State's approval, Straus felt it would not be wise to accept, as 'any transaction with the Turkish government involving money was open to suspicion of improper methods and bribery. Had I as arbitrator made a decision unfavourable to the Turkish government, I should certainly have fallen under such suspicion.'[32] Straus therefore declined to act as arbitrator, but offered the Sultan his free services as mediator, which were accepted. The case was brought before a committee of arbitrators, two for each side, and finally Professor Rudolf von Gneist, a famous German jurist and parliamentarian, was chosen — on Bismarck's recommendation, it was said — to act as sole arbitrator on those points where the others did not reach agreement.

Gneist, who had once acted as arbitrator between Great Britain and the United States in the dispute over the North-Western Frontier,[33] and later was prominent in the fight against antisemitism, gave his award on February 25, 1889, which 'was a great surprise. One expected an award of hundreds of millions in favour of Turkey.'[34] But the claims of Turkey were not quite so big. The main claims were for the repayment of the guarantee fund of 13 million francs plus interest — a total of 40 million

---

[32] O. S. Straus, *Under Four Administrations*, p. 94.
[33] A. D. White, *Aus meinen Diplomatenleben* (Leipzig, n. d.), pp. 98-99.
[34] *Neue Freie Presse,* April 21, 1896.

francs; and for payment of the annual rental of 8,000 francs per kilometer as from 1872, totaling 20 million francs, thus making a grand total of 60 million francs. But the Company had counterclaims: for the construction of the line Jamboli-Schumla; for the cost of plant and rolling stock of the abandoned line Banjaluka-Novi; for compensation of losses caused by Turkey not having built harbour, pier and other facilities, as required under the contract. The company also contested the claim for the rental payment as stipulated for the lines which Turkey had undertaken to build but had not carried out. The final award obliged the company to pay an amount of $26\frac{3}{4}$ million francs to the Turkish government in final settlement. Against this the Porte had to pay to the company $12\frac{1}{2}$ million francs under the primary arbitration award, so that the actual cash payment due to the Porte was reduced to $14\frac{1}{4}$ million francs.[35] That this amount would have been still smaller had von Gneist not been tied by the terms of the arbitration clause is shown in a hitherto unpublished letter of March 7, 1889, from von Gneist to Hirsch in which he wrote (in German):

> I may proceed on the assumption that in the matter of this greatly complicated affair the question of honour is of deepest concern to you, for it is a fine trait in the nature of man that, progressively with his acquisition of wealth, his regard for the importance of his good name increases. It became a source of great satisfaction to see that in a matter of great responsibility and in a time of bitter prejudice, I was enabled in my award repeatedly to emphasize the probity of your course...
> The inevitable consequence is that the operating company must be held responsible as the depository of the entire deposit from the beginning, and remained so with all the harsh consequences which follow from the high interest rate. If, as umpire, I had freedom of action, I would have fixed upon 9 percent interest, had my hands not been tied by article X of the submission to arbitration. If that liberty had been taken by me, however, my award would have been null by reason of exceeding my authority.[36]

Nevertheless, as a commentator on those days stated, '[Public] opinion on the rapid accumulation of fortunes is never flattering.'[37] Gneist's award did not silence the hostile pamphleteers, nor did it prevent writers today from basing themselves on such 'one-sided' sources. Unavoidably legends arose about the fortune made on this Turkish railway deal by Hirsch, which was indeed substantial. The Türkenlose were given to the 'entrepreneur' Hirsch as a payment of 254.5 million francs, but yielded him as 'banker' 280-290 million francs. Deducting the cost of construction of approximately 1,200 kilometers at 150,000 francs totalling 180 million francs, this left a profit of 100-110 million francs. To this must be added 50 million francs of operating profits during the ten years, during which no rental was paid to the Turkish government, making a grand total of 160-170 million francs according to Morawitz.[38]

[35] Dimtchoff, p. 51.
[36] Kohler Papers.
[37] *Neues Wiener Tageblatt*, April 22, 1896.
[38] Morawitz, p. 422.

This figure apparently included 10 million francs for sundry income. If we calculate on 1,280 kilometers then the income would be 12 million francs less.[39]

There is no indication of the size of the 'refund' to the Porte and its functionaries on the revision of the concession in 1872, to which *The Times* alludes.[40] (It is the only source which does so). It may have been included in the legendary 100 million francs of 'baksheesh' which Hirsch was said to have paid in this business;[41] no doubt a substantial sum of such customary 'overhead expenses' must be deducted from the profit.

Whatever the profit was, it was hard earned. It was a compensation for twenty years' unceasing hard labour. 'It would be unjust to forget the greatness of the conception, the tremendous hard work, diligence and intelligence, and particularly the most remarkable persistence, shown by this little banker from Brussels, in order to plan, direct and almost single-handed complete such an important and useful enterprise, in the midst of bitter hostilities and most serious difficulties in a semi-barbarian country such as Turkey then was.'[42] Nobody before him had the courage to tackle this monster-undertaking that might have ended differently.[43] 'He brought to a triumphant conclusion... a civilizing influence of very first rank... A foolhardy promotor had grown into a leader and a predominant money power on the grandest possible scale.'[44]

But it was left to Hallgarten, whose chapter on the Oriental Railways is one long catalogue of Hirsch's malfeasance, to write the most appropriate appreciation of Hirsch's historical role: 'It is by no means easy to do justice to Hirsch... but it is certain that he by his policy has helped to open up the Balkans and put the bulk of his profits into charitable undertakings, largely for Jewish purposes. Thus he stands out *as the most important* and possibly also most typical of *entrepreneurs* who, as private capitalists, with the best means available at that time, partly anticipated and partly took advantage of the sudden transition to a great-power backed economic imperialism.'[45]

The place of these entrepreneurs was subsequently taken by the big joint-stock banks, in which the private bankers, the Protestant and Jewish *haute banque*, appear as shareholders and board members.

Operating a railway line in Turkey in those days involved the company in daily experiences peculiar to the 'local scene,' a few of which are recorded in a contemporary travelogue.[46] Thus, de Laveleye records, an appeal to justice was illusory. When once the railway company added a small shed to a station in the country, the neighbouring land-owner claimed that it was half upon his land; the boundaries were

---

[39] Cf. p. (38) above.
[40] *Times,* August 21, 1888
[41] Benedikt, p. 119.
[42] Morawitz, p. 422.
[43] *Neues Wiener Tageblatt,* April 4, 1896.
[44] Emden, p. 322.
[45] Hallgarten, Vol. I, pp. 245. Our italics.
[46] de Laveleye *The Balkan Peninsula,* pp. 308, 311, 312, 313.

badly marked. The Turk demanded £L.T. 400 for the land which was worth 8-12 shillings at the most. So the company tore down the shed. But the local judge imposed upon the company a fine of £L.T. 120, of which he got the largest share. On another occasion, a Catholic prelate with his co-adjutors and suite went to Adrianople, and majestically took seats in a reserved compartment, but refused to pay for the tickets, claiming to be travelling on a holy errand. The conductor dared not turn the passengers out by force, but the bill subsequently sent by the company was never paid. Or, again, a Captain of the Port in Constantinople demanded several free passes on the Oriental Railway, but got only one. Aggrieved, he denied ships access to the Golden Horn railway pier and had, eventually, to be 'pacified.' Nor was it easy, even in later days, to obtain payment from the government for the transportation of troops and similar services.

There was, however, also another aspect to the railway undertaking. Thus we find in the Austrian State Archives a note by the Austro-Hungarian ambassador to Turkey, Count Zichy, dated March 8, 1878, recommending that an Austrian badge of merit *(Goldenes Verdienstkreuz mit Krone)* be conferred upon the stationmaster of the Oriental Railways at Adrianople, Mr. Carl Heuser, a Bavarian, for services rendered in supplies and military information.[47]

With the accounts of the operating company thus settled, Hirsch could now think of divesting himself of a burden which he had never intended or expected to carry. An offer to the Berliner Diskont Gesellschaft for a large parcel of the shares in the operating company led eventually, in April 1890, to Hirsch's complete sale of the control of the company (188,000 shares) to a group led by the Deutsche Bank under Georg von Siemens and the Wiener Bankverein under Moritz Bauer.

(According to the *Kölnische Zeitung* of December 27, 1888, an international group represented by the Austrian State (Staatseisenbahn Gesellschaft) was seriously interested in Hirsch's shares. But Hirsch may not have forgotten having been once snubbed by these gentlemen. From a despatch of the Austrian Ambassador in Constantinople to Vienna (No. 470, February 27, 1887, State Archives), we learn of news from Paris, to the effect that the Russians had approached Hirsch with an offer for his holding in the Oriental Railways which they wanted to have as a means of pressure against Bulgaria: the fact that Hirsch did not accept the Russian offer may be taken as another proof against Hallgarten's allegation of collusion between Hirsch and the Russians.)

Following the initial contact by Alfred v. Kaulla of the Württembergische Vereinsbank (a relative of Hirsch) with the Porte, von Siemens contracted for the construction of the Anatolian Railway as a first steep to a wider project of the Baghdad Railway. The Deutsche Bank, 'not wanting to leave the Asia Minor lines in the air,' grasped this opportunity to acquire and secure their link with the West.[48] The syndicate established the Bank für Orientalische Eisenbahnen at Zürich, as a holding

---

[47] Alex Novotny, *Quellen zum Studium der Geschichte des Berliner Kongresses* (1957), Vol. I, p. 219.
[48] Helfferich, *Georg von Siemens,* Vol. III, p. 49.

concern for these shares, as well as for a debt of 49 million francs due to Hirsch from the Turkish government under the 1885 loan and the 1888 arbitration award.

Now Hirsch retired, and not only from the Oriental Railways, but from business in general. He may have been influenced in this decision by the death of his son Lucien, who had passed away in 1887 at the age of 31. Apart from an active social and sporting life, racing, and hunting, his main pre-occupation for his remaining years became the Enterprise of Philanthropy.

CHAPTER VI

THE ENTERPRISE OF PHILANTHROPY

I

'NOT even his most violent opponents deny that 'Hirsch's philanthropy exceeded that of Peabody and the other Americans.'[1] But 'his philanthropy was not important so much because of its amounts, but because of the practical approach: economic rehabilitation.'[2]

The opponents could not, however, be silenced, even after his death. They could not deny the quantity or the quality of his benefaction; but they could question the motives. This was shown best in the obituary notice in the 'officiöse' (semi-official) Viennese 'Fremdenblatt' which was known to be close to certain government circles. After stating that Hirsch's name would always remain coupled with the calamities he caused, the article went on to state that in the later years Hirsch took pains to show that there had been a total change in the aims he pursued. On retiring from business he had expended such large sums for charitable purposes to justify a wider consideration of his life. The memory of the company promoter had sunk more and more into the background, and was replaced by that of the philanthropist who showed as much energy in dispensing his great fortune for his purposes as he had formerly manifested in making it. He felt that the mere fact of being a millionaire was not sufficient to secure him the position in the world he aspired to. It was this conviction which made his name one of the best known in Europe. It was, according to this and similar opinions, a mixture of 'Gewissensbisse,' of pangs of conscience, and of social ambition which made Hirsch the outstanding philanthropist of his time.[3]

If our interpretation of Hirsch's character is correct, it is difficult to think of him as subject to pangs of conscience, the more so as there was, objectively speaking, little reason for such pangs. True, he was socially ambitious and probably did not object to the 'additional glory' that was a by-product of his philanthropy, but such social ambition was never the mainspring of this activity.

Hirsch was a dynamic personality, an entrepreneur on the largest scale. Once he had made so much money that money as such and what one can buy with it had lost its attractions, his dynamics, his energy, his 'creative impulse,' needed a different outlet, and found it in philanthropy. And here he acted not like a great benefactor dispensing charity, but as the great entrepreneur tackling a great new enterprise.

It was probably first and foremost the influence of his wife Clara that directed Hirsch to this enterprise. She had come from a family active in Jewish public affairs

---
[1] *Neue Freie Presse,* April 21, 1896.
[2] *Neues Wiener Tageblatt,* April 22, 1896.
[3] *Fremdenblatt,* April 22, 1896, cited in *The Times,* April 23, 1896.

and according to Sara Straus, it was she who guided the Baron's interest to philanthropy, particularly to his fellow Jews;[4] she was his inspirer and associate in the Argentinian venture. (In her widowhood, 1896-1899, she spent $15 million on charities and left bequests totalling $10 million). It was after the death in 1887 of his son Lucien, at the age of 31, that Hirsch stated: 'My son I have lost, but not my heir; humanity is my heir.'[5]

There may have been additional, minor, factors influencing Hirsch's ideas and actions. One was the occasional social discrimination that he experienced and took more as an offence to his Jewish dignity than as a personal slight. Another was, the desire 'to show the Rothschilds.' As his remarks to Herzl about rich Jews show, he apparently did not care much for them. There seems to have been a latent antagonism and competition between Hirsch and them: in business (as we saw in the Südbahn affair), in Jewish activities (such as the Chovevei Zion scheme) and socially.[6]

The interpretation by his opponents of Hirsch's motivation in his philanthropy seems to be of doubtful validity for yet another reason: his large-scale planned benefactions started before there was any need for him to show remorse. In 1873 he gave to Alliance Israélite a million francs for schools in European Turkey (Hirsch, after moving to Paris at the beginning of the Seventies, joined A.I.U. and was elected to its Central Committee in 1876).[7] Nor was the purpose of his large spectacular philanthropic schemes, i.e., *Jewish* economic rehabilitation, liable to silence his antisemitic critics or to buy the favours of an anti-Jewish snobbish society.

True, he gave freely to non-Jewish charitable institutions. He helped many individuals, among them some Austrian aristocrats.[8] Though 'his colours were well-known upon the turf,' it was not equally well-known that 'he raced,—as he said—for the London hospitals.' The gross proceeds of this racing, without deduction of expenses, were distributed among the hospitals, and in 1892, when his fleet filly, La Flêche, won the Oaks, the St. Leger and the One Thousand Guineas, but greatly to his disappointment missed the Derby, his donations from this source alone approximated £40,000.[9]

This combination of sport and charity probably pleased him as much as it did London Society, where, in general, he seems to have found more kindred spirits than anywhere else. But that was sport; that was not the serious business of philanthropy. He could, had he so wanted, have had his name perpetuated by some public institutions endowed by him. But he did not care for this kind of immortality, for this way of buying his way into Society to placate his critics. In his philanthropy he was as ruthless, or rather single-minded, as he was said to have been in the pursuit of

---

[4] *Jewish Encyclopedia.*
[5] Adler-Rudel, 'Baron Hirsch,' p. 39; cf. *The Times,* April 29, 1896.
[6] Hans Tietze recalls that Baron Nathaniel Rothschild, to whom the patronage of Princess Pauline Metternich had opened the doors of the salons of Vienna's high society, kept his own doors closed to other Jews. See *Die Wiener Juden* (Vienna 1933), p. 235.
[7] *Ibid.*
[8] *Neue Freie Presse,* April 21, 1896.
[9] *Ibid.*

Enterprise of Philanthropy

a business. He spent the bulk of his donations, which seem to have exceeded $100 million, on Jewish economic rehabilitation, partly through education and vocational training, and primarily in agricultural settlements in the Argentine, Brazil, Canada and the United States. Ancillary funds, for loans to small tradesmen and others, served the same purpose.[10]

A rich literature exists on the subject of the activities of the various funds set up in Paris, New York, Montreal and Vienna, as well as on his main foundation, the Jewish Colonization Association, but there is as yet no critical but objective, 'definitive' evaluation. Nor has any attempt been made to evaluate the impact of Hirsch's educational institutions upon the Jewish renaissance of this century or their effect in Eastern Europe, the Balkans or Jerusalem, in the U.S., Canada or Argentine. Here we must limit ourselves to the evidence of one former student of the Baron de Hirsch Agricultural School at Woodbine, N. J., A. D. Goldhaft, whose Vineland Poultry Laboratories have contributed greatly to the development of the poultry industry both in the Jewish settlements of New Jersey and in Israel. Goldhaft writes:

> To me as a boy Baron de Hirsch was only a name, as I suppose he is to all of us, a kind of historic name that even resounds down to this day, for the Baron de Hirsch Fund and the Jewish Agricultural Society that it supports, still goes on.
>
> Baron de Hirsch was a person ahead of his time as a philanthropist. In the history books they say that most of his attempts of 'solving' the Jewish problem turned out to be failures, and that hundreds of millions of dollars were wasted. But I wonder if such things can ever be measured. Perhaps some of the settlements that he set up failed to have a spectacular success, and most of them failed in time, but my life was helped by his work, as I suppose were many others.

The present study is concerned with the 'great entrepreneur' and it is not our intention to enter into the details of Hirsch's manifold humanitarian activities.[12] But we may briefly indicate the scope and extent of these philanthropical activities, 'and his particular approach to them.

Not much is known about Hirsch's fortune. In the first report of his death a Viennese evening paper stated that the Turkish venture and other financial transactions had yielded him a fortune of 1,500 million francs.[13] But the next day the morning paper estimated his assets at 500 million francs, adding that in the three years before his death, 1892-1895, he had given away 100 million francs, and his wife 200 million francs.[14] According to Adler-Rudel his assets were estimated at between 14 and 30 million sterling.

As Oscar S. Straus said 'It is impossible to form an accurate estimate of the amount of money Baron de Hirsch devoted to benevolent purposes. That, including the large

---

[10] Cf. Adler-Rudel, p. 53.
[11] A. D. Goldhaft, *The Golden Egg*, pp. 90-91.
[12] These details may be found in Adler-Rudel's Profile of the Baron.
[13] *Neues Wiener Abendblatt*, April 21, 1896.
[14] *Neues Wiener Tageblatt*, April 22, 1896.

legacy of $45 million left to the Jewish Colonization Association, it exceeded $100 million, is an estimate justified by the amount given by him from time to time to the foundations referred to in the article. There were, besides, many gifts to individuals of which there is no record.'[15]

But an interesting picture sometimes emerges of the man and his work from the pages of the contemporary press, which add to the information obtained from the not always complete records of the institutions supported or created by him for sponsoring the specific task which he considered important.

EDUCATION IN THE NEAR EAST
HIRSCH AND THE ALLIANCE ISRAELITE UNIVERSELLE

The beginning of Hirsch's large-scale 'organized' philanthropy coincided with that of his Oriental Railway venture. As Chouraqi sees it, it was one of the manifestations of Hirsch's brilliance as an industrialist that he foresaw the need for trained manpower to secure the future of his undertaking.[16] And thus he built schools as he built railway stations. Or, as we would say today, he recognized the need for infrastructural investment as a first step towards development.

But there was a deeper-seated force which drove him to action. In 1873 he wrote to A.I.U., of whose educational work he thought highly: 'During my repeated and extended visits to Turkey I have been painfully impressed by the misery and ignorance in which the Jewish masses live in that Empire... progress had by-passed them, their poverty stems from lack of education, and only the education and training of the young generation can remedy this dismal situation.'[17] And he offered A.I.U. a fund of one million gold francs to be used for improving the situation of the Jews in Turkey, by the establishment and operation in Constantinople of schools for their young people, by providing vocational training facilities and by providing stipends for training abroad.[18]

This was the beginning. From that year on the Hirsch couple responded to the calls of A.I.U. in such a way that it was said 'Their gifts make possible the greatest undertakings.'[19] Leven's record of the Alliance's activities in those days, from the Balkans to Asia Minor and North Africa, is a record also of Hirsch's numerous additional contributions for the building and operation of schools, of Clara's contributions for the feeding and clothing of school-children, apart from those for hospitals and similar projects,—contributions which total many hundred thousands of francs.

Things did not always go smoothly. The idea of vocational training was new and was resisted for a while by the ultra-conservative elements in Salonica who did not consider arts and crafts as educational aims.[20]

---

[15] 'Baron Maurice de Hirsch,' *Jewish Encyclopedia.*
[16] Andre Chouraqi, *L'Alliance Israélite Universelle et la Renaissance Juive* (1965), p. 49.
[17] N. Leven, *Cinquante Ans,* Vol. II, pp. 23-24.
[18] Chouraqi, p. 49.
[19] *Ibid.,* p. 156.
[20] *Jewish Chronicle,* August 6, 1878.

Enterprise of Philanthropy 67

It is for this vocational training scheme of A.I.U. that Hirsch from 1879 onwards, annually contributed 50,000 francs, and after 1882 undertook to cover A.I.U.'s annual deficits, totalling hundred thousands of francs. Finally, in 1889, Hirsch established an endowment with A.I.U. of ten million francs, the annual income of which, 400,000 francs, was to be used, equally, for covering the annual deficit and for the expansion of vocational education. His total contribution to A.I.U. for educational purposes must, therefore, have been not less than $5 million (about 15 million francs).

In 1876 Hirsch was elected to A.I.U.'s Central Committee, but being too busy himself to attend to the duties connected with this position, he delegated Emmanuel Felix Veneziani (1825-1889) as his deputy. Veneziani, manager of a bank and chairman of A.I.U.'s committee in Constantinople, became Hirsch's advisor, agent and almoner. From 1883 he was a member of the Central Committee in his own right.[21]

UNRRA ANTICIPATED

Hirsch was deeply involved in Near Eastern affairs by his railway venture, and, through his close connection with A.I.U., equally involved with Jewish affairs in this region. Hence the outbreak of the Bulgarian revolt in 1875-6 and the subsequent Russo-Turkish War of 1877, entailing suffering particularly for the Jewish population, 'the innocent by-standers,' quickly moved him to take action. Although nominally it was A.I.U. which, as the 'fire-brigade' to act in any Jewish disaster, was on the scene also here, the reading of the contemporary records, such as the *Jewish Chronicle,* give the impression of a veritable 'one-man' Relief & Rehabilitation Agency in operation: Hirsch, represented by his able lieutenant Veneziani, who was assisted by his two brothers, was everywhere that aid was required. He opened an ambulatorium of 200 beds at Sofia[22] and a 400 bed hospital at Adrianople;[23] and a *Times* despatch speaks of the splendid work of Hirsch's agent, Veneziani.[24] One day he was organizing relief for the Jewish refugees in Varna,[25] the next in Schumla.[26]

In gratitude for these large benefactions, the Jewish authorities in Constantinople decreed that all male children born that year (1877-78?) be named Hirsch (Zvi?),[27] and the Sultan received Veneziani in order to transmit his thanks to Hirsch.[28]

When the war was over, the repatriation of the Jews of Bulgaria and Roumelia, who had been the victims of the war and of local persecution, became a pressing task. Veneziani, with his unrivalled local experience, easily found common language with all the sections of the population, with the Turkish authorities and with the ec-

---

[21] Chouraqi, p. 57.
[22] *Jewish Chronicle,* August 25, 1876.
[23] *Ibid.,* October 5, 1877.
[24] *The Times,* October 15, 1877.
[25] *Jewish Chronicle,* November, 23, 1877.
[26] *Ibid.,* December 28, 1877.
[27] *Ibid.,* March 22, 1878.
[28] *Ibid.,* June 14, 1878.

clesiastical leaders of the Christian population. His task was made easier by the non-sectarian largesse of Hirsch.[29] So we learn of the thanks of the non-Jewish Bulgarian population transmitted to Hirsch.[30]

The Alliance Bulletin for January 1879 states that Hirsch had spent several hundreds of thousands of francs on relief for the destitute and wounded during the recent war.[31] And his gift of £40,000 to the Empress of Russia during the war of 1878 for war charities must be added to this total.

There followed the Turkish-Greek conflict, and the trouble in Crete, with Hirsch's aid readily forthcoming for the, primarily Jewish, sufferers.[32] Money and clothing were provided to the 2,000 Jews whom a fire in a suburb of Constantinople had made homeless;[33] and to the distressed in Asia Minor.[34]

It is a never-ending catalogue which is only in part reflected in the pages of the *Jewish Chronicle* and other Jewish journals of that period.

EDUCATION IN THE 'NEARER EAST'
THE BARON HIRSCH STIFTUNG, VIENNA

It was for the sake of his enterprise that, after the Congress of Berlin, Hirsch made Vienna the centre of his activities. The papers report on his intended settling in Vienna, as indicated by a number of large contributions, such as 100,000 gulden (200,000 francs) for the Austrian Patriotic Fund for war-invalids[35] and 10,000 gulden, plus an endowment for maintenance, of the Jewish girls' orphanage in Budapest.[36] Hirsch never actually settled in Vienna, but lived at the Castle of Eichhorn in Moravia, and at his hunting lodge at St. Johann in Hungary. He soon took a deeper interest in the Jewish question in the Monarchy. The interest and experience gained in his educational enterprise in the Near East was now extended to the 'Nearer East,' i.e., the eastern provinces, Galicia and Bukowina, of the Austrian Empire, of which he had meanwhile become a citizen. It was Vienna's chief-rabbi, Dr. Adolf Jellinek, who had drawn Hirsch's attention to a problem, which was basically not much different from that encountered in the Turkish Empire. The Israelitische Allianz in Vienna, a sister organization of A. I. U., had already started to set up an educational network in Galicia with some financial assistance from Hirsch. Ten years after he had 'settled' in Austria, in 1888, to mark the fortieth anniversary of Francis Joseph's accession to the throne, he set up the Baron Hirsch Kaiser Jubiläums Fund, with 12 million gold francs (kronen)[37] for the purpose of establishing modern educa-

---

[29] *Ibid.*, September 12, 1879.
[30] *Ibid.*, April 26, 1878.
[31] *Ibid.*, February 7, 1879.
[32] *Ibid.*, April 12, 1878; May 17, 1878.
[33] *Ibid.*, September 19, 1879.
[34] *Ibid.*, August 26, 1880.
[35] *Ibid.*, September 25, 1878.
[36] *Ibid.*, February 7, 1879.
[37] Adler-Rudel, p. 40; Chouraqi, p. 136; Leven, Vol. II, p. 368.

Enterprise of Philanthropy

tional facilities, such as kindergartens, play-grounds, primary and vocational schools and training schemes, the free supply of schoolbooks, food and clothing for poor school-children, subsidies to teachers, and free loan funds for artisans and farmers. The schools were to be open, as in Turkey, also to non-Jewish children.

The project at first was not well received by government, apparently owing to the opposition by both the protagonists of the Polish and the German language in that region. Nor did the prevalent orthodox Jewry welcome the gift of a Trojan Horse from the Western assimilated world. So it was only after four years that the scheme was finally sanctioned. By 1899 fifty schools were in operation,[38] of which by the outbreak of the war in 1914, forty-five were still open. Tens of thousands of Jewish children and thousands of adults benefited from a modern education in primary and vocational schools. Thousands were helped to make a productive living by the aid of the free loan funds. Cases are known of persons of eastern European origin who have been embarrassed all their lives because their parents, out of enthusiasm or gratitude, gave them the first name 'Baron de Hirsch' or 'Baron Maurice de Hirsch.'

The post-war inflation necessarily depleted the Fund, which in 1898 had been augmented when Hirsch's widow, on the occasion of the Emperor's golden jubilee set up the 'Clara von Hirsch-Kaiser Jubiläums Stiftung für Unterstützung von Knaben und Mädchen in Osterreich,' with 8 million kronen, for feeding and clothing of children in the schools of the Allianz and the Baron Hirsch Stiftung, and to render assistance to artisans.

BARON HIRSCH FUND, NEW YORK

While one of the main purposes of A.I.U. had been to fight for the improvement of the legal position, to gain emancipation and civil rights for the Jews in the countries of their residence, Hirsch tried generally to improve their economic level, particularly through vocational education and productivization.

Hirsch's view of being able to improve things 'on the spot' received a first severe shock from the pogroms in Russia in 1881-82, the subsequent anti-Jewish legislation and the wave of emigration. New conceptions of relieving the situation started to ferment in his mind.

He at once contributed one million francs for refugee relief and authorised further large amounts, which totalled 5 million francs, to be spent by Veneziani and Carl Netter,[39] who directed the relief work at Brody at the Austrian-Russian frontier where thousands of refugees had concentrated.[40]

The main stream of the immigration went to the United States and the 250,000 Jews there were able only with the greatest of difficulty to raise the means for receiving and absorbing these masses of destitute immigrants. It was important to prevent their

---

[38] Narcisse Leven, *Cinquante Ans d'Histoire, L'Alliance Juive Universelle,* Vol. II, p. 370.
[39] 1826-1882. Merchant and philanthropist, co-founder and representative of A.I.U.; founder of Mikveh Israel Agricultural School near Jaffa.
[40] Adler-Rudel, p. 41 ff; Leven, Vol. II, p. 417 ff.

concentration, to disperse them over the continent. There were small groups among them seeking a new life on the land as farmers.[41] It was Michael Heilprin, a distinguished writer and community leader, who, opposing unproductive charity and advocating self-help, in January 1888, on the advice of Oscar S. Strauss, solicited Hirsch's help in the setting up of agricultural and industrial settlements. Within a few weeks after mailing this appeal Heilprin died, but his letter had found in Hirsch a kindred spirit, an identity of ideas.

About a year later, in May 1889, the American relief committee was informed by A.I.U., with whom they cooperated, that Hirsch was ready to set up a special fund for aiding the Russian and Rumanian immigrants to the United States. Difficult negotiations on the purpose and the administration followed, during which Hirsch provided 'interim finance' at a rate of $10,000 a month, until finally, in February 1891, the Baron Hirsch Fund was set up.

The delay had been caused by the initial difficulty in reconciling Hirsch's ideas of constructive aid, of effective planning, with the type of charitable relief work to which the American committees were accustomed. Some of them indeed, were afraid that the news of the existence of a well-endowed aid agency might attract even larger numbers of destitute immigrants, the very thing which Hirsch—who had come to see in emigration the only solution for the plight of Russian Jewry—was aiming at.

The aims of the Fund which was started by Hirsch with $2.4 million, subsequently increased to $4 million, were to provide immigrants from Russia and Rumania with free transportation from port of entry to places where they could find employment or self-supporting occupations; to grant loans to such immigrants, on real or chattel security, for establishing themselves as farmers, artisans, etc., with re-training facilities to this end and to help them to support themselves financially during the training period; to provide civic education and English language teaching for the immigrants, as well as vocational education for their youth; for farm instructors assisting the new agriculturists, and such other educational or relief measures, as the Trustees might decide upon from time to time.

Between 1901 and 1933 the Fund's 'Industrial Removal Office' dispersed some 74,000 immigrants over 1,731 different localities in the United States; its affiliate, the 'Jewish Agricultural Society' during that period granted loans of more than $7 million to 10,000 farmers.[42]

The story of the Fund, which was administered with devotion by some of the leading figures of American Jewry of that time, and that of its affiliated Jewish Agricultural Society, has been ably told by Samuel Joseph and G. Davidson respectively.

The Fund still exists. It was particularly active after World War II when displaced persons and survivors of Hitler's holocaust poured across the Atlantic.[43]

---

[41] Cf. G. Davidson, *Jewish Farmers and the Story of the Jewish Agricultural Society* (1943).
[42] Joseph, *History of the Baron Hirsch Fund* (1935), pp. 285 ff.
[43] *New York Times,* June 2, 1965.

Enterprise of Philanthropy 71

BARON DE HIRSCH INSTITUTE, MONTREAL

Somewhat similar, though on a much smaller scale, was the situation in Canada. Here the still small and young Jewish community in Montreal had in 1863 formed the Young Men's Hebrew Benevolent Society which, with the sudden mass immigration of refugees from Russia during the 1880's found itself taxed beyond all possible resources. An appeal to Hirsch in 1890 brought an immediate response, a first cheque of $20,000. The Y.M.H.B.S. subsequently changed its name to the Baron de Hirsch Institute for providing education to the poor Jewish immigrant children and for offering a sheltering home for immigrants and orphans. The Institute also, temporarily, aided in the establishment of agricultural settlements, subsequently assisted by Hirsch and thereafter by I.C.A.

The Institute, which in 1963 celebrated its Centenniel, still carries on as an important social service organization and welfare agency.[44]

I.C.A.—'THE JEWISH COLONIZATION ASSOCIATION'

The deterioration in the early 1880's in the situation of the Jews in Russia, the physical and economic persecution, the untold hardships under proscriptions designed to deprive them of every possible means of earning a respectable livelihood, together with an increasing wave of refugees seeking asylum elsewhere, made a deep impression on Hirsch. For a decade he had devoted much of his money, and much of his time and thought to the economic rehabilitation of the Jews in many countries by what he considered the most effective means for this purpose: modern education and training for productive occupations. He still thought in these terms when, ready to help, he turned his attention to the Russian Jewish problem. He still believed that such measures applied in Russia itself would improve their position, without resorting to emigration. After consultation with some of the wealthy Russian Jews, he delegated the Marquis d'Abzac and Leonce Lehmann[45] to submit to the Russian authorities his proposal to provide 50 million francs for opening technical and agricultural schools for the Jews in the Pale of Settlement. This offer the Russians declined to accept unless the fund were administered by themselves, a condition not acceptable to Hirsch, who now began to see the only solution in planned emigration and re-settlement elsewhere.

In 1889, whilst still looking for land suitable for this purpose, Hirsch was informed by A.I.U. of a letter received from Dr. Wilhelm Loewenthal[46] then engaged in Argentina on a scientific research project, who during his travels there had come across a few hundred Russian Jews working as farmers on leased land, but being exploited by the landlord. Though shocked by the conditions under which they had to labour, he was enthusiastic about the tenacity which kept them going. Hirsch, thus strength-

---

[44] Baron de Hirsch Fund Centennial, Montreal, 1963.
[45] 1836-1892. Distinguished French jurist and A.I.U. leader.
[46] 1850-1894. Professor of Hygiene at Lausanne and Paris.

ened in his old conviction that the Jews could be excellent farmers, instructed Dr. Loewenthal to buy this land from the owner and to provide the settlers with the necessary farm equipment. Thus, in 1890, the first Jewish settlement was established in the Santa Fé province. It was given the name Moisesville.[47] The settlers were soon joined by another group of 900 refugees who had been left stranded in Constantinople on their way to Palestine, and were with Hirsch's aid, sent by A.I.U., to the Argentine where in 1891 they founded the settlement Mauricio.

Dr. Loewenthal eventually returned to Paris, and, through Grand Rabbin Zadoc Kahn, submitted to Hirsch and A.I.U. a scheme for large-scale Jewish settlement in Argentina.[48] Hirsch approved of the idea and soon despatched a commission, consisting of Dr. Loewenthal, the British engineer C.N. Cullen and Colonel Vanvinckeroy, a Belgian, to study soil and other conditions in order to determine the suitability of the envisaged scheme. In March, 1891, they submitted a favourable reply and brought back the approval of the scheme by the Argentine government.

The worsening of the political conditions in Russia had set a new mass exodus in motion. So Hirsch started to act. He sent Arnold White, a British journalist and M.P. to Russia to negotiate with the government on organized emigration.

White, who in his writings in the past had shown anti-Jewish prejudices, was deeply moved by the oppressed masses of Russian Jewry. He had in his mission the support of the most influential High Procurator of the Holy Synod, Konstantin Pobjedonosszev, who in 1887 had received from Hirsch a million francs for his schools. After some hesitations the government eventually agreed to a legalized and organized emigration, and in May 1892 approved the articles of the 'Jewish Colonization Association.' (I.C.A.).

ICA was incorporated in London on September 10, 1891 as a limited company, with a capital of £2 million, divided into 20,000 shares of £100 each. Hirsch himself held 19,993 of these while the remaining seven were held by Jewish leaders in London and Paris.

Hirsch distributed his shares in 1893 among the Anglo-Jewish Association, and the Jewish communities of Brussels, Berlin and Frankfort. Of the shares given to

---

[47] Adler-Rudel, p. 47 ff.

[48] There is no contradiction between Chouraqui's story (p. 53) that it was a man of the A.I.U., Chief-Rabbi Zadoc Kahn, who informed Hirsch of the beginnings of a Jewish colonization in the Argentine, which though living in a state of misery, was imbued with the spirit of perseverance, and Adler-Rudel's that it was A. Loewenthal who had approached the A.I.U. which, in turn, put the plan before Hirsch through Zadoc Kahn.

Entirely different is Max Nordau's version (*Jewish Chronicle,* October 1, 1892), according to which Loewenthal, who had learned of Hirsch's willingness to spend £2 million for the alleviation of the plight of Russian Jewry, had, on board his ship during the home journey, drawn up a plan for their colonization in Argentina. On his arrival in Paris he went straight to his friend Nordau, who through Prof. Jules Oppert and Isidor Loeb, another A.I.U. leader, introduced Loewenthal to Hirsch, who accepted the plan.

Arnold White, Hirsch's emissary to Russia, publicly denied that Hirsch's interest in Argentina originated from Loewenthal's plan, but did not give the alternative source of his plan. (Cf. the acrimonious exchange of letters in *Jewish Chronicle,* June 23, June 30, August 13, August 20, October 1, October 8, October 15, 1897).

the Anglo-Jewish Association, Hirsch retained their voting rights for himself for his life-time (and was elected a vice-president of A. J. A.) in order to direct the affairs of I. C. A. as its chairman.

He had first endowed ICA with £2 million, but later on quadrupled this amount.

Hirsch had chosen this form of incorporation, as he said in an interview, because he felt that he as an individual might not be considered as sufficient guarantee by the Russian government, and therefore had decided to associate all Jewry in this, his biggest and crowning undertaking.[49]

Seventy five years have since passed. ICA's original program, the emigration and re-settlement of 3,500,000 Jews from Russia over 25 years remains unfulfilled. Over the years ICA acquired 750,000 hectares of land in the Argentine, 500,000 of which were cultivated. Here, some twenty colonies were established, in which about 3,500 families were settled. The entire Jewish population in and around these colonies never exceeded 35,000-40,000 people.[50] Many of the settlers and their children eventually moved to town.

Two colonies were established in Brazil, and aid was rendered to the farm settlers in Canada and the United States as well as in Russia itself. ICA supported the vocational education schemes initiated by the late Baron at various centres, as well as the work of the Baron Hirsch Fund in New York. After the War of 1914-18, ICA operated in Bessarabia and Poland and helped in setting up credit societies in Eastern Europe. It also supported the scheme of Jewish colonization in Birobidzhan. It cooperated with other Jewish relief organizations, like the JDC (Joint Distribution Committee), and today assists Israel development.

This is not the place for a critical examination of ICA's record, its failures, its achievements. While Hirsch's vision may not have been realized, ICA's indirect contribution to the renaissance of the Jewish people may have been considerable. Argentine's Jewry, which it helped to build up, has become a source of manpower for Israel. Its schools there, like those of the Baron elsewhere, have helped in the making of modern Jewry. Its seventy fifth anniversary (in 1966) would be a fitting occasion for the writing of such a critical history.

Hirsch took a personal interest in each detail of this work. He had welfare offices operated by voluntary ladies' committees in Cracow, Lemberg, Vienna, and Budapest, spending $60,000 annually, on loans rather than on subsidies, and was proud to hear of cases of successful economic rehabilitation aided by these loans. According to O. S. Straus he donated 'for trades in Vienna and Budapest' $1,455,000 and an equal amount for 'Hungarian poor.' Well known was the gift of his turf-winnings, 1891-94 to the London hospitals, totalling $500,000, apart from $200,000 of direct contributions to them.[51]

---

[49] *Jewish Chronicle*, July 8, 1891, quoting *Jüdische Presse*.
[50] Adler-Rudel, p. 57; M. V. Winsberg (*Colonia Baron Hirsch, A Jewish Agricultural Colony in Argentina* (1963), p. 6) quoted 1,440,000 acres, 12 colonies; *Standard Jewish Encyclopedia* refers to 1,107,500 acres, 18 colonies with 16,600 settlers (1951 figures).
[51] *The American Spirit*, p. 332.

There were endless cases of 'smaller contributions,' such as the $50,000 for the Galician town of Stry which had been destroyed by fire, and therefore the estimate of 800 million francs rather than 500 million (i.e., $160 million) sometimes mentioned as the total may not be exaggerated, particularly if one could include also his contributions to non-Jewish institutions, which, apart from the London hospitals, do not appear in Straus's list. Hirsch's widow on her death in April, 1899, left bequests to charity totalling 50 million francs, among them 10 million francs to the Jewish Colonization Assocation, 6 million francs to the Baron Hirsch Fund, New York, 3 million to that in Vienna, 2 million for schools in Jerusalem, and 9 million to Alliance institutions.

To close this record, an anecdote may be quoted which was told in a Viennese paper on Hirsch's demise.[52] Hirsch had for some time spoken of his early death, and he looked ill on his way through Vienna some months before the event. He then attended a board meeting of the Baron Hirsch Foundation. On this occasion he offered an additional annual contribution of 25,000 florin ($12,500). When asked by one of the members to give this undertaking in writing, he flared up and left offended. The next morning, when the offender called upon him to apologize, he said: 'I am not angry, you were quite right. We are only mortals. Look here, I am studying the Austrian Inheritance Law. A high tax—ten per cent! I am trying to find out how to secure and capitalize my foundations.'

'In 1896, under the heading "The Millions to the Millionaires," *Punch* takes for its text an actual appeal made by the working men of Walworth on the death of Baron Hirsch, à propos of his munificent bequests to his countrymen, and holds up the example for imitation.'[53]

A MONUMENT FOR BARON HIRSCH IN NEW YORK

It was a warm response to Hirsch's acts of philanthropy which caused the Jewish masses to create a saga about his name. A typical case is the story of a monument for him in New York.

Wieninger[54] records that in 1902 a monument was erected in New York's Central Park in honor of the great philanthropist, which shows the following dedication, written by President Theodore Roosevelt: 'Whatever may be said or done, the law of brotherhood and general love of mankind will forever remain the first and irrefutable condition in the life of nations.'

Nothing is known about the existence of such a Hirsch monument in New York. Nor would the rather general and nondescript dedication, if actually found on a stone, specifically indicate that this was a Hirsch memorial. A possible explanation for Wieninger's mystifying statement may be the plan for a monument which was men-

---

[52] *Neues Wiener Abendblatt,* April 21, 1896.
[53] Charles L. Graves, *Mr. Punch's History of Modern England* (1926), Vol. IV, p. 103.
[54] *Jüdische National Biographie,* Vol. III, p. 118. (1928). Wieninger quotes the passage in German as follows: 'Was man auch immer sagen oder tun mag, das Gesetz der Brüderlichkeit und der allgemeinen Menschenliebe wird stets die erste und unabweisbare Bedingung im Leben der Völker bleiben.'

tioned in the following letter to the *New York Times* of May 11, 1900 by Jacob H. Schiff.[55]

> 'My attention has been called to a pamphlet appeal, issued over the names of a number of prominent people, asking for contributions toward a fund with which to erect a monument to the late Baron and Baroness de Hirsch, and I have been repeatedly asked for the reasons which have prompted me to keep aloof from this movement. Some months ago, I was approached by a gentleman, then unknown to me, to become a member of a committee, having for its purpose the initiation of the movement referred to.
> Knowing from my many years' official connection with, and labours on behalf of, the Hirsch Foundation, and from my personal acquaintance with the lamented Baron and Baroness de Hirsch, of the intention, labours and wishes of these great philanthropists, I do not hesitate to say, that nothing could be further from their desires than that the aspirations of their noble lives should be perpetuated through a monument in stone and iron. Indeed, it was the last request of the Baroness de Hirsch that no addresses nor eulogies be pronounced over her grave. The noble woman, no doubt, felt that, if the ideas and endeavours, which she and the Baron had embodied permanently in the princely foundations the world over, which they had instituted, could not secure honour and permanency to their memory, no words or monuments could do this.'

A persual of the *New York Times* and Jewish journals of that time may help to clear up the mystery.

---

[55] Cf. Vol. II/348. His Life and Letters (ed. C. Adler), N. Y. 1928.

CHAPTER VII

BARON HIRSCH AND ZIONISM

I

IN PARIS, on June 2, 1895, Theodor Herzl, who was to become the father of political Zionism and the *Judenstaat,* called on Baron Hirsch,[1] the founder of Jewish colonization in Argentina, a philanthropist on a scale unrivalled hitherto, 'the Jewish Carnegie before Carnegie,[2] who had startled the world by his munificence.

Hirsch's invitation was in response to Herzl's request, and Herzl came with notes carefully prepared for this interview. It was to be inconclusive, though not a failure, as is often thought. It might have been followed up at a later date, but not long thereafter, on April 20, 1896, Hirsch died.

When Herzl heard of Hirsch's death, he reproached himself. 'Of the rich Jews he was the only one ready to do something big for the poor. Maybe, I did not know how to treat him. It is months that the pamphlet [*Der Judenstaat*] is out. I gave it to everybody but him. His collaboration could have helped our cause to a rapid success. I feel that our cause has become poorer. I still thought that I could win Hirsch for our plan.'[3]

Indeed, there was much Herzl and Hirsch had in common in their approach to the Jewish problem, and in some respects Hirsch was ahead of Herzl in national thinking, probably without being aware of it. For this reason a careful examination of the facts does not seem to warrant Maurice Samuel's dictum, however beautifully phrased, that Hirsch 'had immortality within his grasp. Or, perhaps, that, too, is an illusion. Perhaps he was foredoomed by his narrow practicability to possess the strength which would have assured him immortality, and to lack the vision without which it was impossible.'[4] Even a careful historian, like Salo W. Baron, could be misled into speaking of Baron Hirsch '...who refused to help Theodor Herzl in the establishment of a Jewish homeland in Palestine, [yet] was nevertheless prepared to stake his entire fortune on Jewish agricultural colonization in the New World.'[5]

Neither does the article in the *Jüdisches Lexikon* quite do justice to Hirsch in saying that 'he had little understanding for political Zionism, as he was still imbued with the philanthropic ideas of the nineteenth century, and did not believe in a properly organized self-help and a national renaissance.'

---

[1] See Herzl. *Tagebücher,* Vol. I pp. 20 ff.
[2] Abraham Goldberg, *Pioneers and Builders* (1943), p. 438.
[3] *Tagebücher,* Vol. I, p. 369.
[4] *New Palestine,* Herzl Memorial Issue (1929), p. 125.
[5] S. W. Baron, 'The Modern Age,' in (ed.) E. W. Schwartz's *Great Ideas and Ages of the Jewish People* (1956), p. 399.

Nor can we accept as historically correct the statement by Abraham Goldberg in his otherwise most understanding appreciation of Hirsch[6] 'that he failed to see, what Herzl tried to convince him of in vain, that the Jewish renaissance and return to economic and social normalcy can be effected only in one country,—Palestine.' In fact, at the time of their meeting, Herzl himself had not yet accepted this axiom. A week after meeting Hirsch, he noted in his diary: 'The arguments against the choice of Palestine: the proximity of Russia and Europe, the lack of opportunity for expansion, the climate, to which one is unaccustomed. In favor: the powerful legend.'[7] And in the *Judenstaat,* published about six months later, in which the respective advantages of Argentina and Palestine are discussed, he states, 'We shall take what is given us, and what is selected by Jewish public opinion.'[8]

Elkan N. Adler, in fact, tells us that Herzl, when visiting London in November 1895, was not yet set on Palestine, but was swayed in its favour only by the influence of the English Zionists; later, however, the idea of East Africa and Argentina came came up again.[9]

II

Hirsch, says Goldberg, was 'neither a visionary nor a philosopher, but a man of sound and practical common sense.'[10] In contrast to Herzl, who just had started a political, albeit long-term solution for the Jewish question, but was forced by the prevailing circumstances to look for what he styled a 'Nachtasyl' elsewhere, Hirsch was searching for a practical solution, for immediate relief, which would, as he saw it, entail also a political solution.'Perhaps he shared with Herzl the dream of a Jewish Homeland in Palestine. But the suffering and the need were too real and too urgent to wait for political processes. He favoured and financed immediate action for rescue work.'[11]

Hirsch, in an article which he wrote in *Forum* in August, 1891, mentioned as countries under consideration for his settlement scheme Argentina, Australia, and Canada. He also stated that he was awaiting the report of a study mission he had sent to Argentina on the prospects there; but Palestine is not mentioned in this context.

Perhaps Hirsch was prompted in this omission by a letter which Carl Netter in 1882 published in a number of journals, arguing against Palestine as a place for Jewish mass settlement.[12] Netter had been deeply impressed by the sudden onrush of refugees from Russia and Rumania, for which he thought Palestine ill prepared. Did he not know of the hardship suffered in Palestine by the German Templer colo-

---

[6] *Pioneers and Builders,* p. 437.
[7] *Tagebücher,* Vol. I, p. 63.
[8] *The Jewish State* (1896), English edition (1936). p. 30.
[9] T. Nussenblatt, *Zeitgenossen über Herzl* (1929). pp. 11-12, also *Tagebücher,* Vol. I, p. 301.
[10] *Pioneers and Builders,* p. 438.
[11] Centennial Volume, Baron Hirsch Institute (Montreal, 1963), p. 19.
[12] Cf. A. R. Malachi, *Mourning of the Yishuv for Carl Netter,* (Hebrew), *Les Cahiers de l'Alliance Israélite Universelle* XII, Nos. 5-8 (June 1963).

nies, and the failure experienced there by an American settlement? Netter, who had been Hirsch's advisor for many of his educational donations, was apparently unhappy over the reaction to his letter in Palestine, where he particularly valued and supported the Chovevei Zion, the 'Bilus,' whose pioneering spirit he greatly admired. He hurried back to Mikveh Israel, but died soon after his return, before he could undo the damage his letter had caused. In any event, under the prevailing political regime Palestine had to be ruled out as a centre for mass immigration and settlement.

Even Shmaryahu Levin, who with his Zionist fellow students had organized demonstrations against Hirsch's Argentine scheme, admits that at that time the small new settlement in Palestine was passing through a crisis, and that it was impossible in 1891, the year of the expulsion of the Jews from Moscow, to make use of Palestine for the emigrants.[13]

Still, we are told by Bein[14] that Hirsch had been in contact with the Chovevei Zion, the precursors of modern Zionism, and had acknowledged the historical ties with Palestine. But in view of his first-hand knowledge of Turkey, and his unpleasant experiences with the Government of Abdul Hamid, he thought that, for political as well as economic reasons, Palestine was not suited for a permanent and well-secured Jewish colonization.

In later years a similar opinion was held by Lord Nathaniel Rothschild, who had become an ardent follower of Herzl's and who on no account wanted a National Home under Turkish rule[15]—in sharp contrast to his Paris relative, Baron Edmond, the 'Father of the Yishuv,' who preferred philanthropic support for quiet infiltration into Palestine, and who remained antagonistic to Herzl and political Zionism, going so far as to oppose it through Sylvain Levi before the Supreme Allied Council at Versailles in 1919.[16]

Sokolov, too, mentions that Hirsch in his negotiations with the Chovevei Zion was not altogether opposed to Palestine,[17] but wavered between different countries in considering soil, price, income, i.e., economic factors, but not history and national desire. During these negotiations he revealed his idea of creating a Jewish Commonwealth *(Gemeinwesen)* saying that he was preparing the conditions for it.[18]

III

But it was not only the instability of the Ottoman regime as such, the arbitrariness of an autocracy, which made Hirsch hesitate about Palestine, but fear of what would follow the regime's apparently inevitable eventual collapse. Herzl, as we have seen, had considered the proximity of Russia as one of the arguments against Pales-

---

[13] *Youth in Revolt*, p. 258.
[14] A. Bein, *Theodor Herzl* (1940), p. 124.
[15] Cf. Fraenkel, *Herzl Yearbook* III, p. 236.
[16] Cf. S. S. Sabatay, 'An Early Zionist Affair' *Jerusalem Post*, January 1, 1965.
[17] Hirsch seems to have planned a visit to Palestine in summer 1880 (cf. *Jewish Chronicle*, July 2, 1880). The *Israelitische Wochenblatt* advised his travelling incognito 'in order that his mission be successful.'
[18] Sokolov, *History of Zionism*, p. 259.

tine. Hirsch too, as we learn from Elkan N. Adler, '...was profoundly impressed by the belief that Palestine was destined to fall into the hands of Russia. And it was this, and this alone, as he himself assured me, that led him to fix upon Argentina, rather than the Holy Land, as the scene of his great experiment in Jewish agriculture.'[19] Hirsch's fear that Palestine would fall under the domination of Russia, 'the archenemy of the Jewish people,' was not without foundation. In the 1880's Britain's policy in the Middle East was dictated by the need of securing Egypt as a reserve bastion, should Constantinople, as was feared, fall to the Russians. British policy was to prevent such an eventuality at any cost, although popular opinion, led by Gladstone, was often vehemently against the 'unspeakable Turk.' In 1877 even Salisbury, a member of Beaconsfield's Cabinet and 'a strong churchman,' seemed inclined to favour a Russian occupation of Constantinople.[20] The continued British occupation of Egypt led to a deterioration in Anglo-French relations, and to an improvement in Franco-Russian relations, which would have made it even more difficult for the British Navy to aid Turkey in the Dardanelles.[21] With Cyprus, the Suez Canal, and the route to India under British control, there were advocates of a settlement granting Russia the Straits and parts of Asia Minor, and giving Austria control over Salonica and predominance in the Balkans; this was considered preferable to a settlement at the northern gates of India. Salisbury seems to have entertained this idea for a while, and mentioned it to William II at Cowes on August 28, 1895.[22] Later, he seems to have changed his mind.

Hirsch, moving in the diplomatic circles in London where these ideas circulated, and interested as he was in Near Eastern politics, was no doubt, well informed on these trends of political thinking and quite justified in his pessimism about the future of Turkey in Asia Minor, knowing as he did, from personal experience, the fickleness and instability of the Ottoman regime and its uncertain future.

IV

Hirsch expressed this fear of Russia in a memorandum, dated Carlsbad, August 1891[23] one of the few documents by Hirsch still preserved. It was sent in response to

---

[19] Elkan N. Adler, *Jews in Many Lands*, p. 91. cf. also Nussenblatt, *Zeitgenossen*, p. 11.
[20] Cf. Robinson, Gallagher and Denny, *Africa and the Victorians* (1961), pp. 254 ff.
[21] Cf. also Sir Edward Pears, a staunch Gladstonian liberal, who, living in Turkey since 1873, had reported on the Bulgarian and Armenian massacres, and who recalls that the general European abhorrence and political annoyance could no longer tolerate the Turkish misgovernment and outrages; and that the European powers were willing to permit, and even invite, Russia to enter Asia Minor and annex Armenia proper and little Armenia, as far as and including Alexandretta, with special arrangements for Palestine, Syria, and Arabia. The evidence that Britain would have acquiesced in such a solution had it not been for her fear of German penetration, came to the author's attention in 1906, (*Forty Years in Constantinople*, p. 374).

Cf., also, Salisbury to Layard: 'The Arabs and the Asiatics in general will look to the Russian as the coming man. His influence over Syria and Mesopotamia will be very embarrassing.' (Temperley, *Foundations of British Foreign Policy* (1938), p. 394.
[22] Cf. G. P. Gooch, *Recent Revelations of European Diplomacy* (1940), p. 57.
[23] J. de Haas, *Theodor Herzl* (1927), Vol. II, Appendix I. (see Appendix II, p. 122).

an approach by the Chovevei Zion, who, as we learn from the covering note by Adam Rosenberg, a New York leader of that movement, wished to bring about an 'entente' between Baron Edmond de Rothschild and Baron Hirsch, and it concerned the formation of a 'Farmers' Trust Bank' for aiding Jewish settlers in 'Asiatic Turkey.' From this document it transpires that Hirsch, in spite of his objections to a settlement in Turkey, and his economic preference of Argentina, would have been prepared to lend his financial support and political connections to Jewish colonization in Turkey, provided it was based on a plan drawn up by an expert committee in the composition and expenses of which he was ready to participate. Nothing came of this committee, though it is unclear whether this was due, as Rosenberg heard, to 'a purely personal reason between the two barons,' although the funds for the committee's expenses were fast forthcoming, or to the fact that the Chovevei Zion failed in raising their half of the expected expenses. We know however from Ahad Haam that the Alliance Israélite was to set up a Central Committee—presumably for colonization work—and that he was to be a member of a body 'which was to visit Turkey and other countries in Asia in accordance with the wishes of Baron Hirsch.'[24] Later on, in Paris, Ahad Haam 'met also the Deputy Manager of Baron Hirsch's philanthropies, who told him that the idea of settling Jews in Palestine was an admirable one, but that the methods of the Chovevei Zion and their love for publicity made it impossible to cooperate with them in the work.'[25] In his memoirs, Dr. Bodenheimer recalls[26] being told by Dr. Hildesheimer, a Berlin Chovevei Zion leader, of his having attended a conference, such as that referred to in Rosenberg's note, where Hirsch had urged a deputation to Constantinople to press for lifting the Ottoman ban on Jewish immigration. For that a fund of 500,000 francs was needed. Hirsch had promised half, if others would raise the balance. But only 40,000 francs were raised, and Hirsch subsequently withdrew from the Palestine project. In Rosenberg's note accompanying Hirsch's Carlsbad Memorandum a sum of 10,000 francs is mentioned which Hirsch's partners were to, and apparently did, raise for the commission's expenses: quite a different sum. Would 20,000 francs have been sufficient? Is 500,000 francs not an exaggerated amount, unless meant to cover foreseen 'unforeseen expenses' in Turkey? It is quite possible that the project, as Rosenberg had heard, failed because of the antagonism between the two barons. Hirsch, as his memorandum shows, was intrinsically a 'political Zionist.' He wanted a concession, a 'charter' from the Turkish Government; Baron Rothschild believed in quiet infiltration. And we learn from Ludwig Stein[27] that Hirsch was willing to take over the Rothschild colonies in Palestine, although he considered their economic prospects less favourable than of those in Argentina. Of all this Herzl was unaware when he met Hirsch.

---

[24] Leon Simon, *Ahad Haam* (1961), p. 67.
[25] *Ibid.*, p. 71.
[26] M. J. Bodenheimer, *Prelude to Israel* (1963), p. 77.
[27] Cf. Nussenblatt, *Zeitgenossen*, p. 208.

V

There is still another version for the reason which made Hirsch favour Argentina. According to Herman Landau,[28] a Canadian Jewish leader who had tried to interest Hirsch in Jewish colonization in Canada, the decision went in favour of Argentina because upon the failure of a bank (Murietta and Cie.) in which Hirsch allegedly had a large interest, the Baron had to take in payment Argentina land bonds which could apparently be realized only in kind.

This story is not quite convincing, considering that Hirsch decided in favour of Argentina after having received a favourable report from a study mission, and after analyzing the comparative economic advantages of a number of countries prepared to receive mass-immigration. He referred to the advantages of Argentina in his Carlsbad Memorandum, as quality and price of land, and facility of communications. It was these factors which made him decide as he did, and not the alleged holding of Argentine land bonds, or, as is sometimes mentioned, the advice of his friend Edward, Prince of Wales. Moreover, Hirsch had decided on his Argentine venture in 1890, and had formed I.C.A. in 1891, while the difficulties entailing the liquidation of C. Murietta & Company arose in 1892.[28*]

While Hirsch concentrated his efforts and his hopes on the Argentine venture because it permitted a concentrated, large-scale Jewish settlement,—an instinctive 'Judenstaat' policy—he, nevertheless lent his support also to Jewish constructive settlement elsewhere, in Canada and the United States, and was ready to do the same in Palestine. His over-riding consideration was to help Jews escaping from oppression to establish themselves again as free, self-reliant citizens, wherever they could do so.

It was the same motive, in a way, which, in seeking a 'Judenstaat für Judennot,' prompted Herzl to seek a 'Nachtasyl' on the way. If Hirsch, practical as he was and unreceptive to ideologies, did aim at a quick solution, he was probably not unaware of the fact that his first 'deputy' in Argentina, Colonel Albert E. W. Goldsmid, an old Chovevei Zion member, considered these colonies as a 'nursery ground for Palestine.' The way, as he used to say, leads from A[rgentine] to Z[ion].

VI

Thus, when some sources, like the *Oesterreichisches Biographisches Lexikon,* maintain, that Hirsch was not won over to Zionism, the historian can accept such a statement only with a qualification. Modern Zionism, as the word came to be understood, was still unknown when Hirsch died. When Herzl approached Hirsch the idea was still in ferment and not mature. When the two met, no mention was made of the word 'Judenstaat,' nor of Palestine, which, indeed, was not yet Herzl's aim at that time. As Bein, Herzl's biographer, comments[29] Herzl had approached Hirsch too soon.

---

[28] A. A. Chiel, *The Jews in Manitoba* (1961), p. 46.
[28*] Cf. David Joslin, *A Century of Banking in Latin America* (1963), p. 147.
[29] *Theodor Herzl,* p. 130.

'THE GREAT MEN' — LEADERS OF THE ANGLO-JEWISH ASSOCIATION
1. Very Rev. Dr. Hermann Adler. 2. Haham Dr. M. Gaster. 3. Sir Samuel Montagu (later Lord Swaythling). 4. First Lord Rothschild. 5. Baron de Hirsch. 6. F. D. Mocatta. 7. Baron H. de Worms, M. P. (later Lord Pirbright.) 8. (Sir) Benjamin L. Cohen, M. P. 9. Dr. M. Friedlander (Principal of Jews' College). 10. Prof. D. W. Marks. 11. Sir Julian Goldsmid. 12. Sir A. Sassoon. C. 1894

Nor had he approached him the right way, namely, from a practical angle. 'He should have come to this cool, practical man with a more specific plan of action.' But Herzl at that time had only a political vision and no practical plan. He criticized and did not give due weight to Hirsch's achievements which, as Sokolov judiciously puts it, 'had met with the measure of failure and success to be expected by such enterprises.'[30] Herzl wrongly accused Hirsch, 'You breed beggars... This philanthropy debases the character of our people.' As Hirsch had emphasized,[31] his aim was self-emancipation, the re-establishment of the oppressed Jews as a productive, independent citizenry. The difficulties of the early years, which may have prompted Herzl's rather rash prejudgement, would be encountered even today in any colonizing enterprise, however superior its organization might be, if immigration could not be selective.

Herzl's approach to Hirsch suffered apparently from what one might call a 'wrongly compensated inferiority complex.' The *Tagebuch* shows clearly his anxiety to make the right impression on the powerful Hirsch, to appear as an equal, to outsnob the

---

[30] *History of Zionism*, p. 258.
[31] 'My views on Philanthropy,' *North American Review*, 416, (July, 1891) and 'An asylum for the Russian Jews,' *Forum* (August, 1891).

snob, (which Hirsch was not). He bought new gloves, for the interview, but crumpled them up so that they should not appear too new! If Hirsch was a snob he was so vis-à-vis the rich. As he said in an interview with Lucien Wolf, 'If a Jew gets rich, he ceases to be a Jew,'[32] (meaning that he loses the compassion for his poor brothers). And to Herzl he said: 'The rich Jews will give you nothing, they are bad, they display no interest in the sufferings of the poor.' It was then that Herzl exclaimed: 'You talk like a socialist, Baron Hirsch.' These psychological stresses may have made Herzl misunderstand Hirsch. For instance, Herzl mentions that Hirsch's eyes twinkled when he exclaimed that he would go to the Kaiser William II, 'who has been educated to the reception of great ideas.' Herzl interpreted this twinkle as a sign of Hirsch being impressed by his courage to approach William. It did not occur to him that the more cynical Hirsch, as an intimate friend of Edward (VII), was not inclined to share his belief in William's receptiveness for great ideas. The question, thus, is not whether Hirsch was, or was not, won over to the Zionist idea, but what his reaction would have been to Herzlian Zionism had he had a chance to know it. Here we obviously enter a field of conjecture.

VII

It is rather difficult to define Hirsch's attitude to Jewish matters. He was not, like so many of his 'assimilationist' contemporaries, a super-patriot of his country. He was the proverbial 'Weltbürger,' a cosmopolite who had changed his citizenship—a mere convenience—four times. *Ubi bene, ibi patria.* He had his homes in England, France, Moravia and Hungary, and was thinking of one in Argentina as well, where, as he told Lucien Wolf, he might manage the colonization work himself. Thus, strange as abstract ideologies were to his mind, he would have had little understanding for the connotations of 'national movement,' or 'national home.' Though he had a strictly religious upbringing he was not himself religious or traditional. Only on Yom-Kippur did he refrain from hunting in order not to hurt the feelings of his Jewish acquaintances. Nor did religious scruples prevent him from seeking a daughter-in-law in the English aristocracy.[33] Still, Wolf perceived in him a 'genuine racial pride,' a 'thoroughly Jewish heart'; 'his Jewish chauvinism was very marked.' He probably would not have been particularly perturbed had Herzl mentioned the word 'Judenstaat,' though he might have suggested something like 'öffentlich-rechtlich gesicherte Heimstätte,' as more acceptable to many Jewish circles. Had he not himself spoken of a 'Gemeinwesen,' a commonwealth? And, as we read in Bodenheimer's Memoirs,[34] he had originally intended to turn his colonies in Argentine into a Jewish state; he had, in fact, thought of a kind of congress, a convention of all the Jewish communities, for that purpose, but was dissuaded from this idea by his brother-in-law, Baron Ferdinand Bischoffsheim, who feared that such a step might endanger

---

[32] Lucien Wolf, 'Glimpse of Baron de Hirsch, *Jewish Chronicle,* May 8, 1896.
[33] See Margot Asquith, *My Autobiography,* p. 85 ff.
[34] Bodenheimer, *Prelude to Israel,* p. 113.

the newly-won emancipation of the Jews in their home countries. To him a 'state' was still a legal term, and not the outward expression of a national ambition. For this reason he may not have grasped the idea of the 'Judenstaat am Wege,' i.e., political organization and national renaissance, prior to the achievement of the State, although he would have approved of an organization for the purpose of preparing emigration. In our language today 'A Zionist is one who settles in Israel.' But he took an active part wherever Jewish interests were at stake. He used his connections at the Congress of Berlin in 1878 for helping to obtain the emancipation of the Jews in Rumania.[35] He intervened with Sir Henry Drummond Wolff on behalf of the Jews in Persia.[36] Wolff passing through Vienna in October, 1889, on his way to Persia, where he had been accredited as British representative, recalls being entertained by 'the celebrated Baron Hirsch,' who was much interested in the conditions of the Jews there and their amelioration. True, one might say, these are the efforts of a 'shtadlan' (one who intervenes on someone else's behalf). But all his early efforts for the emancipation of Jews in Russia and Rumania eventually became a big drive for what he meant to be an auto-emancipation on new soil. Significant, too, is his answer to a Russian Jewish industrialist, who prided himself on the large number of workers he employed, and on a Jewish hospital he had built. 'I wish,' said Hirsch, 'you employed such a large number of Jews and had built your hospital for the Russians.'[37] In all these Jewish activities Hirsch's wife Clara was a staunch support and source of inspiration. Particularly after the death of her son, as Sokolov mentions,[38] did she find comfort in the idea of establishing a home for the oppressed Jewish people.

Herzl, though instinctively attracted to him, never realized how close Hirsch was to his basic idea, to his analysis of the Jewish problem. As Sacher puts it, Hirsch's 'analysis of conditions in the "Pale of Settlement" had convinced him that mere philanthropy would never solve one of the most persistent problems of Jewish economic life: marginalism.'[39] The remedy: mass-emigration and auto-emancipation. The Jews must become productive again, they must return to the soil. This could be done only in a new land offering the possibilities for mass-immigration and of settling Jews on the land. These were also basic parts of the Zionist credo, and there was in Hirsch's idea a note of the 'avoda azmith,' self-labour postulate of A. D. Gordon. Goldberg rightly says that Hirsch's mistake was in the postulate that only farmers are productive,[40] but we can find the same mistake in more recent Zionist thinking, in the equation of pioneering spirit with agricultural self-labour.

Hirsch's exaggerated 'physiocratic' views are, indeed, surprising in one of the greatest entrepreneurs of the new industrial era. He was emphatically anti-intellectual. He wrote in a letter, that he preferred the lad who tends his father's cattle and field

---

[35] N. M. Gelber, 'The Intervention of German Jews at Berlin Congress,' Leo Baeck Yearbook, 1960.
[36] Sir Henry Drummond Wolff, Rambling Recollections, Vol. II, p. 370.
[37] Oesterreichische Wochenschrift, May 11, 1896.
[38] History of Zionism, p. 256.
[39] Howard Morley Sacher, The Course of Modern Jewish History (1958), p. 510.
[40] Goldberg, Pioneers and Builders, p. 441.

to the one who knew how to write and read. And to Herzl he said that all our troubles were due to Jewish ambition to rise too high. Still, in his *Forum* article he takes pride in the achievements of Jewish doctors, scientists, statesmen, musicians and poets, indicating the contribution Jews can make to the world under conditions of freedom.

Herzl differed. He wanted to bring a sophisticated European society into the home country, without structural changes, without the 'Berufsumschichtung' postulated by the Zionist youth movement, in this respect closer to Hirsch than to Herzl.

Herzl thought that to re-create the 'historical peasant' would be like arming a modern army with cross-bow and arrow.[41] And yet the very same peasant soon appeared as a symbol of the Zionist movement on the certificates of the Jewish National Fund. Thus, says Goldberg, 'without [Hirsch] being aware of it, ...his Jewish philosophy and approach to the Jewish problem were basically Zionistic.'[42]

Similarly, Shmaryahu Levin, once an outspoken and active antagonist, referring to the talk in those years of an autonomous Jewish settlement in Argentina 'a new attempt to bind the Jew to a soil—and not his own' wondered 'whether Baron Hirsch was merely a great philanthropist, or a man with a vast dream of a Jewish national reconstruction.'[43]

Somewhat different is Sokolov's evaluation: 'Hirsch was not a Zionist, nor do we desire to claim him as a national Jew. Had he been asked, whether he recognized the national idea, he would have replied, that he was opposed to it. He was not made interested in abstract ideas. Nevertheless his actions became those of a national Jew.'[44]

And it is the actions that matter. As Goldberg says, 'Hirsch belonged to the small group of Jewish leaders, who helped prepare the advent of a new era in Jewish life.[45]

---

[41] *Tagebücher*, Vol. I, p. 40.
[42] *Pioneers and Builders*, p. 441.
[43] *Youth in Revolt*, p. 265.
[44] *History of Zionism*, p. 252.
[45] *Pioneers and Builders*, p. 443. Recently discovered letters of William II and the Auswärtige Amt to the Grand Duke of Baden show that they thought Hirsch was backing the Jewish colonization in Palestine. Thus William, on September 29, 1898, writing on his sympathies for the Zionist idea, mentions that he followed the Zionist activities, furthered by the 'berüchtigte und allbekannte,' the notorious and well-known Baron Hirsch. And the Auswärtige Amt too, in a letter dated January 26, 1904, refers to the colonization activities in Palestine, backed by rich Jews, like Baron Rothschild and Baron Hirsch. Cf. A. Bein, 'Dokumente über Herzl's Begegnung mit Wilhelm II,' *Zeitschrift für die Geschichte der Juden*, II, 1-2 (1965).

CHAPTER VIII

FRIENDS AND ENEMIES IN HIGH PLACES

FERDINAND OF BULGARIA AND THE BOURBONS

AMONG Hirsch's friends, one was much impressed by Herzl's idea. 'It is a grandiose idea... it has my full sympathy' Prince Ferdinand of Bulgaria told Herzl, and added ...'I was really brought up by Jews; I spent my youth with Baron Hirsch. I am half a Jew, as people often reproach me.'[1] This was said three months after the death of Hirsch of whom a *Times* obituary had recorded that 'he was on intimate terms with Prince Ferdinand of Bulgaria,' a circumstance which, it pointed out, at one time led to much speculation.[2] The Viennese papers remembered on this occasion that the Coburg princes, like the Prince of Wales, were among Hirsch's permanent hunting guests, and that he maintained almost friendly (intimate) relations with the Orleans family.[3] On April 23, 1896 *The Times* reported from St. Petersburg that Prince Ferdinand of Bulgaria, on an official visit there, had left the day before, apparently earlier than anticipated, straight for Paris in order to attend his friend's funeral. Before the ceremony he was closeted with the widow for half an hour.[4]

It is indeed difficult to explain this friendship. Prince Ferdinand of Saxe-Coburg-Gotha, (according to Brockhaus: Coburg-Kohary, 1861-1948) was 26 years old, and an officer in the Hungarian army,[5] when he was elected ruler of Bulgaria on July 7, 1887. His mother, Princess Clementine of Orleans, was a daughter of Louis Philippe.[6] She had married Prince August of Saxe-Coburg-Kohary (1818-1881), a nephew of Leopold I of Belgium, the husband of her older sister. Leopold himself arranged this marriage; one of his friends and advisors was Senator J. R. Bischoffsheim, Hirsch's father-in-law. In his memoirs, Germany's Ambassador to Paris, Prince Hohenlohe, who repeatedly quotes Hirsch's opinion on Turkish affairs, recounts on April 19, 1882: 'Shooting today with Hirsch, in the Versailles preserves, I drove with N. Potocki, Hirsch with the Duc de Penthiève and the Duc de Coburg. A true sign of the times was the sight of the grandson of Louis Philippe [i.e., the Duc de Penthiève] shooting with Hirsch, the German Jew.'[7] Is it Ferdinand who would have been 21 at that time, who is referred to here as 'duke,' or is it rather his brother August

---

[1] Theodor Herzl, *Tagebücher*, July 22, 1896, Vol. I, p. 500.
[2] *The Times*, April 22, 1896.
[3] *Augsburger Abendzeitung*, April 23, 1896.
[4] *Jewish Chronicle*, April 24, 1896; *Oesterreichische Wochenschrift*, April 24, 1896.
[5] Cf. his picture in Honved uniform, p. 87.
[6] 'Bulgaria,' *Encyclopedia Britannica* (1910), Vol. IV.
[7] *Memoirs of Prince Chlodwig Hohenlohe—Schillingfürst* (1906), Vol. II, p. 293.

Prince Ferdinand of Bulgaria

(1845-1907) who seems also to have been friendly with Hirsch. He was mentioned among the mourners at Lucien Hirsch's funeral on April 8, 1887.[8]

Ferdinand '...was a typical Orleans,—every feature of his interesting head disclosed that he was a scion of the French Royal family.'[9] This is the description of him given by R. von Kühlmann, the German diplomat, and later Foreign Secretary, (whose father had been General Manager of the Oriental Railways in Constantinople —'an earlier young man of Türkenhirsch'—a fact which made his son tainted to Hallgarten[10]) when the latter visited Sofia in 1914. Kühlmann found Ferdinand a brilliant *causeur*, who recalled the valuable advice on Balkan politics he had received from Kühlmann's father. 'And Ferdinand's mother,' says Kühlmann, 'who had inherited the family's political gifts, for a while financially supported the not always stable Bulgarian throne.'[11]

---

[8] *Jüdische Presse*, Berlin, April 21, 1887.
[9] Richard von Kühlmann, *Erinnerungen* (1948), p. 443. cf. Sir Valentine Chirol (*Fifty Years in a Changing World* (1927), p. 127): 'His features, and more especially his nose, betrayed his partly Jewish descent... Something in his manners and pose reminded me that he was not only a Kohary, but also a great-grandson of Phillipe Egalité.' And that old hand in the British Consular Service, A. G. Hulme-Beaman, writes (*Twenty Years in the Near East*, London, (1898), p. 185): 'Prince Ferdinand is altogether a Bourbon in appearance.' Prince Francis Joseph Kohary, the last of his line, was father-in-law of Ferdinand's grandfather, Duke Ferdinand August George of Saxe-Coburg (1785-1850).
[10] Hallgarten, *Imperialismus vor 1914* (second edition), Vol. II, p. 278.
[11] Kühlmann, *Erinnerungen*, p. 503.

On a second visit to Sofia during World War I when Kühlmann accompanied Wilhelm II, Ferdinand offered to sell his guest some valuable tobacco land for private investment at a low price. Wilhelm considered this offer as an attempt to bribe him.[12] Ironically, Ferdinand's predecessor on the throne of Bulgaria, Alexander of Battenberg, 'was held to have been under the influence of Hirsch and the Austrians';[13] he was anti-Russian, and, therefore, forced out. And we are left to wonder to what extent Hirsch was a king maker in the case of Ferdinand.

Hirsch indeed had been known to be a supporter of the monarchist restoration movements in France and Spain.[14] According to Dennis Brogan 'the great Austrian Jewish banker, Baron Hirsch, subscribed handsomely to a cause dear to the leaders of Paris society, [i.e., the movement led by General Boulanger]. Who knew? It might open doors hitherto closed to him, though he was a friend of the Prince of Wales.'[15]

Hirsch's behaviour becomes even clearer in Walter Frank's story—based on unpublished documents in the Political Archives of the German Foreign Ministry—that the Count of Paris contributed 800,000 francs to Boulanger's election fund, 500,000 of which were given by Hirsch, who in return for this gift was promised entry into High Society.[17] On November 20, 1888 Count Münster, the German Ambassador to Paris, reported home that Rothschild remained cool to the Orleans entreaties to come to terms with Boulanger, but that Hirsch was not averse to putting a few millions on this card.[17] And there is the more recent version by Guy Chapman,[18] according to which Hirsch contributed 2.5 out of the four million francs in the hands of the Royalist Committee in 1888, in return for which gift he was to be elected to the Club of the rue Royale. When he was eventually black-balled, he—as we know from other sources—acquired the premises in which the Club was located and had it evicted.

This incident is reminiscent of the story told about Anselm v. Rothschild who, black-balled by a casino club near Vienna for the usual antisemitic reasons, by way of reprisal, bought a modern sewage disposal unit for the adjoining village and installed it within sight and smell of the casino. He was quickly sent a membership card which was returned, scented with the most expensive perfume—and the sanitary construction went right on.

In any event, Hirsch's support of Boulanger did not endear him to the French government. In a note (in the Austrian State Archives) dated September 23, 1890, the Austrian Embassy in London reported to Vienna on a rumour from Paris, to the

---

[12] *Ibid.*
[13] Langer, *European Alliances and Alignments,* p. 340.
[14] *Jüdisches Lexicon.*
[15] D. W. Brogan, *The Development of Modern France, 1870-1939* (1940), p. 202.
[16] Walter Frank, *Nationalismus und Demokratie im Frankreich der Dritten Republik, 1871-1914* (1933), p. 141.
[17] *Ibid.,* p. 216.
[18] Guy Chapman, *The Third Republic in France, First Phase 1871-1894* (1962), p. 289. Chapman's source appears to be Dansette, *Boulangisme* (1946).

Friends and Enemies

effect that the French government was considering the expulsion of Hirsch from France for his connections with Boulanger. (This was eighteen months after Boulanger had fled to Brussels).

These stories would seem to refer to the years 1888-89. But, as we have seen in the Hohenlohe Memoirs, Hirsch was accepted in Parisian High Society, though not at the Club, even before 1882. His support of Boulanger was actually meant to be support for the cause of Orleans.

His involvement in the affair of Count Harry von Arnim fifteen years earlier may be interpreted in the same way.

In 1873 Hirsch's name was involved in a *cause célèbre,* the scandal and subsequent criminal proceedings instituted by Bismarck against Count Harry von Arnim, former German Ambassador to France. In his 'cloak and dagger' biography of Baron von Holstein, Joachim von Kürenberg tells us how Holstein, officially attached to the Embassy as Secretary, but actually sent by Bismarck to spy on his chief, found incriminating letters addressed to Baron Hirsch, 11, rue Carancbacelle, Nice.[19] Arnim was supposed to have delayed certain negotiations relating to the French war indemnity with the express purpose of benefiting certain speculations on the stock exchange in which he was engaged with Baron Hirsch. As Emil Ludwig saw it: 'There is a ludicrous similarity between the accusations which Bismarck and Arnim, both Pomeranian Junkers, both leading servants of the Empire, each of them guided in business matters by an ennobled Jew, levy against each other.'[20] But apparently no substantiation for this suspicion could be found and, as Bismarck[21] records, no attempt was made in Court to prove Arnim's connection with Hirsch on the above-mentioned grounds.

In retrospect, Arnim's connection with Hirsch seems to have been a different one. Arnim, as we learn from Bismarck, tried to influence the German Emperor in favour of a restoration of the French monarchy and apparently worked against the Thiers government, a policy which conflicted with that pursued by Bismarck. Hirsch, too, as we know, actively supported the Royalist cause. The two men may have been brought together by this common interest which does not exclude cooperation in the financial sphere as well.

This is the meager evidence, direct and inferred, of an intriguing relationship of Hirsch's with the House of Orleans. We may add that Ferdinand's secretary Fürth,[22] a converted Jew, who had previously been Hirsch's secretary[23] appears to have acted as a go-between between Herzl and Hirsch.[24]

---

[19] Joachim von Kürenberg, *His Excellency, The Spectre* (1933), p. 24.
[20] Emil Ludwig, *Bismarck*, (1927), p. 448.
[21] Bismarck, *Gedanken und Erinnerungen* (1898), p. 464.
[22] *Jewish Chronicle*, May 28, 1896.
[23] M. Nordau in *Jewish Chronicle*, August 20, 1897.
[24] Herzl, *Tagebücher*, Vol. I, pp. 213 and 224.

BARON HIRSCH AND HIGH SOCIETY

There was something peculiar, almost pathetic, in Hirsch's relations with the Austrian High Society which may explain why he never established a residence in Vienna, although he had acquired Austrian citizenship in 1878 and had operated with Austrian government support.

Sir Sidney Lee relates that Edward visited Austria in 1891, mainly to enjoy the hospitality of Hirsch, ('the Hungarian Jewish Millionaire) ...thereby ruffling the susceptibilities of the Austrian Court, which looked askance at the Prince's host,...[from] whom, despite his munificent charities, ...high birth on the continent held aloof.' But Edward was 'not disconcerted by the criticism passed in straight-laced circles' on the display of his broad-minded sympathies for one 'who in his view was disparaged by unworthy prejudice.'[25]

And Sir Philip Magnus said of Hirsch: 'He was richer than the Rothschilds, but unlike them never assimilated socially. He was excluded from the Jockey Club, cold-shouldered, or treated, at best, with a mortifying condescension by most archdukes and great magnates, and never received at Court.'[26]

This negative attitude to Hirsch apparently prevailed not only in the Court circles, but also in the financial aristocracy. In his memorial article in the *Wiener Tageblatt* of April 23, 1896, its editor Moritz Szeps, recalled that the Rothschilds, who dominated the Südbahn, and Baron Wodianer, the grandson, as was said, of a Jewish old-clothes merchant of Pressburg, did not consider Hirsch as an equal, and therefore refrained from joining in the Oriental Railway venture.

True, this happened before Hirsch's success and fortune, but Hirsch even then was a wealthy man and a nobleman of the third generation.[27]

An exception may have been his relations with Crown Prince Rudolf, who in 1886 was his hunting guest. But Rudolf was a 'black sheep.'

In Paris, as we see from the Hohenlohe-Schillingfürst Memoirs, Hirsch was in the centre of the diplomatic and High Society. But here, too, he was black-balled by the Cercle de la Rue Royale. (This story, incidentally, circulated in numerous versions, differing even as to location.)

---

[25] Sir Sidney Lee, *King Edward VII* (1925), pp. 574-576.

[26] Sir Philip Magnus, *King Edward the Seventh* (1964), p. 217-219.

[27] We have indeed, a good description of the Vienna of those days. 'There prevailed a widespread mistrust of the great fortunes. The formula of the noted jurist Schey, that one does not make a million without having just touched the penitentiary with one's sleeve, was still current. The Turkish transactions of the Parisian-Viennese Baron Hirsch "exceeded any intrigues ever thought out," and the negotiations about the nationalization of the Nordbahn in 1886, when the privilege (concession) of the Rothschilds expired, disclose a piece of the Orient in Austria.' See Hans Tietze, *Die Juden Wiens* (1932), p. 231 (based on Count Vassily's book on Viennese Society, 1885). 'Baron Albert Rothschild and his Parisian wife, who in 1887 finally received the so much desired "Hoffähigkeit" (acceptance at Court); Baron Nathaniel Rothschild, to whom under the sponsorship of Princess Pauline Metternich,—for many years the Notre Dame de Zion of Viennese Society—all salons were open, while his own remained closed to other Jews; exotic financial adventurers like Baron Hirsch, champion of Jewish philanthropy; colourless sons of outstanding fathers, like H. Königswarter; original figures, like Baron Edward Todesco... were the prominent figures of Viennese Jewry in the Eighties.' *Ibid.*, p. 235.

Friends and Enemies 91

Only in London was there no discrimination. Here the enthusiasm for the turf and for hunting which Hirsch, according to Held, had inherited from his father, made him a congenial member of a society, which, under the leadership of the Prince of Wales, was free from racial prejudices against Hirsch. But were the prejudices in Vienna racial or rather personal?[28]

The Austrian aristocracy consisted of two elements, the old landed aristocracy, the former feudal lords, and the new military, administrative and financial knights. There was a chasm between them, and their social relations were ruled by laws unfathomable by the ordinary man. As Rudolf Sieghart recalled, 'bürgerliche' commoners, members of the old phanariot families, like the Baltazzi Brothers, were accepted as equals in the High Society, which remained closed to other barons of high finance.[29] The Rothschilds, while strictly maintaining their Judaism, were accepted in the same High Society, which remained closed to other financiers, even if they were baptized for several generations.

The two, the old and the new aristocracy, met in the board-room, not in the salon. Since the middle of the century, an increasing number of the old feudal family names had been on the board of the financial and industrial corporations. Their function there was partly 'decorative,' to increase public confidence in the new corporations among a basically snobbish bourgeoisie. But partly these families, having received large amounts of cash from the land reform, (Grundentlastung, 1848) were looking for lucrative investments.[30] Thus on the boards of 1,005 Austrian companies (banks, railways, industries), registered between 1867-1873, were one duke, fourteen princes, 105 counts, 37 barons and 47 other aristocrats.[31] At the same time, many of the new financial barons acquired real estate as a status symbol.

Hirsch sat with members of the old aristocracy, like Larisch and Zichy, on the board of 'Der Anker' and other corporations; but at that time—before 1870—his headquarters were at Brussels, which partly explains the absence of social contacts. Later, in January, 1892, some of them, such as Count Kinsky, were Hirsch's guests, together with Edward, at Wretham Hall, Norfolk. At the Congress of Berlin in 1878, Hirsch was accompanied by his associate, Altgraf Salm, another member of the old aristocracy, chairman-designate for the Turkish Rumelian Railway Company. Hirsch carried his opprobrious reputation to Vienna from Constantinople where he was considered almost an enemy. The Viennese society refused to accept as equal a man who had allegedly spent 100 million francs on bribes, the recipients of which allegedly included the Austrian chancellor von Beust and Turkish cabinet ministers

---

[28] It is interesting to note that the book *'Society in London'* by a Foreign Resident, (pseudonym for Escott), 1885, does not mention Hirsch. It only mentions the Oppenheim & Bischoffsheim establishments as the 'two other [than the Rothschild's] chief monuments, which London affords to the Hebraic ascendancy.' Hirsch probably acquired Bath House in London after that time, and met Edward only in 1886. But was he not prominent there even before, or possibly only as a member of the Bischoffsheim establishment?
[29] *Die letzten Jahre einer Grossmacht* (1932), p. 256.
[30] Cf. Jacquemyns, Vol. III, p. 358.
[31] Steiner, *Die Entwicklung d. Mobilbankwesen in Osterreich*, p. 278.

such as Daoud Pasha and Mahmud Pasha.[32] What the Viennese society apparently did not want to admit openly was the fact that Hirsch was only one of the many who had to pay their way in the Ottoman Empire (or anywhere else, for that matter) in order to carry out their projects.

Hirsch's involvement in the *affaire* von Arnim (1873), and the way in which he was vilified and libeled in connection with the suicide of Count Wimpffen, the Austrian Ambassador to Paris in 1882, indicate how his meteoric ascent in international economic affairs, his then gigantic enterprise, had made him an easy target for 'unfriendly comments.'

Nor should one forget his cynical outlook, or his personality, as described by Drumont and Emden, which hardly helped to endear him to the provincial Viennese Society.[33]

CROWN PRINCE RUDOLF AND EDWARD, PRINCE OF WALES

There were two more illustrious personages with whom Hirsch was on friendly, and even intimate terms; Rudolf von Habsburg and Edward, Prince of Wales, who became King Edward VII in 1901, five years after Hirsch's death.

Crown Prince Rudolf met 'the French financier', Baron Hirsch at a shooting party in September 1886, and introduced him thereafter to his friend, the journalist Moritz Szeps, whom Hirsch helped financially to start a new (liberal) Viennese daily.[34]

In December 1886 Hirsch had obtained an introduction to the Prince of Wales from Rudolf, allegedly in consideration of a loan of 100,000 gulden.[35] After Rudolf's tragic death in 1889 it was said in Vienna that his debt was waived in return for nobility conferred upon Hirsch's natural sons whom his widow had adopted.[36]

Little else is known about this relationship, to which there are only occasional references,[37] owing apparently to its short duration. Moreover Rudolf, in face of the straight-laced court, had to be circumspect in being seen publicly in the company which he preferred.

Not so Edward. 'The only shock ever administered by the Prince in Hungary to a society which was admittedly almost shockproof was caused by his attempt to introduce Baron Hirsch into its midst.'[38] Thus Magnus quotes Count Geza Andrassy

---

[32] Benedikt, p. 119-120. Dimtchoff, p. 32, 35.

[33] Feelings, however, seem to have been mutual. It is significant that Hirsch did not offer any shares in the Jewish Colonization Association (I.C.A.) to the Jewish community in Vienna. Sigmund Mayer, (*Ein jüdischer Kaufmann, 1831-1911*, (1911)) had heard from Dr. Plotke, one of the German I.C.A. directors, that the I.C.A. people in Paris had no high opinion of Viennese Jewry, and particularly not of its *haute finance*. Was this attitude not inherited from I.C.A.'s founder?

[34] Bertha Szeps, *My Life History* (1938), p. 108.

[35] Magnus, p. 217, quoting Lonyay's book on Rudolf, *The Tragedy of Mayerling* (1958). Lonyay's version reads as follows: 'In January [1877] he [Rudolf] had obtained a loan of 100,000 gulden from the banker Baron Hirsch, in return for an act of friendliness he had performed earlier on, in December, when he invited the banker to meet the Prince of Wales.' (p. 177).

[36] Letter from Dr. Wechsberg, Vienna, to Kohler, January 24, 1922.

[37] Professor Heinrich Benedikt, quoted in the Foreword to the present book.

[38] Magnus, p. 191, n.

Crown Prince Rudolf of Austria

to Sir Michael Adeane. Edward was one of the first royal personages who had perceived the social changes which the new capitalist age had brought about. He favoured the 'ascension' of financiers whose company he enjoyed. By 1905 the House of Lords counted 35 bankers among its members.[39] The Prince was wise enough to consult and profit from the advice of such experts as the Rothschilds, Maurice Hirsch, and Ernest Cassel.[40] Most of the Prince's friends were rich men, and among them the Prince discovered a special affinity with Jews.[41]

Hirsch had visited the Prince on his way through Paris to Cannes at the Hotel Bristol on April 1, 1890, at tea-time, and on the following day the Prince lunched at Hirsch's house. Passing through Paris again on April 19 on his way home the Prince

---

[39] Andre Maurois, *Edouard VII et son Temps* (1933), p. 280.
[40] Magnus, p. 65.
[41] *Ibid.*, p. 106.

saw Hirsch twice. During the following London season Hirsch became part of the Prince's entourage, a frequent guest at Sandringham and the country houses of the Prince's friends. He himself had rented Bath House in Piccadilly, a shoot near Newmarket, and a country house near Sandringham where he entertained lavishly.[42] Later that year Edward kept his promise to be Hirsch's guest at his hunt at St. Johann on the Austro-Hungarian border, arriving at Vienna on October 5 with a party including Lady Randolph Churchill, Lady Lilian Wemyss, Lord Dudley, Horace Furquart, Lord and Lady Curzon and the Arthur Sassoons. A day later the Prince gave a luncheon at the Grand Hotel for Hirsch and the King of Greece, and after lunch the party left by special train for St. Johann 'while the Austrian archdukes gasped.'[43] The Prince found his few Austrian and Hungarian fellow guests congenial, although not aristocratic, and the unpretentious house most comfortable. He spent twelve days there (October 6-18, 1891). In five days 11,300 heads of game had been bagged, a record hunt for which Hirsch had engaged several hundred beaters.[44] Edward's love of variety in his vacation tours had been gratified and he was apparently pleased to have at the same time been able to demonstrate frankly his regard for his host 'to whom he felt attracted by his philanthropic ardour and by his enthusiasm for sport and the turf,' however much ruffling thereby the susceptibilities of the Austrian Court, which looked askance at the Prince's host.[45]

Some years later, in October 1894, the Czarevitch, later Nicholas II, was somewhat bewildered by the company found at Sandringham. It included, apart from turf enthusiasts, also Baron Hirsch who on this occasion 'was less interested in horses or even in railway contracts, than he was in philanthropic plans to succour the oppressed Russian Jews.'[46]

It was the Prince who had introduced Hirsch to his friend and counsellor in racing matters, Lord Marcus Beresford. In 1890 the latter bought for Hirsch the yearling filly La Flèche, which two years later scored the rare triumph of winning four classic prizes, and the Prince rejoiced in the triumph of his friend.[47] By the time Hirsch died the Prince had grown a little tired of this man whose idealistic enthusiasms he had not always shared.

As is only to be expected, there was a lot of gossip about the relation between the two men and their motives. According to the Viennese, Edward's stables were financed by Hirsch.[48] Some of the stories can still be traced in the journals, and even in the diplomatic records of those days. Thus the *Westminster Gazette's*[49] report that the Prince had inherited one million pounds, was denied in the *English Mail*[50] a

---

[42] *Ibid.*, p. 218.
[43] *Ibid.*, p. 221.
[44] *Ibid.*; Sir Sidney Lee, *King Edward VII*, Vol. I, p. 574.
[45] Lee, p. 574.
[46] Magnus, pp. 242-243.
[47] Lee, *King Edward VII*, Vol. I, p. 574.
[48] Cf. Wechsberg Letter.
[49] April 30, 1896.
[50] May 7, 1896.

King Edward VII, when Prince of Wales

few days later. And even some years later, we read a note from Cambon, the French Ambassador to the Court of St. James, telling Delcassé that Hirsch had advanced to Edward at least fifteen million francs, for which his sister, the Empress Frederica had guaranteed. William II, visiting London on the occasion of Edward's coronation, had tried to settle the matter. It seems, so Cambon said, that the English Rothschilds had taken over the guarantee of the Empress.[51] But, as we know from another source,[52] Hirsch in a verbal or written instruction to his wife and executor had waived this debt, and in this sense the *Westminster Gazette* was not far wrong. But it is difficult to understand what brought the story up again, five years after Hirsch's death.

Elsewhere we have pointed out the historical improbability of the story that Hirsch had British support at the Congress of Berlin as a *quid pro quo* for his loans to Edward. More mischievous are stories like the one of Hirsch as amorous intermediary between Edward and a lady, which Frank Harris tells with his notorious imagination.[53]

---

[51] French Documentary Series 2, Vol. I, 100, (February 23, 1901).
[52] Letter from Dr. Wechsberg, Vienna, to Kohler, January 24, 1922.
[53] Frank Harris, *My Life and Loves* (1927), Vol. III, p. 30.

Are We as Welcome as Ever?

When Edward died, in 1910, the last to see him was his friend, Sir Ernest Cassel, with whom 'he had formed the most masculine friendship of his life,'[54] and whom he allegedly made his executor. Hirsch had been the first to recognize Cassel's great gifts.

Max Beerbohm, in a cartoon in his *Fifty Caricatures,* shows Cassel, two Rothschilds, Lord Burnham and Baron Hirsch before the door of Edward's successor. It carries the title 'Are We as Welcome as Ever?' As Hirsch's death had preceded Edward's by more than thirteen years, the symbolic intent of the cartoon is obvious: Would there be a place in the new era to come for the great financiers of enterprise, like Hirsch who had opened the Balkans, or like Cassel who deserved so well of Egypt's development? The curtain had fallen on an entire epoch.

[54] Magnus, p. 258.

THE DETRACTORS

Would not—one is bound to ask—a man so eager for public recognition have reacted more sharply against the endless chain of defamation and vilification? It seems from some letters quoted by Dimtchoff that Hirsch occasionally answered some of his accusers; later he may have given it up as a hopeless task. But it is striking that he never brought to the public's attention that remarkable testimony which a man of the undoubted standing of von Gneist had volunteered, a publication which, incidentally, might have changed some historical writing since. But Hirsch at that time, as Moritz Szeps wrote[1] had entered the second period of his life. He no longer cared for the judgment of the world, he cared only for the dire needs, the suffering, and the unhappiness in the world.

It is indicative that on the first news of his death a French paper reported him to have been murdered by anti-semites.[2] Did he not receive threatening letters often enough? Hirsch after all lived in the Paris of the Dreyfuss Affair, and the Vienna where the Christian-Socialists, the lower middle class under Lueger, had become the leading party, and rivalled with the German nationalists in anti-semitism. To all of them Hirsch was an easy and welcome target for libel and slander. One of the most typical cases was that of Wimpffen, the Austrian Ambassador in Paris, who had committed suicide on December 30, 1882 and had left a note in which he asked Hirsch to take care of his family and remove them from Paris. The anti-semitic journals in Germany and Vienna published a fake letter, allegedly left by Wimpffen, in which he accused Hirsch of having bribed him, as he had bribed Beust, Daoud and Mahmud Nedim Pasha, Count Zichy and others. Only when this letter was reprinted in a Viennese daily, in 1890, did the Austrian government compel the paper to state that this letter was a forgery.[3]

There was no limit to such accusations and vilifications, which found their way from one publication into the other, and were—and still are—sometimes uncritically and in good faith taken over as source material even by qualified contemporary historians.

Thus for instance David Landes, in his *Bankers and Pashas*[4] recalls the fact that '...investment banking often required the collaboration of outsiders,... contact man, —merchant, banker, projector, or even confidence man—who had the ear of the ruler or Minister (note: Hirsch in the Ottoman Empire, Oppenheim in Egypt) ...On the other hand, one may be sure that much influence with governments was bought—tactfully, through gratuities and accommodations, and, crudely, through bribes.' Here Landes refers also as source 'on the dubious methods of Hirsch' to Paul Dehn's *Deutschland und der Orient in ihren wirtschaftspolitischen Beziehungen*,[5]

---

[1] *Wiener Tageblatt*, April 23, 1896.
[2] *Le Figaro*, April 22, 1896.
[3] *Oesterreichische Wochenschrift*, January 1891, No. 1.
[4] London, 1958.
[5] Munich, 1884.

without, apparently, being aware of the anti-semitic and German nationalist bias of the source.

It can be safely assumed that Hirsch, like most of his contemporaries doing business in Turkey, the Balkans or even in the West, had 'to pay his way,' and one should not single him out on this account. Nor should he be blamed for using 'contact men.' After all, the members of the aristocracy who serve on the board of British corporations,—the so-called 'guinea-pigs'—or the well-known American retired generals in a similar position in the United States are in a way the successors of this system. And many respectable law firms or consultant economists make a living as 'lobbyists' in Washington and elsewhere. There is nothing intrinsically wrong if Hirsch used as his 'lobbyists' or negotiators members of the high aristocracy such as Altgraf Salm at the Congress of Berlin, or men like Paul Talabot in 1869, and Ralph Earle, M.P. in 1872, in Constantinople.

Hirsch cultivated members of the High Society and of the Diplomatic Corps and entertained them lavishly. This seems to have been due primarily to a desire to satisfy his 'ego,' without the expectation of an early return on this heavy investment. And it is noteworthy that this investment was particularly heavy after Hirsch had practically retired from business, when he used his connections, if at all, primarily to further his humanitarian projects. In this High Society Hirsch was not just tolerated because of the entertainment offered by him, but also valued because of his intellectual qualities. This is shown in the *Memoirs of Prince Chlodwig Hohenlohe—Schillingfürst,* Germany's Ambassador to Paris, in Volume II of which Hirsch is repeatedly quoted. Hohenlohe met Hirsch in 1874 at the home of the Duc de Decazes, France's Minister of Foreign Affairs. In 1876 Hohenlohe repeatedly quotes Hirsch's opinion on political events in Bulgaria and Turkey.

CHAPTER IX

BARON HIRSCH THE MAN

*I am no well thought-out piece of fiction,
I am a man with all his contradiction.*

Johann Wolfgang von Goethe

WHO WAS BARON HIRSCH?

IT IS difficult, in view of the paucity of sources, to learn enough about Hirsch, the man, to recreate today the picture of a personality who a hundred years ago loomed so large in the international financial and, unwittingly perhaps, political scene of Europe. Defamation and vilification were not less his share than admiration and adulation. His greatest enterprise, the Oriental Railways, was, as previously quoted, in the eyes of Hallgarten, the Rhinegold of a Nibelungen Song, the overture of which were Hirsch's speculations, and which, continued in the Baghdad Railways scheme, ended with the conflagration of Europe as its Twilight of the Gods. It is a story of 'cunning force, robbery and deceit.' Hirsch was a business man, a man of action, not of ideologies. He did not guess that his venture would become a *cause célèbre* in international politics, an act almost symbolic for what was to become known as the Age of Imperialism. He only saw the advantages to an expanding world economy which would accrue from such an undertaking.

That Baron Hirsch should have taken up the idea at all, sufficiently shows what manner of man he is. The very qualities—the optimism, the indomitable persistence, the self-confidence—which impelled him to attempt the realization of a scheme, which even ordinarily courageous men regarded with misgivings, are the best guarantee of coming success. In other hands the scheme, even if it had been launched, would have probably made shipwreck at an early stage of the voyage.[1]

These words in which the *Jewish Chronicle* lauded Hirsch's Argentine colonization scheme, could have been written equally well on his Oriental Railway venture.

How can we understand the many contradictory statements about Hirsch, of which we have here given but a few examples? How do we reconcile the picture of the ruthless 'robber baron' with that of the greatest philanthropist in his time? Was he a modern kind of Robin Hood, who took from the rich to give to the poor? Should we resign ourselves to what a distinguished contemporary, O. S. Straus, said on the news of his death: 'Baron Hirsch cannot be measured by ordinary standards; his

---

[1] Editorial article, *Jewish Chronicle*, April 11, 1892.

activity was both varied and colossal, whether as financier, organizer, railroad contractor, diplomat, statesman, man of the world and philanthropist.' While this beautiful appreciation may help us in our evaluation of Hirsch, it does not help us in knowing him, in understanding what appears to have been a complex and colourful personality.

Looking for other evidence, we find a rather interesting description of Hirsch, doubly interesting because its author is the ill-famed Edouard Drumont, whose *La France Juive* belongs to the classics of anti-semitic literature. After violent attacks on Hirsch for closing his hunting grounds at Petit Versailles to the public (who previously used it as recreation grounds) and for employing only German workers and German equipment on his Oriental Railways, Drumont continues on Hirsch himself as follows:

> Hirsch, in Paris, compared with Rothschild, in a way enjoys a preferred position. Hirsch is the Baron, while the others together are the barons. In contrast to Rothschild who likes to appear merely as representative of others, Hirsch likes to be in the foreground, and gladly leaves his associates behind, 'in an inferior semi-dark-

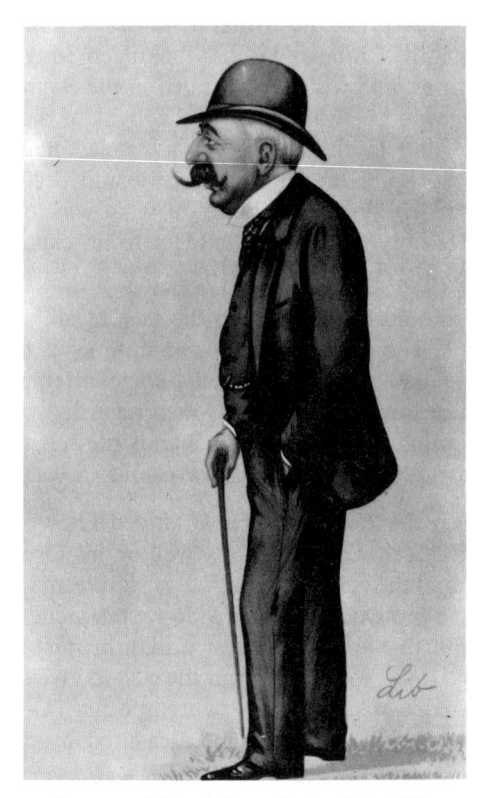

Cartoon of Hirsch from *Vanity Fair*, 1890

ness.' He does not display the conceited supercilious attitude of Rothschild, whom hardly anybody dares to address in company; as a cheerful *arrivé* he shows more frankness and is a better integrated and rounded personality, and is therefore less ridiculous than the other Jewish aristocrats. His arrogance is mitigated by his bad jokes and *bonhomie*. Of a fresh colour, a bit bloated, he feels happy when not suffering from his liver pains. He likes to play the good-natured one with a tendency to malicious teasing...

This behaviour, in contrast to that of the Rothschilds, is easily understandable. The latter inherited their position from their ancestors who had acquired it. Thus they believe themselves to belong to the aristocracy, while Hirsch believes that the aristocracy belongs to him, being of his likes. And, indeed, Hirsch did himself create his position in Society. He calculates exactly and knows the purchase price of each moral qualm. And he is the third in league of those despisers of the human race of our days, Bismarck and Gambetta, with the difference that nothing can mitigate his despising of mankind!![2]

Considering the source of this description one might detect in it a note of admiration rather than of defamation. Certain basic traits in Hirsch's character seem to have been correctly analyzed and described.

As Theodor Herzl said after his famous interview with Hirsch on June 2, 1895, 'On the whole a pleasant, intelligent, simple, natural man,—vain, *par exemple,*—but I could have worked with him.'[3] And Paul H. Emden, who, if he did not know him personally, probably knew many who did, writes of Hirsch, 'Great as he had become, he had not been able to get rid of many human weaknesses which detracted from his inner worth and at times made him look petty and comical.'[4] Striking among these peculiarities was his misleading manner of behaving like a *nouveau riche,* or *arrivé.*[5]

LIVING BETWEEN TWO WORLDS

True, Baron Maurice de Hirsch, the 'descendant of a family which had held a patent of nobility for three generations, and a fortune equally old, himself amassed a fortune, largely as a builder of railways.'[6] In spite of this background, or because of his own remarkable achievement, he had the characteristics of a self-made man.

'In politics,'—as the obituary in the *Jewish Chronicle* (April 24, 1896) notes —'de Hirsch took no active part, but his views inclined to the sturdy radicalism of the self-made man.' And the article quotes the anecdote, reported by a correspondent of the *Daily Chronicle,* of Hirsch saying, after listening to a Socialist orator in Hyde Park: 'I agree with every word he said.' We remember also Herzl's exclamation, 'You talk like a Socialist, Baron Hirsch,' in the historical interview of June 2, 1895. And

---

[2] Translated from *Das Verjudete Frankreich,* 7th German edition (n.d.), Vol. II pp.71-72.
[3] *Tagebücher,* Vol. I p. 28.
[4] *Money Powers of Europe,* p. 323.
[5] *Ibid.*
[6] Jacob H. Schiff, *His Life and Letters* (1928), Vol. II, p. 81.

we know of Hirsch's financial support, on Crown Prince Rudolf's introduction, of Moritz Szep's liberal *Wiener Tageblatt*.

On the other hand, the article on Hirsch by L. J. S. in the *Jüdisches Lexikon* records that he was in his political conviction ultra-conservative and supported liberally monarchistic movements in France and Spain (i.e., the Orleans). And we know of Hirsch's inclination to spend his time in High Society.

The year of Hirsch's birth, 1831, is in a way symbolic of these contradictory trends in his character. It was equidistant in time from the Congress of Vienna of 1814, the Restoration of the old feudal system and its privileges, and from 1848, the year of the liberal revolutions, which were the beginning, also, of the process of Jewish emancipation.

Hirsch was, like his parents, a proud member of the nobility and they had a 'vested interest' in the maintenance of their privileged position. At the same time as conscious, and even orthodox Jews, if for no other reason, they were anxious for the success of the liberal trends, which finally promised equal civil rights to the Jewish citizens.

They themselves, in spite of their noble status, had in the past suffered from this inequality before the Law and were exposed to social discrimination. The subsequent reaction may have had a share in molding Hirsch's character.

It should be noted here that in contrast to other financial barons who acquired estates rather as status symbols, Hirsch's ancestors had acquired landed property first and treated it as an economic asset, not as a hobby, before they became ennobled.

Hirsch passed away in 1896, eighteen years after the Congress of Berlin, which had marked the birth of the Age of Imperialism, as well as the beginning of the Balkanization of the World, and eighteen years before 1914, the conflagration which consumed the World of 1878, together with the remnants of 1814.

If the making of Hirsch's fortune was an intrinsic part of the beginning of that period, its application, and the spirit which prompted it, conformed with the ideas to which a New Age was to give birth.

A CITIZEN OF THE WORLD

The distrust and the rejection which Hirsch met in some places, and particularly in Viennese Society, may have had a deeper root: he did not belong, he was not 'bodenständig.'

It is rather significant to see how he was viewed by his contemporaries and historians.

According to O. S. Straus he lived the larger part of his life in Austria. Margot Tennant, meeting him in London in 1886, speaks of him as an Austrian, and Sokolov even makes him heir to an Austrian title. The *Oesterreichische Biographisch Lexikon* states that in 1871 (1878?) he had acquired Austrian citizenship. Lucien Wolf in the *Encyclopaedia Britannica* calls him German by birth, Austro-Hungarian by domicile. The *Universal Pronouncing Dictionary* calls him an 'Austrian financier,' and Tietze the 'Parisian-Viennese Baron Hirsch.' Sir Sidney Lee speaks of the 'Hungarian Jewish millionaire,' and S. G. Mears of the 'noted German.' Morawitz speaks admiringly of the 'petit banquier de Bruxelles,' and Cameron, less admiringly, of the 'international financial adventurer, operating mainly from Brussels.' And in the mid-'nineties we find him appearing in a group-photograph of the leading figures of English Jewry (cf. p. 82).

From Held we know that he had changed his nationality repeatedly: German (Bavarian), Belgian, French and finally Austrian, though we doubt the allegation that the desire to escape income tax or death duties prompted these changes, as residence rather than nationality is the basis for taxation.

But let us see where Hirsch actually resided. From various sources we can reconstruct the following table of his main whereabouts.

HIRSCH'S WHEREABOUTS

1831-1844	Munich
1844-1847	Brussels
1848-1851	Munich
1851-1855	Brussels
1855-1869	Munich, Brussels, Paris (cf. Sara Straus)
1869-1871	Constantinople
1872-1887	Paris, Moravia, Hungary (cf. Held)
1887-1896	London, Paris, Moravia, Hungary
1896	died in Hungary

Only for the years of his retirement from business do we know something about his movements between his various residences throughout the year. The winter he usually spent in Paris, with some breaks at the Riviera. In the early spring he moved to London for the season, and then for the summer to his estate of Beauregard in Versailles. August-September were spent at Eichhorn castle in Moravia, October and part of November at his hunting lodge of St. Johann on the Hungarian frontier.[7] His London residence was the famous Bath House in Piccadilly. In England he also owned a hunting lodge near Newmarket, and leased country houses from time to time.

We learn about the splendour of his Paris palais in Rue d'Elysée from the *Monographie*, an art album devoted to it, published in 1906, and from the description in Herzl's Diaries.[8] And we know of his estate at Beauregard from the Hohenlohe Memoirs, as well as from Dumont's outbursts.[9]

---

[7] *Neue Freie Presse*, April 12, 1896; Held in *Monographie*. Herzl, *Tagebücher* Vol. 1, p. 21.
[8] He had bought three houses in the Rue d'Elysée from the family of the Emperor Napoleon for a sum exceeding 2,300,000 francs (*Jewish Chronicle*, December 13, 1878).
[9] In an anti-Jewish article by the Paris correspondent of the *Morning Advertiser* (quoted in *Jewish Chronicle* of June 11, 1875) Hirsch is blamed for having purchased the palace of the Duchesse d'Alba in Paris, and the 'magnificent pleasance' of Beauregard, as well as for having leased all the shooting in state forests around Paris—St. Germain, Fontainbleau, Rambouillet, etc.

Eichhorn castle, on the crag of a mountain near Brünn in Moravia (20,000 hectares) was a historical site, being the only castle that had withstood the Swedes in the Thirty Years' War. Hirsch had bought it in 1885 for £230,000 from the Princess of Ypsilanti.[10] In Moravia he also owned an estate near Rossitz. Hirsch sold his hunting estate at St. Johann because he had to pay the neighbouring peasants 40,000 florins annually as 'Wildschaden,' i.e., for damages done by his flocks of deer. Instead he bought the estate of O'Gyalla (near Neuhäusl) in Hungary—he called this purchase a stupidity of his—and started to build the Chateau Gereuth there, a palais rather than a hunting lodge. At this estate of 88,000 acres he hoped to entertain Prince Edward and the French President in the coming season.[11] And here he died.

In Vienna, significantly, he never acquired a permanent residence, but usually spent only a few days there on his way from or to Paris. Of interest is the story that Francis Joseph made him a member of the Hungarian (and not the Austrian) Upper-House,[12] which surely implies his holding Hungarian citizenship.

It is difficult to understand how Hirsch could have been called an Austrian—except for his passport—or how he could have lived the largest part of his life in Austria. In our estimate, he may have spent part of the summers of half of his life on his estates in Moravia and Hungary, and part of them at Beauregard. But it is equally difficult to provide an alternative definition. Hirsch was a cosmopolitan in the finest sense of the word. He himself used this designation jokingly in an interview with Lucien Wolf.[13] 'Ubi bene, ibi patria.' And until the rise of the new Germany and of nationalism after 1871, there existed a kind of European unity, largely promoted with French capital. Banks in the various domiciles were inter-related across the national boundaries; finance was truly international. Hirsch, born with a practical bent and not burdened with ideologies, found himself at home in this 'Free Trade Area,' moving rapidly from one of its corners to another.[14]

Restlessness was Hirsch's basic characteristic, the need for work, for activity.[15] The death of his son Lucien must indeed have accentuated this trait. And after his retirement from business, voluntary though it was, sport and philanthropy became the outlet for his 'nervous energy.'

We thus have the picture of Hirsch, as a 'Na Venad,' a footloose migrant, restless himself, who—possibly subconciously aware of this inner restlessness—advocates 'rooting in the soil,' i.e., agriculture, as a means of bringing peace also to the Wandering Jew.

---

[10] *The Times*, April 21, 1896.
[11] *The Times*, April 25, 1896.
[12] *Jüdische Presse*, Berlin, February 2, 1888.
[13] Lucien Wolf, *Oesterreichische Wochenschrift*, May 29, 1894.
[14] Hirsch's contemporary, the famous 'Prince of Journalists,' Blowitz, a Bohemian of Jewish extraction, for many years *The Times* correspondent in Paris, was called by Bismarck a 'Frenchman,' by the French 'un journalist allemand.' According to his recent biographer, Frank Giles, 'This failure to establish any nationality seems to be the essence of internationalism.'
[15] *Neues Wiener Tageblatt*, April 22, 1896.

The Man 105

Cartoon from *Moonshine*, 1892

SOME PERSONAL TRAITS

Hirsch's appearance, we read in an obituary notice, was not that of a financier but rather that of a sportsman. He was tall, of slim figure, fine deportment and elastic movements; he had a healthy complexion, intelligent looks and a touch of grey in his hair. He was fond of walking.[16] He was parsimonious and frugal, where his person was concerned, and of bourgeois moderations. He ate simple food, while entertaining his guests lavishly. His hospitality was not that of an upstart, but that of a grand seigneur.[17]

There were many anecdotes in circulation about his parsimony: how he often made his purchases in Vienna which was cheaper than Paris; how he avoided sending telegrams where letters were sufficient; how he hired cabs from a stand around the corner, where they were a fraction cheaper; how he avoided eating at the Grand Hotel where he was staying, as 'he couldn't afford it.' He was particularly critical

---
[16] *Ibid.*
[17] *Neue Freie Presse; Neues Wiener Abendblatt,* April 21, 1896.

of expenditure, even that of his agents, when the expense account of his charities was involved. And he was always suspicious of being exploited.

But he had a dry sense of humour. Seeing cheap melons on the market, he commented: 'mine cost me 500 francs a piece.'[18] This sense of humour ultimately turned bitter and sardonic.[19]

He was a tremendous worker. Coming home late from a party, he could keep his secretaries busy into the morning, dictating letters. Of his legendary, tremendous, correspondence, alas, few items survived.

STATUS SEEKING

Some commentators refer to Hirsch's almost pathetic weakness for civic honours and positions. Thus Hallgarten refers to the highest Turkish decoration, the Grand Cordon of the Osmanje Order which Abdul Hamid II, persuaded by bribed courtiers, had conferred upon Hirsch, though he detested him thoroughly and once almost had him arrested and 'removed' (Hirsch had saved himself by taking refuge on board an Austrian vessel). However, the notice of Hirsch's funeral mentioned only two decorations—the Grand Cordon of the Franz Joseph Order and Commandeur de Légion d'Honneur,[20] but not the alleged Turkish decoration. But neither does it mention the Order of the Italian Crown of which he was made a Commander.[21]

We know that in the early years of his Turkish venture Hirsch had been appointed Belgian Consul-General in Constantinople. He was also a member or perhaps even Commissioner General[22] of the Commission for the Austrian Pavilion at the Paris World Exposition, (1878) where, at his expense, (60,000 gulden) he provided the beautiful facade of the pavilion.[23] Another member, Count Zichy, had opposed Hirsch's appointment, first refusing to sit together with him because he claimed together with others to have traced the layout for the Oriental Railways before Hirsch came into the picture, but had not received any compensation from Hirsch. Eventually he gave in and even attended the celebrations given by Hirsch on the occasion of the Exposition.[24]

Hirsch was anxious to obtain nobility for his offspring. We are told that his son Lucien (died October 20, 1888) was the first Jew to obtain a Belgian barony.[25] Hirsch also tried hard (and apparently successfully) to obtain nobility for his natural sons, Arnold and Raymond de Forest, but was less successful in the case of Lucien's natural daughter Lucienne, who later married the banker E. Balser.

---

[18] *Neues Wiener Tageblatt,* April 22, 1896; *Neue Freie Presse; Neues Wiener Abendblatt,* April 21, 1896.
[19] Emden, p. 320.
[20] Cf. *Jewish Chronicle,* June 27, 1879, and January 18, 1878.
[21] *Jewish Chronicle,* August 3, 1888.
[22] *Ibid.,* November 24, 1876.
[23] *Ibid.,* May 24, 1878.
[24] *Neues Wiener Tageblatt,* April 22, 1896.
[25] Was he not heir to the Bavarian title?

The Man

As the obituaries in the Viennese press noted, Hirsch lately had always been seen accompanied by two young boys, whose mother had been English,[26] or American.[27] Their name was given as Forreste-Bischoffsheim. The younger of the two, Raymond (1880-1912) died young, the older (b. 1879) now known as Count of Bendern, lives in Vaduz, Liechtenstein. The *Semi Gotha* of 1912[28] claims that on his mother's side Arnold, holder of a twenty year old barony which in 1900 was confirmed for Great Britain by Royal Decree, hailed from old French aristocracy, de Forrestier. And we learn from the 1956 *Who's Who* of his education at Eton and Oxford, his army and war service, and his membership of Parliament. In 1932 he became a naturalized citizen of the Principality of Liechtenstein, which made him a hereditary count and Diplomatic Counsellor. A London society weekly, after referring to the sporting achievements of this good-looking and wealthy Liberal M.P. tells us that he was rejected by the Reform Club.[29] This was allegedly because of the role he

Hirsch family tomb in Paris

[26] *Neues Wiener Abendblatt,* April 21, 1896.
[27] *Neue Freie Presse,* April 22, 1896.
[28] p. 146.
[29] *The Bystander,* February 12, 1913.

played in the agitation for land reform, which the wealthy and respectable Whig landowners abhorred. And Lloyd George and Winston Churchill, who had sponsored his membership, resigned from the Club.

There seems also to have been some litigation or dispute between the two brothers on the one side and the Paris municipality on the other, concerning the palace of Beauregard, which Hirsch allegedly had left to Paris.

Other sources allege that it was Hirsch's widow who had adopted the two boys, some thought after Hirsch's death, but more likely before, as the mention of the name Forreste-Bischoffsheim would seem to indicate. They were also among her heirs. Here we have only a small and insufficient clue to the character of a woman who would justify a biography of her own, a woman over-shadowed all her life by a husband to whom she was not only companion and, often enough, secretary, but probably also a sober counsellor.

IN RETROSPECT

No revolution is made without revolutionaries, without the men who have the idea and the ideal, without the men who carry the flag over the barricades.

So it was with the Industrial Revolution which in the early part of the 19th century spread from England to Western Europe and thence and thereafter to East and South. It was a revolution not so much of industry, but largely one of communication, prompted by the inventions of the age—the locomotive, the steamship, the telegraph, and the telephone—and their industrial application. Not even in the 'civilized West' was it always simple to introduce these new systems of communications. To bridge the gap between West and East—a gap to be measured in centuries rather than miles—was an idea in some of the great minds of that time; but it was an undertaking which, with all the pitfalls to be expected in a fairly unknown and semi-barbaric country, would have discouraged any but the most intrepid entrepreneur.

Progress and development, as Schumpeter has shown half a century ago, depend on the entrepreneur who knows how to employ technical innovations and to conquer new markets. To do this he must know how to convert savings into risk capital. And for this he will have to rely on the speculative instinct of the masses usually with the prospects of high returns. If these hopes are disappointed, the entrepreneur who may have been merely over-optimistic, is often enough accused of dishonesty. But frequently there are only fine distinctions between honesty and dishonesty, dependent often merely upon the light of local traditions. It was in the Vienna of the 1860's that a chairman could answer a challenger at a shareholders' meeting, that 'Die Moral steht hier nicht auf der Tagesordnung, (Morals are not on the agenda here).'[1] The economic historian looking back on periods of rapid growth is bound to distinguish carefully between the methods by which it was achieved, which involves a moral (value) judgment, and its effect on the national economy, which is an economic evaluation.

---

[1] Steiner, *Entwicklung des Mobilbankwesens in Oesterreich,* p. 180.

A spontaneous testimonial by an authority such as von Gneist is a sufficient judgment for Hirsch's honourable moral conduct. But the dictum from Vienna, quoted above, indicates the *Zeitgeist* in which he was operating, and explains the suspicion to which he was exposed.

True, Hirsch was, as some authors call him, a 'speculator.' He operated successfully in the sugar and copper market. We saw that his in-laws, the Bischoffsheims, were apprehensive of his daring ideas and schemes. Life was for Hirsch an adventure, a high adventure, in business, in sport, in philanthropy. The ordinary business of the banks of his time, the placing of foreign loans, however profitable, was pettifogging, boring to him, and of minor interest. He was stimulated by challenges, by risks, but reduced speculative risks by careful study and preparation. He in fact admonished his partner Langrand-Dumonceau against undue risks. Like money making, money spending was high adventure on a large scale, his colonization scheme intrinsically a challenge to Russian despotism. Such was Baron de Hirsch.

In this work an attempt has been made to collect from very wide fields the stones for assembling a mosaic from which the picture of Baron Maurice de Hirsch would emerge. Many stones are still missing, many had to be rejected after a critical examination. The picture is still incomplete, but its main features emerge clear enough.

This monograph is not an apologia, or an attempt to whitewash Baron de Hirsch, but rather an attempt at sifting the often contradictory evidence and arriving at the historical truth. Many times we have shown the historical questionability of the stories in circulation among his contemporaries, whether friendly or hostile. A veritable saga grew up around his powerful personality, even during his life time and still more after his death. Such a saga can be helpful to the historian as well as dangerous, both guiding and misleading.

We hope that this work will prove helpful to any future historian whom the discovery of further material may one day enable to write a full biography worthy of Baron de Hirsch—a great figure in the economic history of Europe in the nineteenth century, as well as in the history of the Jewish people on the way to their renaissance.

MARGOT ASQUITH*

I had another vicarious proposal. One night, dining with the Bischoffheims, I was introduced for the first time to Baron Hirsch, an Austrian who lived in Paris. He took me in to dinner and a young man whom I had met out hunting sat on the other side of me.

I was listening impressively to the latter, holding my champagne in my hand, when the footman in serving one of the dishes bumped my glass against my chest and all its contents went down the front of my ball-dress. I felt iced to the bone; but, as I was thin, I prayed profoundly that my pink bodice would escape being marked. I continued in the same position, holding my empty glass in my hand as if nothing had happened, hoping that no one had observed me and trying to appear interested in the young man's description of the awful dangers he had run when finding himself alone with hounds.

A few minutes later Baron Hirsch turned to me and said:

"Aren't you very cold?"

I said that I was, but that it did not matter; what I really minded was spoiling my dress and, as I was not a kangaroo, I feared the worst. After this we entered into conversation and he told me among other things that, when he had been pilled for a sporting club in Paris, he had revenged himself by buying the club and the site upon which it was built, to which I observed:

"You must be very rich."

He asked me where I had lived and seemed surprised that I had never heard of him.

The next time we met each other was in Paris. I lunched with him and his wife and he gave me his opera box and mounted me in the Bois de Boulogne.

One day he invited me to dine with him *tête à tête* at the Café Anglais and, as my father and mother were out, I accepted. I felt a certain curiosity about this invitation, because my host in his letter had given me the choice of several other dates in the event of my being engaged that night. When I arrived at the Café Anglais Baron Hirsch took off my cloak and conducted me into a private room. He reminded me of our first meeting, said that he had been much struck by my self-control over the iced champagne and went on to ask if I knew why he had invited me to dine with him. I said:

"I have not the slightest idea!"

BARON HIRSCH: "Because I want you to marry my son Lucien. He is quite unlike me, he is very respectable and hates money; he likes books and collects manuscripts and other things and is highly educated."

MARGOT: "Your son is the man with the beard, who wears glasses and collects coins, isn't he?"

BARON HIRSCH *(thinking my description rather dreary)*: "Quite so! You talked to him the other day at our house. But he has a charming disposition and has been a good son; and I am quite sure that, if you would take a little trouble, he would be devoted to you and make you an excellent husband: he does not like society, or racing, or any of the things that I care for."

* *My Autobiography* (Penguin Books ed, London 1936), pp. 85-89.

MARGOT: "Poor man! I don't suppose he would even care much for me! I hate coins!"
BARON HIRSCH: "Oh, but you would widen his interests! He is shy and I want him to make a good marriage; and above all he must marry an Englishwoman."
MARGOT: "Has he ever been in love?"
BARON HIRSCH: "No, he has never been in love; but a lot of women make up to him and I don't want him to be married for his money by some designing girl."
MARGOT: "Over here I suppose that sort of thing might happen; I don't believe it would in England."
BARON HIRSCH: "How can you say such a thing to me? London society cares more for money than any other in the world, as I know to my cost! You may take it from me that a young man who will be as rich as Lucien can marry almost any girl he likes."
MARGOT: "I doubt it! English girls don't marry for money!"
BARON HIRSCH: "Nonsense, my dear! They are like other people; it is only the young that can afford to despise money!"
MARGOT: "Then I hope that I shall be young for a very long time."
BARON HIRSCH *(smiling)*: "I don't think you will ever be disappointed in that hope; but surely you wouldn't like to be a poor man's wife and live in the suburbs? Just think what it would be if you could not hunt or ride in the Row in a beautiful habit or have wonderful dresses from Worth! You would hate to be dowdy and obscure!"
"That," I answered energetically, "could never happen to me."
BARON HIRSCH: "Why not?"
MARGOT: "Because I have too many friends."
BARON HIRSCH: "And enemies?"
MARGOT *(thoughtfully)*: "Perhaps. . . . I don't know about that. I never notice whether people dislike me or not. After all, you took a fancy to me the first time we met; why should not other people do the same? Do you think I should not improve on acquaintance?"
BARON HIRSCH: "How can you doubt that, when I have just asked you to marry my son?"
MARGOT: "What other English girl is there that you would like for a daughter-in-law?"
BARON HIRSCH: "Lady Katie Lambton, Durham's sister."
MARGOT: "I don't know her at all. Is she like me?"
BARON HIRSCH: "Not in the least; but you and she are the only girls I have met that I could wish my son to marry."
I longed to know what my rival was like, but all he could tell me was that she was lovely and clever and *mignonne,* to which I said:
"But that sounds exactly like me!"
This made him laugh:
"I don't believe you know in the least what you are like," he said.
MARGOT: "You mean I have no idea how plain I am? But what an odd man you are! If I don't know what I'm like, I am sure *you* can't! How do you know that I am not just the sort of adventuress you dread most? I might marry your son and, so far from widening his interests, as you suggest, keep him busy with his coins while I went about everywhere, enjoying myself and spending all your money. In spite of what you say, some man might fall in love with me, you know! Some delightful, clever man. And then Lucien's happiness would be over."
BARON HIRSCH: "I do not believe you would ever cheat your husband."
MARGOT: "You never can tell! Would Lady Katie Lambton marry for money?"
BARON HIRSCH: "To be perfectly honest with you, I don't think she would."
MARGOT: "There you are! I know heaps of girls who wouldn't; anyhow, *I* never would!"
BARON HIRSCH: "You are in love with someone else, perhaps, are you?"

It so happened that in the winter I had fallen in love with a man out hunting and was counting the hours till I could meet him again, so the question annoyed me; I thought it vulgar and said, with some dignity:

"If I am, I have never told him so."

My dignity was lost, however, on my host, who persisted. I did not want to give myself away, so, simulating a tone of light banter, I said:

"If I have not confided in the person most interested, why should I tell *you*?"

This was not one of my happiest efforts, for he instantly replied:

"Then he *is* interested in you, is he? Do I know him?"

I felt angry and told him that, because I did not want to marry his son, it did not at all follow that my affections were engaged elsewhere; and I added:

"I only hope that Mr. Lucien is not as curious as you are, or I should have a very poor time; there is nothing I should hate as much as a jealous husband."

BARON HIRSCH: "I don't believe you! If it's tiresome to have a jealous husband, it must be humiliating to have one who is not."

I saw he was trying to conciliate me, so I changed the subject to racing. Being a shrewd man, he thought he might find out whom I was in love with and encouraged me to go on. I told him I knew Fred Archer well, as we had hunted together in the Vale of White Horse. He asked me if he had ever given me a racing tip. I told him the following story:

One day, at Ascot, some of my impecunious Melton friends—having heard a rumour that Archer, who was riding in the race, had made a bet on its result—came and begged me to find out from him what horse was going to win. I did not listen much to them at first, as I was staring about at the horses, the parasols and the people, but my friends were very much in earnest and began pressing me in lowered voices to be as quick as I could, as they thought that Archer was on the move. It was a grilling day; most men had handkerchiefs or cabbages under their hats; and the dried-up grass in the Paddock was the colour of pea-soup. I saw Fred Archer standing in his cap and jacket with his head hanging down, talking to a well-groomed, under-sized little man, while the favourite—a great, slashing, lazy horse—was walking round and round with the evenness of a metronome. I went boldly up to him and reminded him of how we had cannoned at a fence in the V.W.H. Fred Archer had a face of carved ivory, like the top of an umbrella; he could turn it into a mask or illuminate it with a smile; he had long thin legs, a perfect figure and wonderful charm. He kept a secretary, a revolver and two valets and was a god among the gentry and the jockeys. After giving a slight wink at the under-sized man, he turned away from him to me and, on hearing what I had to say, whispered a magic name in my ear.

I was a popular woman that night in Melton.

Baron Hirsch returned to the charge later on; and I told him definitely that I was the last girl in the world to suit his son.

It is only fair to the memory of Lucien Hirsch to say that he never cared the least about me. He died a short time after this and someone said to the Baron:

"What a fool Margot Tennant was not to have married your son! She would be a rich widow now."

At which he said:

"No one would die if they married Margot Tennant."

BARON VON ECKARDSTEIN*

One of the richest men in Europe then was Baron Hirsch, known generally as "Turkish Hirsch"; because he had made most of his money building the Oriental Railways for the Sultan. He came originally from Munich, and his principal place of business was in Brussels. But he was generally to be found either at Bath House in Piccadilly, at his magnificent Hotel in Paris, or at his Castle on the Hungarian frontier. The Prince used to visit the Castle for the shooting, and though I was often invited, I could only accompany him once.

"Turkish Hirsch" used to do us very well. He was a product of three cultures, and, towards the end of his life, lapsed into an almost incomprehensible lingo in which he mixed up English, French and German. For example, at this Castle of St. Johann, there was a terrace commanding a magnificent view of the Carpathians. He would bring a new arrival out on this terrace and say, with a wave of his hand, "And those sind die Karpaths." One day, on a new English visitor arriving, I saw the Prince take him out on the terrace, and say, with a wave of the hand, "And those sind die Karpaths." Baron Hirsch was there, but seemed to have no idea why we laughed.

Hirsch was a queer mixture of generosity and greed. I found him once kept in the pouring rain outside a club by a squabble with a cabman over sixpence. "Why not pay him and come in out of the wet? You'll catch cold and be laid up for weeks," I said. "That's all very well," said Hirsch, "but I have my principles."

One evening, at Monte Carlo, he had given a dinner for the Prince, and we all of us afterwards went on to the Casino. He had reserved us a special roulette table at which he took a seat himself; but he generally staked only five-franc pieces and never more than a gold louis, which he did with such a trembling hand that no one could help noticing it. As I was on chaffing terms with him, I asked him, on leaving, why he got in such a stew over five francs. "It's not on account of the five francs," said he, "but for fear that playing might be the beginning of my going down hill. For no fortune, not even mine, is big enough to last if the devil of gambling once gets hold of one."

* *Ten Years at the Court of St. James'* 1895-1905 (London, 1921), pp. 53-54.

O. S. STRAUS*

Then the bubble burst! Under my instructions I had assured the Turkish authorities that with their acceptance of the amendments of our Senate the negotiations in the matter would be concluded, and all that would be necessary to give effect to the treaty was the proclamation of the President. Instead, however, it was thought best again to submit the terms to the Senate, as fourteen years had elapsed since the negotiation of the original treaty. Thereupon some of our leading missionaries, at the instigation of prominent Armenians who had been naturalized in America and returned to Turkey, opposed ratification, and no further action was taken. It was a very discouraging situation, for many annoying cases constantly came up, some of a rather serious nature.

I might add that ten years later, when I was again minister to Turkey, I was instructed to renew negotiations, but the Ottoman Government was now unwilling to negotiate at all on this subject, and we were left without any treaty of naturalization.

There were one or two interesting special matters that came up during this mission. Toward the end of 1887 Baron Maurice de Hirsch came to Constantinople to adjust some financial differences with the Turkish Government. His railway, connecting Constantinople with European cities, was about completed. The Turkish Government claimed that he owed it 132,000,000 francs, a claim growing out of kilometric guarantees and other concessions.

One day while I was calling on the Grand Vizier, Kiamil Pasha, he asked to introduce some one to me, and forthwith I met a tall and slender man in his fifties, dark eyes sparkling with spirit and energy, clean-shaven except for a full black moustache, dressed rather dudishly in a cutaway coat, white vest and white spats—Baron de Hirsch. I was glad of this opportunity, for I had often heard of him and his great philanthropic activities. We had a pleasant conversation about things in general.

A few days later I took dinner with the Sultan. He spoke to me about Baron de Hirsch and the claim of Turkey against him. The Turkish Government was hard-pressed for funds—its chronic condition. The Sultan explained that for some time efforts had been made to arrive at some settlement, and that it was now proposed to arbitrate. The Baron had suggested first the French and then the Austrian ambassador as arbitrator, but neither was satisfactory to His Majesty; he, however, had much confidence in my judgment and impartiality, so that he had counter-suggested my name to the Baron, which was satisfactory to the latter; and they had agreed to pay me an honorarium of one million francs.

I assured the Sultan that I was much complimented by his request, but I would have to consult the Secretary of State. He told me he had already requested the Turkish minister at Washington to inquire the views of the Department, and that Mr. Bayard had said there was no objection to my acting as arbitrator. But I said I would have to communicate with Mr. Bayard personally and would let His Majesty hear from me in the course of a few days.

I cabled Mr. Bayard and learned, as the Sultan had said, that there was no objection to my

* *Under Four Administrations.* (Boston, 1925), pp. 92-96.

acceding to the latter's wishes and accepting the honorarium if it appeared to me advisable. Upon giving the proposal careful consideration, however, I felt it would not be wise for me to comply with the Sultan's request, much as I should have liked to please him. Any transaction with the Turkish Government involving money was open to suspicion of improper methods and bribery. Had I as arbitrator made a decision disappointing to the Turkish Government, I should certainly have fallen under such suspicion, and I deemed it improper to assume an obligation which might throw the American legation into a false light.

I advised Secretary Bayard accordingly and frankly told the Sultan I could not accept. I added, however, that while I would not accept an honorarium, I should be glad to act as mediator to see whether a satisfactory adjustment could not be brought about between the Baron and the Grand Vizier, which offer the Sultan accepted.

As the negotiations went forward, the Baron and the Grand Vizier had frequent disagreements and altercations. Each of them would come to me with his grievance, and I would give my opinion and bring them together again. Finally there arose a legal question, and this was submitted to Professor Gneist, the famous German authority on international law. Upon his decision the Baron finally paid the Turkish Government 22,000,000 francs.

During these negotiations, which lasted several months, an intimate friendship developed between the Baron and his wife and Mrs. Straus and myself. They often took family dinner with us. They were declining official invitations because of the recent death of their only child, Lucien. The Baroness was an exceptionally fine woman, learned and able, whose principal aim in life seemed to be to find ways of being most helpful to others. In the quarters of the poor, both Jew and Gentile, her short, trim figure, dressed in deep mourning, was familiar. Her face had an attractively benign expression. A story regarding her activities in connection with the construction of her husband's railroad was characteristic of her.

In a village near Constantinople a number of houses belonging to the poor had to be torn down to make way for the railway station. The work was to be done with the understanding that the Turkish Government would compensate these people, but evidently no such consideration was forthcoming. A number of those thus dispossessed came to the Baron to complain, but he answered that it was the Government's responsibility, not his. On hearing of this the Baroness informed her husband that she did not propose to let the railroad cause unhappiness to people, that it would probably be a long time before the Government paid the compensation, if ever, and that she insisted on paying these people out of her own private fortune so that they could at once build new houses and be happy. Then and there she carried out that programme.

The Baron spoke to me of his own benefactions and said he purposed during his lifetime to devote his fortune to benevolent causes. His philanthropy up to that time had been bestowed mainly in Russia, but he was desirous of doing something for the Russians who, because of the oppression resultant from the Ignatieff laws, were emigrating to America. They had been persecuted and were poor, and he wanted to enable them to reestablish themselves.

I was familiar with the conditions of these Russian immigrants, because prior to my coming to Turkey I had been in close relationship for several years with Michael Heilprin, author of a number of scholarly works and one of the chief editors of Appleton's Encyclopaedia. He worked untiringly on behalf of these new arrivals, collecting money for them and aiding them personally in numerous ways. I think his untimely death was due primarily to his generous expenditure of energy in this way. I mentioned Heilprin to the Baron and said I would write him for suggestions how best the immigrants might be helped.

When I heard from Heilprin I forwarded the letter to the Baron, together with a list of men who had done most in the way of benevolent work for the Jews of New York. Prominent on that list were Meyer S. Isaacs, president of the United Hebrew Congregations; Jesse Seligman,

Four Encounters

president of the Hebrew Orphan Asylum; Jacob H. Schiff, who was connected with a number of our charitable enterprises; and my brother Isidor. The Baron subsequently communicated with Mr. Isaacs and some others, and out of their arrangements grew the Baron de Hirsch Fund and the Baron de Hirsch Trade School. Later the Baroness, upon conferring with Mrs. Straus, endowed the Clara de Hirsch Home for Working Girls.

Neither my wife nor I wish to claim any credit for the founding of the de Hirsch benevolent institutions. We were simply the medium through which these came into being. We never even suggested the nature of them. We only gave the requested information regarding the need for such institutions.

LUCIEN WOLF*

They were only glimpses. In all, I saw the famous Baron three times, and only on one of those occasions did I have a really long talk with him. I derived, however, a very definite impression of him from these fleeting interviews, and it may not be uninteresting to jot it down while it is still fresh in my memory. The first time I met him was two years ago. He received me in a large and handsome room at Bath House, Piccadilly, his palatial *pied-à-terre* in London. Through the corners of the half-veiled windows, looking out on a parterre of flowers, with the Green Park beyond, the sunbeams entered in brilliant filaments and danced about the gilt frame of a gorgeous, but otherwise comfortable, armchair in which the Baron sat. Portly, robust, and good-looking, he seemed to carry his sixty odd years well. The weight of his millions sat lightly on his broad shoulders, and the eyes which looked at me from midway between the huge iron-grey moustache, and the carefully brushed up circlet of silver-grey hair had all the twinkle and cheeriness of a temper for which this world had lost none of its savour.

My first impression was one of pleasant disappointment. I had expected to meet something of a *poseur*. All I had heard had prejudiced me against the Leviathan philanthropist. It seemed to me that he must be the archtype of Renan's Ecclesiastes, perhaps a little subdued by Gentile culture, a little aggravated by the arrogance which comes of huge wealth, but a man with all the Jewish sense of the value of *réclame* and otherwise wholly without specific Jewish sentiment. The first grasp of his hand showed me that I was mistaken. To begin with, he was certainly not a *poseur*. If he was older and less distinguished looking than his portraits, on the other hand he was infinitely more genial. Moreover, he was exceedingly Jewish both in manner and conversation, and he made no effort to disguise it.

True, I had an advantage which the ordinary Gentile interviewer does not enjoy. It takes a Jew to understand a Jew, and no Jew, whatever his social position, puts on "side" to another Jew, unless, of course, he is deficient in sense of humour, or is a Sephardi. We were not long in finding this common ground. Scarcely was I seated than the Baron asked me in what language I preferred to talk, English, French or German. I told him it was all the same to me, and reminded him of what De Blowitz said to the Queen of Roumania when she asked him what nationality he was: "Mon dieu, Majesté, je n'en sais rien; je suis né en Bohème et je vis en France ou j'écris en Anglais."

"I might almost say the same thing," I added, "for I just missed being born in Bohemia, I was educated in France, and I practise journalism in England."

The Baron looked up sharply. His eyes twinkled as they settled on my nose. Something seemed to dawn upon him, for, nodding his head and puckering up his brows he said, hesitatingly, "You are a—a Hebrew—Not so?" I smiled assent. "Ah! que nous sommes cosmopolites!" he exclaimed.

The ice was broken. To me it seemed that the Baron was delighted with the opportunity for a regular *schmuse,* as the Hebrew *argot* hath it. We chatted for over an hour about his Argentine Scheme and Jewish matters generally, he talking throughout in that inimitable Jewish vein, which is a compound of shrewdness and quiet humour, of irony and pathos with here

* "Glimpses of Baron de Hirsch," *Jewish Chronicle,* May 8, 1896.

and there a flash of genuine racial pride. That his heart was in his great scheme and that it was a thoroughly Jewish heart, I am convinced. I shall not soon forget the tenderness with which he said, as he looked at one of my photographs: "Dear me! How interesting it is to see these old Jewish faces under the Argentine sun. See this sad-faced man carrying his bundle of sticks, still clad in his long Polish coat; and these little Hebrew cowboys who have passed from the Ghetto to the open country of the New World!" His Jewish *chauvinisme* was very marked. Talking of the persecution in Russia, he said to me with impressive earnestness, "When my Scheme is a success it will bring shame to the cheek of every Russian. The time will come when I shall have three or four hundred thousand Jews flourishing on their homesteads in the Argentine, peaceful and respected citizens, a valuable source of national wealth and stability. Then we shall be able to point to them and contrast them with their brethren who have been demoralised by persecution. What will the Jew-haters have to say then? I have made up my mind," he added, "not to stop in this work. If my energies or my fortune could accomplish it, believe me, the whole Jewish population of Russia would be taken out of the country to-morrow."

He seemed to me to be under no illusions with regard to the Scheme. "So far I have been experimenting," he said. "I have turned to the right and to the left, and now if I have not yet hit upon the ideal thing, at any rate I know what not to do." Of the Argentine he said: "It is not precisely a land in which *Milch und Honig fliesst,* but it gives a magnificent return for honest labour." He thought very highly of his emigrants. "You have no conception," he said, "of the good will with which they take to the soil. The predictions of our enemies that the Jews would never go back to agriculture have been falsified. The Russian Jew has grit, industry, sobriety; he is eager for work. No matter what he has been at home, he takes readily to the spade." He then told me about a family he had sent out, of which the father had been a professor, and the daughters were well educated girls, accomplished musicians and linguists, and who were then all following the plough at Entre Rios. "Yes," he added, "they give me the greatest hope." His chief difficulty, he told me, had all along been to find willing and congenial associates. "Poor Jews," he said, "will do anything for me, but they cannot offer me any guarantees; middle-classes—people with their twenty or thirty thousand roubles—are contented and apathetic: the rich—well, when a Jew becomes rich, you know, he is no longer a Jew." He said this between a sigh and a smile and then, following out an obvious train of thought, remarked, after a pause, "I suppose I shall spend all my money in this movement, and then I shall go out and manage it myself."

He told me a great deal more about the Colonisation Scheme which I need not repeat here. Most of the facts are now known and, moreover, my object is not to describe the Scheme, but to give some idea of the personality of its founder.

The other two occasions on which I saw Baron de Hirsch were more fleeting. Walking across the park one Sunday morning, after a meeting of the Council of the Anglo-Jewish Association, I met him in the brilliant crowd which throngs the vicinity of the statue of Achilles at the height of the London season. He recognised me most kindly, and, after a few cordial banalities, passed on. Last year I called on him in Paris. I only remained with him a few moments. He asked me with a smile whether I had come to interview him again. I said no, but added, that one of these days I should like, if he would allow me, to catechise him about the feelings of of a millionaire.

"It would make what we journalists call 'very good copy,'" I remarked.

"All there is to say," he answered, "I can tell you now. The poor think that money will buy everything; the rich know that it won't."

The sentiment is not a new one, but the interest of it—the unfathomable pathos of it—lies in its application.

APPENDIX II

BARON DE HIRSCH'S MEMORANDUM ON PALESTINEAN COLONIZATION, 1891*

As representing the New York Chovevi Zion, Shovey Zion, and others offering co-operation in the Palestinean work, I met in Paris S. P. Rabinowitz, editor of the *Keneseth Yisroel* and translator of Graetz's history into Hebrew, who was waiting for Baron de Hirsch's answer to a petition presented by the representatives of the Russian Chovevi Zion, which was then at variance with Baron de Rothschild. Rabbi Mohilever and Dr. Hirsch Hildesheimer were the spokesmen of the Chovevi Zion.

"Although pressed by the Russian Chovevi Zion, through Mr. Rabinowitz and Dr. Hildesheimer, to add my voice to their petition, I refused to do so, stating it as my view that the Palestinean cause must stand or fall with Baron Rothschild; and that the Chovevi Zion should, therefore, at all events, co-operate with him, whether with or without Baron de Hirsch. I did, however, assist in aiding the London and Parisian Chovevi Zion in bringing about at that time an entente between Barons de Hirsch and Rothschild; the result of this, I believe at least in part, was that Baron de Hirsch's answer which was, at first expected to turn out absolutely in the negative, assumed the form given below, from a copy I received from Drs. Sonnenfeld and Schwarzfeld, Baron de Hirsch's General Agent and Secretary, respectively.

"On the strength of this document, a conference was convened in Paris at the office of the Alliance Israélite Universelle, Rue de Trévise, about the middle of September, 1891, participated in, to the best of my recollection, by Grand Rabbin Zadoc Kahn, M. Erlanger, on the part of Baron de Rothschild, and by Isidor Loeb on the part of Baron de Hirsch, and Rabbi Mohilever, Dr. Hildesheimer, S. P. Rabinowitz, Col. Goldsmid and myself, as representing the Chovevi Zion.

"This conference decided to raise 10,000 francs for the expenses of the Commission referred to in Baron de Hirsch's document. I accompanied Rabbi Mohilever and Dr. Hildesheimer back to London, where we conferred on the matter with the Russo-Jewish Committee at the office of Mr. Samuel Montagu and with Lord Rothschild (who was seen by Rabbi Mohilever and Dr. Hildesheimer). The Russo-Jewish Committee donated two hundred pounds sterling for the purpose. During my first stay in Palestine (from about the beginning of October to the middle of December, 1891), I received information from Dr. Hildesheimer that the 10,000 francs were fast materializing. I also undertook to have duly contributed the sum of $2,000, then deposited by the New York Chovevi Zion with Baron de Rothschild.

"On my return to Paris, at the end of December, 1891, I was informed by M. Erlanger that the matter had been wholly dropped. The reason of the breakdown, so far as I could ascertain, was a purely personal one between the two barons."

(Signed)   Adam Rosenberg.

---

* *Jacob de Haas, Theodor Herzl* (New York, 1927), Vol. II. pp. 287-294.

Hirsch's Memorandum

The document reads:

MEMORANDUM

Concerning the project of Russian Emigration and the creation of a (Agra) Farmers' Trust Bank in Asiatic Turkey.

I have taken note of the minutes of the meeting held at Paris, July 29, 1891, and composed:

On the one part of several members of the Central Committee of the Alliance Israélite Universelle, with Mons. Zadoc Kahn, Grand Rabbin of France, as their spokesman, and on the other part by delegates of Russian Societies in favor of Palestinean Colonization.

These latter proposed to and, in fact, did obtain from the Alliance its approbation and its moral support in favor of a project having as its object:

(a) The creation of Russo-Jewish colonies in Asiatic Turkey, particularly in Syria and Palestine.

(b) The establishment of a Farmers' Trust Bank in order to facilitate such colonization by all available means.

I have been called upon at Paris by several of the delegates of the Russian Societies who orally put before me their idea and their project; they have, besides, so as to gain my assent and support, addressed to me a letter accompanied by a memorandum, setting forth the plan of the enterprises projected. I have taken cognizance thereof.

On the occasion of their call, I explained to the delegates the reasons why it is not possible for me to share their point of view, or to approve without reservation, the project of colonization in Asiatic Turkey. They do not ignore that, if they wish to follow my advice, they ought partly to modify the standpoint hitherto taken by them exclusively, namely, that of religious memories and historical traditions. However grand and honorable these traditions may be, they do not constitute a sufficiently solid basis wherewith to secure the immigrants in their new fatherland against new vicissitudes and new misfortunes. The delegated gentlemen know that I think it to be the duty of all who have in view the real welfare of our coreligionists only to entertain the project of colonization in Asiatic Turkey with the express proviso of a provisional and very careful investigation of which I shall speak later. After having expressed to them my opinion I added that I am quite disposed, in order to prove to them my great desire to be helpful to them, to assist them in the negotiations to be undertaken at Constantinople, adding to theirs delegates of my own choice, who are to enter on the spot in an investigation of the localities more seriously to be considered for an eventual choice, as well as to obtain of the Turkish government the best possible terms.

One cannot, indeed, start colonizing haphazardly, and the movement should be preceded by a preliminary serious and careful investigation.

First of all, then, a commission should be appointed, composed of experts, three or five for example; their mission would be, in the first place, to choose those localities and lands most suitable for colonization purposes, next to put themselves in touch with the authorities in order to acquire the selected lands on the best possible terms. Surely, if the principle of colonization in Asiatic Turkey be granted, that should be the way to go about it; only thus will those charged with the selection of the lands and wishing to assume the responsibility of this work, have the opportunity to inform themselves exactly by personal investigation of the means whereby they subsequently can conduct the negotiations with a full knowledge of the subject.

This provisional investigation, urgently needed as it is insofar as colonization, pure and simple, is concerned, is not less so as regards the establishment of a Farmers' Bank.

According to the project submitted to me by the Russian delegates, this Bank should serve:

I. To advance interest bearing loans on good security in form of mortgages, to wit:

(a) To new colonists whose own means are insufficient to provide for cultivating their lands, planting and sowing, and such other farm work as is necessary up to the time of harvesting or reaping; (b) To the already installed colonists to aid them in improving and enlarging their lands.

2. To provide a shelter and living for the destitute that will seek employment as farm laborers in the colonies or on the private farms.

3. To enable the purchase of lands in Asiatic Turkey on the part of Jewish colonists coming from Russia.

4. To direct the hitherto so ill-regulated and planless emigration movement towards the latter country in a safe and systematic manner.

This program is excellent in theory, but, before deciding upon the creation of such an institution and fixing a priori its different departmental functions, it will be very necessary to know whether the organic conditions of that colonization work necessitates so extensive a program.

It should first be known what will be the area and consequently the importance of the lands to be acquired; before all, it should be ascertained whether it is not possible by means of an understanding with the government, to obtain lands for cultivation through concessions without payment of a purchase price.

If this latter alternative should eventuate, a Farmers' Trust Bank would certainly lose much of its interest.

In these circumstances, and until these preliminary questions have been settled satisfactorily, it appears premature to discuss the subject of a Farmers' Trust Bank, and especially, to follow the Russian delegates into the details of its functional organization. The above suffices to demonstrate the necessity of a serious preliminary investigation of the project of colonization in Asiatic Turkey. It may be well for me briefly to point out, in the following, the chief reasons that have convinced me that to be sure of success, colonization ought to be tried, in the first place, in the new world, and, especially, in the Argentine Republic.

And, first, from the agricultural viewpoint and that of economic life, the superiority of this latter country may be thus shown. No one is unaware that agriculture in Turkey does not prosper. The causes are known.

In the Argentine Republic, on the contrary, the soil is of a proverbial fertility; the climate is excellent; thanks to the financial crisis, at present prevalent in that country, one could buy there considerable lands at remunerative prices. The Argentine Republic is the true land of the future; there thousands of millions have hitherto been spent for railway constructions, river enlargements, harbor works; all that has been done at large cost and all this exists; the new colonists will profit thereby under exceptionally advantageous conditions.

Aside from the agricultural and economic status, the political social life aspect of the colonies in Argentine, I maintain, offers the Jews a point of concentration which they will hardly find elsewhere. The area of this country is nine times that of France, while its population does not reach the figure of four millions. Consequently there is room and a future for an unlimited number of Jews.

From the moment that Jews emigrate, it should be done with the view, not of gaining only a few years of tranquillity and respite, but with the firm purpose of securing for their posterity rest and stability in the future. Are they sure those that propose to direct the Russian emigrants towards Asiatic Turkey, that these very ones will see any useful result from their labors, and their efforts crowned with success? Are they not afraid to expose them once more to collisions, soon or late, with their present persecutors, the Russians? Have they considered that they thus tend to disperse the emigration movement, instead of concentrating?

The central idea, then, the principal whence I believe the work of emigration ought to start, is as much as possible concentration. But, as I have said at the start, if the deputation of the Russian Societies persist in their project, I am quite disposed to place at their disposal both my influence and my active co-operation with the Imperial Ottoman government.

I merely feel bound to demonstrate to them the necessity of having their project preceded by a preliminary careful investigation and the superiority of colonization in the Argentine Republic above all other hitherto proposed systems.

This preliminary investigation is for me a question of so high importance that it outweighs all others; it is, moreover, an absolute condition of my prospective intervention, I must be sure of it.

Since this note has been drawn up, I was visited by M. J. Navon, who, as you know, has had relations with M. Erlanger of the Alliance on the subject of immigration into Asiatic Turkey. I have had a long talk with him and I am well convinced, although he is ostensibly very enthusiastic about the immigration into Asiatic Turkey, that at bottom he would not hesitate to give the preference to the Argentine Republic, had he not beforehand embarked upon the other project. The conversation I had with M. Navon is summed up as follows:

I have made him understand the danger entailed in conducting haphazardly the immigration movement into Asiatic Turkey, as well as to treat at random with the government, without having before investigated, in the most careful manner and on the spot, the localities eventually most suitable for colonization. M. Navon believes and, it appears to me rightly so, that provided Palestine be waived, the Turkish government will accept a limited number of Jewish immigrants and furnish them gratuitously, or nearly so, the necessary lands. I for my part would prefer to have these lands acquired for private ownership.

To resume, M. Navon understands the absolute necessity for the sending of a commission of three to five members who shall be charged with thoroughly investigating the question of the lands to be selected and asked of the Turkish government.

These delegates should act as much in the name of the Alliance as in my own name. M. Navon preferred that it be in my name especially. I admit I feel some hesitation to present the matter as coming largely from me, for the reasons above set forth; nevertheless, I shall do my share, if such become indispensable, not wishing to spare, as I have said, neither my influence nor my active co-operation. These delegates will have to place themselves in touch with the persons competent to select the proper lands for colonization. They will have to visit these lands, inspect them with care, examine also which is the best organization to be given to the immigration, in a word, draw up a veritable plan of campaign, as I have done for the immigration to the Argentine Republic through the labors of Dr. Loewenthal. Their plan once fixed, they will, lastly, have to negotiate with the Turkish government, in order to fix the terms of purchase, those of duration, taxation etc.

This most highly important investigation ought to be made in an extremely conscientious manner. The delegates and the members of the Central Committee of the Alliance who have signed the minutes of the meeting of July 29, 1891, will now have to make their choice, in constituting this commission, of truly capable men, well posted on the matters that they will have to examine, and proof against the intrigues by which they will not fail to be surrounded. As to the delegates to be chosen by me, I reserve it to myself to appoint them; after I shall have been informed of the delegates chosen by the Alliance and by the Russian Societies I shall act thereon.

I shall furnish these delegates the necessary instructions and references.

MAURICE DE HIRSCH.

Carlsbad, August, 1891

With reference to this document, the author has received the following statement from M. Bigard, the Secretary of the Alliance Israélite Universelle, under date of December 21, 1926:

On July 29, 1891, a meeting was held in Paris for the purpose of discussing questions of emigration at which meeting there were present besides several members of the Central Committee of the Alliance Israélite, Dr. Mohilever of Bialystok and Dr. Hildesheimer of Berlin. Baron de Hirsch was at Carlsbad at the time. The suggestions made at the meeting were submitted to him; the delegation had requested especially the organization of a movement of Russian emigration towards Asia Minor, after the sending of a commission of experts. Baron de Hirsch set forth in a detailed note the reasons why Turkey in Asia and especially Palestine seemed to him to be unadvisable as lands for emigration. He added that if they persisted in the project it would be requisite, and this absolutely, to have it preceded by a thorough preliminary study. In a letter which he addressed on August 3, 1891, to the German Central Committee for Russian Jews in Berlin, he declared on the other hand:

"I point out the danger there is in sending emigrants into Asia and Turkey; I know that land better than anybody, and better than anybody also I am in a position to judge of the misery and deceptions which await the colonists who would be sent there haphazardly."

The project, moreover, had no further sequel.

CHRONOLOGY

BARON MAURICE DE HIRSCH

1831	born at Munich December 9
1841	death of grandfather, Jacob von Hirsch—Inheritance?
1844	sent to school at Brussels
1848	returns to Munich
1849/50	successful speculations
1851	enters Bischoffsheim & Goldschmidt, Brussels
1854	Bischoffsheim & Goldschmidt participate in first Turkish loan
1855	Marries Clara Bischoffsheim, moves to Munich
1856	father, Joseph von Hirsch, and Bischoffsheim & Goldschmidt join in establishing *Bayerische Ostbahn*
1856	son, Lucien, born
1858 (?)	returns to Brussels, joins Bischoffsheim & Goldschmidt (?)
1858	joins board of Der Anker, Vienna, cooperating with Langrand-Dumonceau
1859	joins board of *Association Générale d'Assurances* with Langrand-Dumonceau
1860 (ca.)	establishes Banque Bischoffsheim-de-Hirsch, Brussels, with brother-in-law, Ferdinand
1860	Russian Railway venture, Moscow-Ryazan
1863	joins *Allg. Maatschappij;* Dutch Railway venture
1864	Bischoffsheim & Goldschmidt co-founders of Bank of Constantinople
1868	began construction of East-Hungarian Railway, jointly with Bischoffsheim & Goldschmidt, etc.
1869	Oriental Railway Concession; settles in Constantinople
1870	Bischoffsheim & Goldschmidt's Egyptian loan
1871	building his Palais in Rue d'Elysée, Paris
1871	issue of *Türkenlose*
1871	gift of one million francs to Alliance Israélite Universelle for schools in Orient
1870/72	progress of work on railway
1871/72	Banque Bischoffsheim-de-Hirsch merged into Banque de Dépôts des Pays Bas
1872/73	merger with Banque de Paris et des Pays Bas
1873	revision of concession agreement
1875	completes restricted railway contract
1878	Congress of Berlin
1878	transfers Betriebsgesellschaft from Paris to Vienna
1885	death of father, Joseph von Hirsch
1885	appoints delegation to Russian Government concerning situation of Russian Jews; contributes 500,000 francs to Boulanger cause
1886	meets Crown Prince Rudolf and Edward, Prince of Wales; finances Szeps's *Wiener Tageblatt*

1886 (ca.)	meets Margot Asquith
1886	Baron Rothschild starts financing colonies in Palestine
1887	death of son Lucien; meets O. S. Straus in Constantinople
1888	von Gneist Arbitration Award. First train: Vienna-Constantinople. Carl Netter's letter opposing Palestine for mass immigration.
1889	contributes 2.5 million francs to Boulanger cause. Cercle de Rue Royale incident (?)
1889	sells out Betriebsgesellschaft to Deutsche Bank / Wiener Bankverein, which in
1890	sets up Bank für Orientalische Eisenbahnen
1891	establishes ICA; Fund for Galician Schools, Vienna; Baron Hirsch Fund, New York; Carlsbad Memo on Palestine.
1895	meets Theodor Herzl
1896	dies on April 20, at O'Gyalla, Hungary
1899	death of Clara de Hirsch

BIBLIOGRAPHY

ADLER, ELKAN N., *Jews in many Lands*. London, 1905.
ADLER-RUDEL, S., 'Moritz Baron Hirsch. Profile of a Great Philanthropist,' *Yearbook* VIII, Leo Baeck Institute. London, 1963.
Admiralty War Staff, Intelligence Division, *Handbook of Turkey in Europe*. London, 1917.
Alliance Israélite Universelle, *'Le Droit de l'Homme et l'Education, (Actes du Congrès Centenaire de l'AIU)* Paris, 1961.
ASQUITH, MARGOT, *My Autobiography* (Penguin Books ed.). London, 1936 (Orig. ed. 1920).
BAMBERGER, LUDWIG, *Erinnerungen* (ed. P. Nathan). Berlin, 1899.
Baron de Hirsch Institute, Montreal, *Centennial* 1863-1963. Montreal, 1963.
BARON, S. W., 'The Modern Age' in *Great Ages and Ideas of the Jewish People*, ed. L. D. Schwartz. New York, 1956.
BARTIER, N., Fondateurs et Créateurs de Crédit Communal de Belgique,' *Bulletin Trimestriel du Crédit Communal de Belgique*. Brussels, October 1960.
Bayerische Staatsbank, Die, von 1780-1955. Munich, 1955.
BEIN, ALEX, 'Dokumente zu Herzls' Begegnung mit Wilhelm II,' *Zeitschrift für die Geschichte der Juden*. Tel-Aviv, II, 1-2, 1965.
—, *Theodor Herzl*. New York, 1940.
BENEDIKT, HEINRICH, *Die wirtschaftliche Entwicklung in der Franz-Josephs Zeit*. Vienna, 1958.
BISMARCK, OTTO VON, *Gedanken und Erinnerungen*. Stuttgart, 1898.
BLAISDELL, W. H., *European Financial Control in the Ottoman Empire*. New York, 1929.
BLOWITZ, OPPER DE, *Une course à Constantinople*. Paris, 1884.
BODENHEIMER, K. N., *Prelude to Israel*. New York, 1963.
BOUVIER, JEAN, *Le Crédit Lyonnais*, 1863-1882. 2 vols. Paris, 1963.
—, *Le Krach de l'Union Générale* 1878-1883. Paris, 1960.
BROGAN, SIR DENIS *The Development of Modern France*, 1870-1939. London, 1940.
BRUNNER FREDERICK H., 'Juden als Bankiers—Ihre Weltverbindende Tatigkeit,' in *Zwei Welten*. Tel-Aviv, 1962.
BUSCH, MORITZ, *Bismarck, Some Secret Pages of his History*. 3 vols. London, 1898.
CAIRNCROSS, A. E., *Home and Foreign Investment*, 1870-1939. Cambridge, 1953.
CAMERON, RONDO S., *France and the Economic Development of Europe*, 1800-1914. Princeton, 1961.
CHAPMAN, GUY, *The Third Republic in France, First Phase*, 1870-1894. London, 1962.
CHIEL, S. A., *The Jews in Manitoba*. Toronto, 1961.
CHIRAC, A., *Les Rois de la République*. Paris, 1883.
CHLEPNER, S. B., *L'Etranger dans l'Histoire Economique de la Belgique*. Brussels, 1932.
CHOURAQI, ANDRE *l'Alliance Israélite Universelle et la Renaissance Juive*. Paris, 1965.
COLLINS, MAURICE, *Wayfoong, The Hongkong and Shanghai Banking Corporation*. London, 1965.
CORTI, EGON C., *Leopold I*. Vienna and Leipzig, 1922.
Creditanstalt-Bankverein, *Ein Jahrhundert*. Vienna, 1957.

DAVIDSON, GABRIEL, *Our Jewish Farmers, The Story of the Jewish Agricultural Society*. New York, 1943.
DEHN, PAUL, *Deutschland und Orient in ihren wirtschaftlichen Beziehungen*. Munich and Leipzig, 1884.
DIMTCHOFF, R. M., *Das Eisenbahnwesen auf der Balkan-Halbinsel*. Bamberg, 1894
DRUMMOND-WOLFF, SIR HENRY, *Rambling Recollections*. 2 vols. London, 1908.
DRUMONT EDOUARD, *La France Juive—Essai d'histoire contemporaine* (16th ed.). Paris, 1886.
EARLE, E. M., *Turkey, The Great Powers and The Baghdad Railway, A Study in Imperialism*. New York, 1923.
ECKARDSTEIN, BARON VON, *Ten Years at the Court of St. James*, London, 1921.
ELLIOT, SIR HENRY G., *Some Revolutions and other Diplomatic Experiences*. London, 1922.
EMDEN, PAUL, *Money Powers of Europe in the Nineteenth and Twentieth Century*. London, 1936.
ENGELS, FRIEDRICH, *Die Briefe von, an Eduard Bernstein*. Berlin, 1925.
ESCOTT, T. H. S., 'A Foreign Correspondent,' *Society in London*. (Eighth ed.) London, 1885.
FEIS, H., *Europe, The World's Banker*, 1870-1914. New Haven, 1930.
FRAENKEL, JOSEPH, *Lucien Wolf und Theodor Herzl*. The Jewish Historical Society of England. London, 1960.
FRANK, WALTER, *Nationalismus und Demokratie in Frankreich der Dritten Republik*, 1871-1914. Hamburg, 1933.
FRIEDJUNG, H., *Das Zeitalter des Imperialismus*. 2 vols. Vienna, 1922.
FÜRSTENBERG, CARL, *Lebensgeschichte eines deutschen Bankiers*, 1870-1914. Berlin, 1931.
GELBER, N. M., 'The intervention of German Jews at the Berlin Congress,' *Yearbook V*, 1960, Leo Baeck Institute. London, 1960.
GILES, F., *Blowitz, A Prince of Journalists: The Life and Times of Henri Stefan Opper de Blowitz*. Leventon, 1963.
GOLDBERG, A., *Pioneers and Builders*. New York, 1943.
GOLDHAFT, A. D., *The Golden Egg*. New York, 1957
GOOCH, G. P., *Recent Revelations of European Diplomacy*. London, 1940.
GRAVES, CHARLES L., *Mr. Punch's History of Modern England*. 4 vols. London, 1922.
GRUNWALD, K., 'The Bankers of Galata', *Riv'on l'Bankauth [Banking Quarterly]*, 6. Tel-Aviv, 1962.
—'The Sarrafs, Bankers of Iraq,' *Hamizrach Hehadash* XI, 3. Jerusalem, 1961.
GRUNWALD, MAX, *Samuel Oppenheimer und sein Kreis*. Vienna, 1913.
—'Deszendententafel der Familie Wertheimer,' *Mitteilungen zur jüdischen Volkskunde*. Vienna, 1912.
GUEDALLA PHILIP, *Palmerston*. London, 1926.
HAAS, JACOB DE, *Theodor Herzl*. 2 vols. New York, 1927.
HALLGARTEN, G. W. F., *Imperialismus vor 1914* (Second Edition) 2 vols. Munich, 1963.
HARRIS, FRANK, *My Life and Loves*. 3 vols. Nice, 1927.
HASLIP, JOAN, *The Sultan—The Life of Abdul Hamid II*. London, 1958.
HELFFERICH, KARL, *Georg von Siemens*. 3 vols. Berlin, 1921.
HERSCHLAG, I. Z., *Introduction to the Economic History of the Middle East*. Leyden, 1964.
HERZL, THEODOR, *Tagebücher*. 3 vols. Berlin, 1921.
—*The Jewish State* (1896). London, 1936.
HOHENLOHE-SCHILLINGFURST, PRINCE CHLODWIG, *Memoirs*. 2 vols. London, 1906.
HÜMMERT, L., 'Die finanziellen Beziehungen jüdischer Bankiers und Heereslieferanten zum Bayerischen Staat in der ersten Hälfte des 19. Jahrhunderts.' (Ph. D. Dissertation). Munich, 1927.

Bibliography

JACQUEMYNS, G., *Langrand-Dumonceau, Promoteur d'une Puissance Financière Catholique*. 4 vols. Brussels, 1960.
JAPHET, SAEMY, *Recollections from my Business Life*. London, 1931.
JENKS, H. LELAND, *The Migration of British Capital to 1875*. London, 1927.
JOSEPH, SAMUEL, *History of the Baron Hirsch Fund. The Americanization of the Jewish Immigrant*. Philadelphia, 1935.
JOSLIN, DAVID, *A Century of Banking in South America*. London, 1965.
KANITZ, F. V., *Donau, Bulgarien und der Balkan*. 3 vols. Leipzig, 1877.
KATZNELSON, R. (ED.), *Juden im deutschen Kulturbereich*. Berlin, 1959.
KAUCH, I., 'Jonathan Raphael Bischoffsheim.' *Revue de Personnel, Banque Nationale Belgique*. Brussels, January, 1950.
KAYSERLING, M., *Gedenkblätter*. Leipzig, 1892.
KINDLEBERGER, C. P., *Economic Growth in France and Britain 1860-1960*. London, 1964.
KÜHLMANN, R. V., *Erinnerungen*. Heidelberg, 1948.
KÜRENBERG, JOACHIM VON, *His Excellency, The Spectre*. London, 1933.
LANDES, D. S., *Bankers and Pashas—International Finance and Economic Imperialism in Egypt*. London, 1958.
LANGER, W. L., *European Alliances and Alignments, 1871-1890* (Second Edition). New York, 1962.
LAVELEYE, E. DE, *The Balkan Peninsula*. London, 1887.
LEE, SIR SIDNEY, *King Edward VII*. London, 1925.
LEVEN NARCISSE, *Cinquante Ans d'Histoire, L'Alliance Juive Universelle*. Vol. I, Paris, 1911; Vol. II, Paris, 1920
LEVIN, SHMARYAHU, *Youth in Revolt*. London, 1927.
LONYAY, RUDOLF, *The Tragedy of Mayerling*. London, 1950.
LUDWIG, EMIL, *Bismarck*. London, 1927.
MAGNUS, SIR PHILIP, *King Edward the Seventh*. London, 1964.
MALACHI, A. R., 'The Yishuv's Mourning for Carl Netter,' (Hebrew) *Cahiers de l' A.I.U.*, XII, 5-8. Jerusalem, June, 1963.
MAUROIS, ANDRE, *Edouard VII et son Temps*. Paris, 1933.
MAYER, SIEGMUND, *Die Wiener Juden, 1700-1900*. Vienna, 1917.
MEARS, S. G., *Modern Turkey*. New York, 1924.
MEYERS, GUSTAVUS, *History of the Great American Fortunes*, (1909). New York, 1936.
MIDHAT BEY A. H., *The Life of Midhat Pasha*, London, 1903.
Monographie du Palais des feu le Baron et la Baronne de Hirsch (Décorations intérieurs et extérieurs, 4 pp. and 60 plates). Paris, 1906.
MORAWITZ, CHARLES (KARL), *Les Finances de la Turquie*. Paris, 1902.
—*50 Jahre Geschichte einer Bank, (Anglo-Austrian Bank)*. Vienna, 1913.
New Palestine, Herzl Memorial Volume. New York, 1929.
NOVOTNY, ALEXANDER, *Quellen und Studien zur Geschichte des Berliner Kongresses*, I, Graz, 1957.
NUSSENBLATT THEO., *Zeitgenossen über Herzl*. Brünn, 1929.
PALMADE GUY P., *Capitalisme et Capitalistes Françaises au XIX Siècle*. Paris, 1961.
PEARS, SIR EDWARD, *Forty Years in Constantinople*. New York, 1916.
—*Life of Abdul Hamid*. London, 1917.
PEARSON, HESKETH, *Dizzy*. The Life and Personality of Benjamin Disraeli. London, 1951.
PIRBRIGHT, LORD, ('Von einem Engländer'), *Die Osterreichisch-ungarische Monarchie und die Politik des Grafen Beust*. Leipzig, 1870.

POULGY, G., *Les emprunts de l'Etat Ottoman*. Paris, 1915.
PRYS, JOSEF, *Die Familie von Hirsch auf Gereuth*. Munich, 1931.
—'Zum Anteil der Familie von Hirsch im Kampfe um die bayerische Judenemanzipation,' *Zeitschrift für die Geschichte der Juden in Deutschland*. Berlin, 1935.
RADOLIN, JOSEF MARIA VON, *Aufzeichnungen und Erinnerungen aus dem Leben des Botschafters*. 2 vols. Leipzig, 1928
RECHBERGER, W., *'Zur Geschichte der Orientalischen Eisenbahn,'* (Ph. D. Dissertation). Vienna, 1960.
RICH, N. & M. K. FISHER, *The Holstein Diaries*. Vol. II. Cambridge, Mass., 1957.
ROBINSON, RONALD and JOHN GALLAGHER with ALICE DENNY, *Africa and the Victorians— The Climax of Imperialism in the Dark Continent*. New York, 1961.
ROTH, CECIL, *The Magnificent Rothschilds*. (Pyramid Edition). London, 1962.
SACHER, HOWARD MOORLEY, *The Course of Modern Jewish History*. New York, 1958.
SCHIFF, JACOB H., *His Life and Letters,* (ed. C. Adler). 2 vols. New York, 1928.
SCHNEE, H., *Die Hochfinanz und der moderne Staat*. 4 vols. Berlin, 1953-1963.
SCHWARZ, STEPHAN, *Die Juden in Bayern im Wandel der Zeiten*. Munich-Vienna, 1936.
SIEGHART, RUDOLF, *Die Letzten Jahre einer Grossmacht*. Berlin, 1943.
SIMON, SIR LEON, *Ahad Haam*. London, 1961.
SOKOLOV, NAHUM, *History of Zionism*. London, 1922.
STAVRIANOS, L. S., *The Balkans since 1453*. New York, 1958.
STEINER, F. G., *Entwicklung des Mobilbankwesens in Osterreich*. Vienna, 1913.
STERN, SELMA, *The Court Jew*. Philadelphia, 1954.
STRAUS, O. S., 'Baron Moritz de Hirsch,' in *Jewish Encyclopedia*. New York, 1913.
—*The American Spirit*. New York, 1913.
—*Under Four Administrations*. Boston, 1925.
STRAUS, SARA, 'Clara von Hirsch' in *Jewish Encyclopedia*. New York, 1913.
SUPPLE, HARRY E., 'A Business Elite: German-Jewish Financiers in 19th Century New York,' *Business History Review*, XXXI, 2. Harvard, 1957.
SZEPS-ZUCKERKANDL, BERTA, *My Life-History*. London, 1938.
TAYLOR, A. J. P., *The Habsburg Monarchy*. (Penguin Edition). London, 1964.
TEMPERLEY, HAROLD W. R., *Foundations of British Foreign Policy*. Cambridge, 1938.
TIETZE, H., *Die Wiener Juden*. Vienna, 1933.
TREUE, WILHELM, *Vorbemerkungen des Herausgebers 'Tradition'*, No. 4. Munich, 1965.
VELAY, A. DU., *Les Finances de la Turquie*. Paris, 1903.
WEIZMANN, CHAIM, *Trial and Error*. London, 1949.
WESTWOOD, J. N., *History of the Russian Railways*. London, 1964.
WHITE, A. D., *Aus meinem Diplomatenleben*. Leipzig, n. d.
WINSBERG, MORTON S., *Colonia Baron Hirsch, A Jewish Agricultural Colony in Argentina*. Gainsville (Flo.), 1963.
WOLF, LUCIEN, 'Glimpses of Baron de Hirsch,' *Jewish Chronicle*. London, May 8, 1896.
YOUNG, G., *Constantinople*. London, 1926.
—*Corps de Droit Ottoman*. Vol. IV. Oxford, 1906.
ZIMMERER, HEINRICH, 'Europäische Turkei,' in Helmholt's *Weltgeschichte*, Volume IV. Leipzig, 1920.

IMPORTANT NEWSPAPER ARTICLES, ETC.

Jewish Chronicle. April 24, 1896.
Neues Wiener Abendblatt. April 21, 1896.

Bibliography 133

Augsburger Abendzeitung. April 23, 1896.
Neue Freie Presse. April 21, 1896.
Neues Wiener Tageblatt. April 22, 1896.
Nues Wiener Tageblatt, Finance Section, April 22, 1896.
The Times. April 22, 1896.
The Times, 'The Bulgarian Railways.' August 21, 1888.
The Times. May 23, 1896.
Fremdenblatt. April 22, 1896.
Jewish Chronicle. Various dates.
'Österreichische Wochenschrift. Various dates.
Die jüdischePresse. Berlin.
Le Figaro. April 22, 1896.
The Bystander. February 12, 1913.
Berliner Boersen Zeitung Nov. 6, 1884.

Jewish Encyclopedia
Enclyclopedia of Social Sciences, 1932, Volume 7. (E. Tscherikower, 'Baron Hirsch.').
Encyclopedia Judaica
Jüdisches Lexikon
Pronouncing Dictionary of Biography & Mythology, 4th edition. Philadelphia, 1915.
Österreichisches Biographisches Lexikon
Wienigers Jüdische National-Biographie, III, Cernauti, 1925.
PIERER, H. A., *Universallexikon.* Altenburg, 1843

INDEX

Abdul Aziz, Sultan of Turkey, 30, 47, 67
Abdul Hamid, 78, 106
Abzac, Marquis d', 71
Adeane, Sir Michael, 93
Adler, Elkan N., xv, 77, 79
Adler-Rudel, S., xii, xv, 65
Ahad Haam, 80
Albertis & Co., 37
Algemeene Maatschappij vor Handel en Nijverheid, 24
Ali pasha, 39
Alliance Israélite Universelle, 11, 64, 65, 66-67, 68, 69, 70, 80, 122
Andrassy, Count Julius (Gyula), 40, 53, 54-55, 56, 92
Anglo-Austrian Bank, 25, 32, 35, 36, 37, 39
Anglo-Jewish Association, 72, 73
'Anker, Der,' Insurance Company (see 'Der Anker'),
Arnim, Count Harry von, 89, 92
Asquith, Margot (née Tennant), 9, 9 n., 102
Association Générale d'Assurances, 21, 22, 25
Augsburger Abendzeitung, 12
Austrian Patriotic Fund, 68
Austrian State Railways, 29, 33, 55, 56, 61

Balkan Railways, 33
Balser, E., 106
Baltazzi, 91
Bamberger, Amalia (née Bischoffsheim) (mother of Heinrich and Ludwig Bamberger), 14
Bamberger, Amalia (née Hirsch) (wife of Heinrich Bamberger), 14
Bamberger, Heinrich, 14, 15, 22
Bamberger, Ludwig, 14, 16, 17, 38
Bank für Orientalische Eisenbahnen, 61
Banque de Belgique, 15
Banque de Crédit Foncier et Industriel, 22, 23
Banque de Paris ed des Pays-Bas (Paribas), 13, 14, 37, 38, 46, 57
Banque des Dépôts des Pays Bas, 15, 37
Banque, Franco-Egyptienne, 13
Bär, Dr., 9
Baron de Hirsch Agricultural School, 65

Baron de Hirsch Institute, Montreal, 71
Baron de Hirsch Trade School, 119
Baron Hirsch Fund, New York, 69, 73, 119
Baron Hirsch Kaiser Jubiläums Fund (see Baron Hirsch Stiftung), 68
Baron Hirsch Stiftung, Vienna, 68
Baronof, 56
Battenberg, Alexander of, 88
Bauer, Moritz, 61
Bayerische Hypotheken-und Wechsel-Bank, 5
Bayerische Ostbahn Aktiengesellschaft, 5, 18
Bayerische Staatsbank, 3, 5, 6, 6 n., 18
Bayerische Vereinsbank, 7, 7 n.
Bein, Alexander, 81
Belgian Railways, 24
Bellova, 52-53, 57
Benedikt, Professor Heinrich, xi, xv, xvi, 52
Beresford, Lord Marcus, 94
Berliner Diskonto Gesellschaft, 61
Bernays, Rabbi Isaac, 9
Bernstein, Eduard, 42
Beust, Count Friedrich Ferdinand von, 30, 37, 40, 51, 91, 97
Biedermann, Clarissa, 13
Bischoffsheim, Amalia (née Goldschmidt), 13
Bischoffsheim, Clara (see Hirsch)
Bischoffsheim, F., & de Hirsch, 15, 18, 20, 22, 23, 24, 25, 35
Bischoffsheim, Family, 11, 13, 20, 21, 29, 37, 91 n., 113
Bischoffsheim, Ferdinand, 18, 20, 21, 83
Bischoffsheim, Goldschmidt & Co., 11, 13, 15, 16, 17, 18, 32, 46
Bischoffsheim, Henry, 13, 14
Bischoffsheim, Jonathan Raphael, 13, 15, 22, 26 36, 86
Bischoffsheim, Louis Raphael, 13, 15, 16, 36
Bisemont, Count, 23
Bismarck, Prince Otto v., 17-18, 30, 47, 48, 53, 81, 101
Bleichröder, Goson v., 46, 47
Bloch, Dr. Joseph S., xi
Blount, Edward, 35
Bodenheimer, M. J., 80, 83

135

Index

Bodenkreditanstalt, Wien, 32, 36
Böhmische Unionbank, 56
Bontoux, Paul Eugene, 52, 56, 57
Boulanger, General, Georges, 88, 89
Bouvier, Jean, xii, 37, 38, 57
Brestel, Baron von, 37
Brogan, Dennis, 88
Brouwer de Hogendorp, Florentin de, 20, 24, 35
Brussels, Hirsch's education in, 11
—return to, 11
Bucher, Moritz, 47
Budde, 33

Cahen d'Anvers, 13, 46
Cairncross, A., xvii
Calice, Baron, 49
Cambon, Jules, 95
Cameron, Rondo E., xvi, 29, 38, 41, 103
Camondo, Baron, 46
Cassel, Sir Ernest, 14, 32, 93, 96
Central Archives of German Jewry, xiii
Cercle de la Rue Royale, 90
Cezanne, 35
Chapman, Guy, 88
Charles VI, 9
Chirac, Auguste, 56
Chouraqi, Andre, 66
Chovevei Zion, 64, 78, 80, 122
Churchill, Lady Randolph, 94
Churchill, Winston, 108
Coburg, Duc de, 87
Coburg-Kohary, August, 86-87
Coburg-Kohary, Ferdinand (see Ferdinand of Bulgaria)
Compagnie des Chemins de Fer Liègeois-Limburgois, 24
Comptoir d'Escompte de Paris, 57
Comptoir (Nationale) d'Escompte, 13
Congress of Berlin, 28 n., 44, 54, 55, 68, 84, 91, 95, 98, 102
Congress of Vienna, 102
Crédit Communal, 15
Crédit Générale Ottoman, 32, 37
Crédit Lyonnais, xii, 38, 46, 54, 57
Crédit Mobilière, xvi, 24, 26, 29, 37, 46
Crimean War, 29
Cullen, C. N., 72
Curzon, Lady, 94
Curzon, Lord, 94

Daoud Pasha, 30 n., 31, 32, 33, 42, 52, 92, 97
Davidson, G., 70
Debt Publique Ottoman, 46, 47

Decazes, Duc de, 98
Dechamps, 23
de Decker, 23
Dehn, Paul, 31, 98
Delcassé, 95
'Der Anker' Insurance Company, 21, 22, 91
Deutsche Bank, 14, 61
Deutsche Reichsbank, 14,
Dimtchoff, Radoslave M., 31, 33, 43, 51, 97
Dreyfuss Affair, 97
Drummond-Wolff, Sir Henry, 21, 31, 84
Drumont, Edouard, 100
Dudley, Lord, 94
Dutch State Railways, 24, 26

Earle, Ralph, 25 n., 39, 48, 98
East-Hungarian Railway, 13, 20, 25
Edward, Prince of Wales (Edward VII), xv, 44, 54, 81, 83, 86, 88, 90, 91, 92-96
Eichhorn, Castle of, 68, 103, 104
Eichthal, Aron Elias von (née Seligmann), 3, 5
Emden, Paul, 11, 11 n., 12, 18, 101
Engels, Friedrich, 42
Erlanger, Emile, & Cie, 37, 57, 122, 125

Feis, H., 41
Ferdinand, of Bulgaria, 86
Forest, Arnold de, 106, 107-108
Forest, Raymond de, 106
Forreste-Bischoffsheim (see also Forest), 107, 108
Franco-Prussian War, 38, 39
Frank, Walter, 88
Frederica, Empress of Germany, 95
French Eastern Railways, 26
Fuad Pasha, 30, 31
Furquart, Horace, 84
Fürth, 89

Gau-Königshofen, 1
Gereuth, 2, 4
Germain, Henry, 38, 57
Gladstone, William, 28 n., 51
Gladstone, William (British Primeminister), 79
Gneist, Professor Rudolf von, 58-59, 97, 109
Goldberg, Abraham, 77, 85
Goldhaft, A. D., 65
Goldschmidt, House of, 21
Goldschmidt, Leopold, 15
Goldschmidt, Maximilian, 16
Goldschmidt, Minna Caroline (née de Rothschild), 16

Index

Goldschmidt, Regina (née Bischoffsheim), 15-16
Goldschmidt, Salomon H., 11, 13
Goldschmidt-Rothschild, Bank, 16
Goldsmid, Col. Albert E. W., 81, 122
Goltz, Baron von Der, 50
Gordon, A. D., 84
Grunwald, Kurt, 1 n.
Grunwald, Max, 1 n., 9 n.

Hallgarten, G. W. F., xvi, 43, 44, 60, 87, 106
Harris, Frank, 95
Hartwick, Engineer, 49
'Haute Banque', 37, 46, 60
Heilprin, Michael, 70, 118
Held, Gustav, xi, riii, xv, 7, 8 n., 11, 18, 91, 103
Hentsch, Edouard, 35
Herzl, Theodor, xviii, 9, 10 n., 76, 78, 80, 81-82, 85, 86, 89, 101, 103
Heuser, Carl, 61
Hildesheimer, Hirsch, 80, 122, 126
Hirsch, Caroline (Guttel), 9
Hirsch, Clara von (née Bischoffsheim)
 —marriage to Hirsch, 5, 11
 —meeting with Hirsch, 11
 —dowry of, 12
 —engagement to Hirsch, 16
 —philanthropy, 51, 63-64, 65, 66, 69, 75, 84, 86, 108, 118, 119
Hirsch, Emil von, 5, 7
Hirsch, Jacob von, 2, 3, 8, 11, 12
Hirsch, James von, 40, 44
Hirsch, Joel Jacob von, 3, 4, 6, 8
Hirsch, Joseph von, 4, 5, 11, 12, 18
Hirsch, Lucien von, 8, 18, 62, 84, 87, 104, 106, 113-114, 118
Hirsch, Moses, 1, 2
Hirsch, Zenaide (née Polyakoff), 44
Hohenlohe-Schillingfürst, Prince Chlodwig, 86, 89, 90, 98, 103
Holstein, Baron von, 89
Holstein Diaries, 47
Horse-Racing, 64, 73, 94
Hulme-Beaman, A. G., 87

ICA—see Jewish Colonization Association
Ignatieff, Nicolai P. (Count), 41
International Land Credit Company, 23, 31
Isaacs, Meyer S., 118
Israelitische Allianz, Vienna, 68

Jacquemyns, G., xii, xvi, 20, 21, 23, 25, 32
Jellinek, Dr. Adolf, 68

Jenks, H. L., xvi, 25
Jewish Encyclopedia, 9 n.
Jewish Colonization Association (ICA), xv, xviii, 65, 71-73, 81, 92
Jewish Chronicle, 67, 68
Joint Distribution Committee, 73
Joseph, Samuel, 70
Judenstaat, 76, 77, 81
Jüdisches Lexikon, 76

Kahn, Rabbi Zadoc, 72, 122, 123
Kanitz, F. von, 45, 48
Kaschau-Oderberg Railway, 25
Kaulla, Alfred v., 61
Kinsky, Count Eugen, 35, 91
Kohler, Max J., xi, xiii, xiv, 8 n., 18
Kohler Papers, 5 n., 9 n.
Kollenscher, Max, xv
Kölnische Zeitung, 42
Königswarter, House of, 21, 90 n.
'Krach' (1873), 26, 38
Kühlmann, Richard von, 87
Kürenberg, Joachim von, 89

Landau, Herman, 81
Länderbank K. & K. Priv., 56
Landes, David S., 97, 98
Langrand-Dumonceau, Count, xii, 20, 21-25, 30, 30 n., 31, 56, 109
Larisch, Count Johann, 91
Laveleye, Emil de, 32, 45, 51, 53-60
Layard, (Sir) Henry, 29
Lee, Sir Sydney, 90, 102
Lehmann, Leonce, 71
Leven, Narcisse, 66
Levi, Sylvain, 78
Levin, Shmaryahu, 66, 78, 85
Liège-Luxembourg Railway, 26
Lloyd George, David, 108
Loeb, Isidor, 72, 122
Loewenstein-Wertheim, Prince, 3
Loewenthal, Wilhelm, 71, 72, 125
Ludwig I of Bavaria, 5
Ludwig II of Bavaria, 5
Ludwig, Emil, 89

Maatschappij tot Exploitatie van Staatspoorwegen (see Société d'Exploitation des Chemins de fer Neerlandaise), 24
Magnus, Sir Philip, 90, 92
Mahmoud Nedim Pasha ('Mahmoudoff'), 31, 39, 41, 42, 43, 51, 52, 92, 97
Maximilian II of Bavaria, 3, 5

Mayer, Karl von, 35
Mazerat, 46
Mears, S. G., 102
Mendel, Alexander, 24, 25
Metternich, Prince, 30
Metternich, Princess Pauline, 64, 90 n.
Mercier, 21, 22, 25, 46
Midhat Bey, see Midhat Pasha, 52-53
Midhat Pasha, 41, 45, 52
Mijatovich, Count, 40
Moharrem, Decree of, 46
Mohilever, Rabbi, 122, 126
Moisesville, 72
Montagu, Samuel, 122
Montefiore, Moses, xv
Morawitz, Charles (Karl), 32, 38, 49, 59, 102-103
Moscow-Riazzan Railway, 20, 24
Munich, 3, 4
Münster, Count, 88
Murietta & Cie, 81

Navon, M. J., 125
Netter, Carl, 69, 77
Nicholas II, 94
Nordau, Max, 72 n.

Oesterreichisches Biographisches Lexicon, 81
Offenheim case, xvi
Omar Fewzi Pasha, 45-46
Oppenheim, House of, 91 n., 98
Oppenheim, Jacques Evers, 21, 37
Oppert, Jules, 72
Oriental Railway, xv, xvi, 12, 61, 90, 99, 100, 116
—Concession, 20, 21, 24, 25, 26, 28, 31, 33
—terms of, 34
—alteration of, 39-41
—conclusion of, 58
Orient Express, 49
Ottoman Bank, 13, 32, 37, 46, 47, 54, 57
Ottoman Concession, 24, 25, 26
Ottoman Government
—H's obtaining of railway concession from, 18, 19, 28
—organization of *Türkenlose,* 36 ff.

Palmerston, 29
Paris, Count of, 88
Paris-Lyon-Mediterranée Railway, 35
Pears, Sir Edwin, 50
Penthièvre, Duc de, 86
Pereire Brothers (Emil and Isaac), 33

Pete, Betts & Crampton, 24
Pirbright, Lord (Baron Henry de Worms), 31
Planegg, 3, 4, 5
Pobjedonosszev, Konstantin, 72
Polyakoff, Jacob, 43 n.
Polyakoff, Lazar, 43 n.
Polyakoff, Samuel, 43 n.
Potocki, N., 86
Poulgy, G., 41
Pressel, Wilhelm von, 35 and n., 48
Prost, Adolphe, 26
Primker Justizrath (Councillor), 46
Prys, Josef, 1 n., 9 n.,

Rabinowitz, S. P., 122
Riche Frères, 25
Ristich, 55
Roosevelt, Theodore, 74
Rosenberg, Adam, 80, 122
Rothschild, Anselm v., 88
Rothschild, Edmond de, 78, 80, 100, 101, 122
Rothschild, Hannah de, 12
Rothschild, House of, 5, 18, 21, 47, 64, 90, 91, 93, 95, 96, 101
—Constantinople Railway, 29, 32, 34-35, 56
Rothschild, Nathaniel, 78
Royale Belge, 22
Rudolf, Crown Prince of Austria, 90, 92, 102
Rustchuk-Varna Railway, 24, 29

Sacher, Howard M., 84
Salisbury, Lord, 79
Salm-Reiffenscheidt, Franz von, 54, 91, 98
Samuel, Maurice, 76
San Stefano, Treaty of, 54
Sassoon, Arthur, 94
Schiff, Jacob H., 75, 119
Schnee, Heinrich, 1 n.
Schwarzfeld, 122
Seidler, 35
Seilliére, F. A., 37
Seligman, Jesse, 118
Sieghart, Rudolf, 91
Siemens, Georg von, 61
Société d'Exploitation des Chemins de Fer Neerlandaise (see Maatschappij tot Exploitatie van Staatspoorwegen), 35
Société Générale de Belgique, 15
Société Générale pour Favoriser le Commerce et l'Industrie, 13, 24, 35, 37
Société Impériale des Chemins de Fer de la Turquie en Europe, 35
Société John Cockerill, 15

Index

Société Nationale des Chemins de Fer Vicinaux, 15, 19
Sokolov, Nahum, 10, 18-19, 31, 78, 82, 84, 85, 102
Sonnenfeld, 122
South-Austrian Railways, 33, 34, 35
Springer, Max, 35, 37
Stein, Ludwig, 80
Stern, Selma, 1 n.
St. Johann, Hungary, 68, 93, 103, 104, 116
Straus, Oscar S., xiii, 9, 9 n., 11, 12, 16, 18, 31, 51, 58, 65, 70, 73, 99, 102
Straus, Sara, 11, 18, 103
Sulzbach, Goldschmidt & Co., 37
Szeps, Moritz, 90, 92, 97, 102

Taafe, Count Eduard, 56
Talabot, Paulin, 35, 39, 98
Tedeschi, Baron (see Todesco), 31, 90 n.
Tennant, Margot (see Asquith)
Tietze, Hans, 102
Todesco (see Tedeschi)
Treue, Wilhelm, 44
Türkenlose, xvi, 36-39, 42, 48, 51, 59
Turkish-Roumelian Railways, 54

Ungarische Länderbank, 56, 57
Union de Crédit de Bruxelles, 15
Union Générale, 56, 57

Van der Elst & Cie., 24, 30, 32
Vanvinckeroy, Colonel, 72
du Velay A., 37, 38
Veneziani, Emmanuel Felix, 67, 69

Victoria, Queen of England, 13
Vindabona Mortgage Insurance Company, 22, 23

Waring, Charles, 25
Wassermann, David, xiii
Weizmann, Chaim, xv
Wemyss, Lady Lilian, 94
Wertheimer, Samson v., 9
Wertheimer, Zacharias Wolf, 9
White, Arnold, 72
Wiener Bankverein, 36, 37, 46, 61
Wieninger, 74
William II of Germany, 79, 83, 85 n., 88, 89
William-Luxembourg Railway, 17-18, 26
Wilmar, Baroness Ainis de, 18
Wilson, Thomas, 28 n.
Wimpffen, Count, 92, 97
Wodianer, Baron, 33, 55, 90
Wolf, Lucien, 11, 83, 102, 104
Württemberg, Grand Duke of, 3
Württembergische Vereinsbank, 61
Würzburg, 1, 2, 3, 4, 5, 7
de Wynkele, Jules van, 26

Yad Vashem (Jewish National Remembrance Authority), xiii, 1
Young Men's Hebrew Benevolent Society, 71
Ypsilanti, Princess, 104

Zichy, Count, 30 n., 61, 91, 97, 106
Zimmerer, Heinrich, 48
Zionism, 7, 76 ff.

ACKNOWLEDGEMENTS

The author and publisher wish to express their gratitude to the following for permission to reproduce certain extracts and illustrations:

Roger W. Strauss, Jr., for an extract from, *Under Four Administrations,* by Oscar S. Strauss, published by Houghton Mifflin Company, New York, 1928, © Roger W. Strauss 1934.

F. H. Brunner, New York, for the frontispiece photograph, the photograph of Baron de Hirsch in Turkish attire, the cartoon, 'Days with Celebrities', published in *Moonshine,* 1892, and the caricature of Baron de Hirsch published in *Vanity Fair,* 1890; all taken from his collection.

Josef Fraenkel, London, for the drawing, 'The Great Men', from his book, *Lucien Wolf and Theodor Herzl,* published by the Jewish Historical Society of England, London, 1960.

Daniel Franck, Paris, for the photograph of the Hirsch family tomb © Daniel Franck, 1966.

William Heinemann Ltd. London, for the caricature 'Are We Welcome as Ever?', by Sir Max Beerbohm, from their book, *Fifty Caricatures,* 1911.

The National Library of Austria, Vienna, for the photograph of Crown Prince Rudolf of Austria.

Paul Popper, Ltd., London, for the photograph of King Edward VIII.

BALKAN RAILWAYS 1885

- OTTOMAN RAILWAYS PRIOR TO 1870
- SÜDBAHNGESELLSCHAFT
- STAATSBAHNGESELLSCHAFT
- ORIENTAL RAILWAYS
- PLANNED ORIENTAL RAILWAYS

0 50 100 km.

Drawn by CARTA, Jerusalem